DAGGERS IN THE FORUM

DAGGERS in the FORUM

The Revolutionary Lives and Violent Deaths of the Gracchus Brothers

KEITH RICHARDSON

'. . . those daggers which Gaius Gracchus boasted he had flung into the forum for the citizens to fight it out . . .'

Cicero, *The Laws*, 3.20.

CASSELL
LONDON

CASSELL & COMPANY LIMITED
35 Red Lion Square, London WC1R 4SG
and at Sydney, Auckland, Toronto, Johannesburg,
an affiliate of
Macmillan Publishing Co., Inc.,
New York

First published 1976

ISBN 0 304 29540 X

Typesetting by Malvern Typesetting Services Limited
Printed in Great Britain by
Richard Clay (The Chaucer Press) Ltd
Bungay, Suffolk

F.676

CONTENTS

INTRODUCTION ix
1 Born Into a Legend 1
2 A Proud Heritage 12
3 Tiberius Goes to War 28
4 The Storm Breaks 40
5 Land for the People 53
6 The Reign of Tiberius Gracchus 67
7 Massacre on Capitol Hill 85
8 A Showdown with Scipio 100
9 Gaius Takes up the Cause 113
10 Revolutionary Power 128
11 Vision of Empire 140
12 The Tide Turns 156
13 End of an Era 166
14 Daggers in the Forum 177
15 The Fatal Legacy 192

SOURCES 201
Lists of Consuls 229
The families 234
Select bibliography 237
INDEX

MAPS
The Mediterranean World 17
Italy 57
The Centre of Rome 91

THE TWO FAMILIES

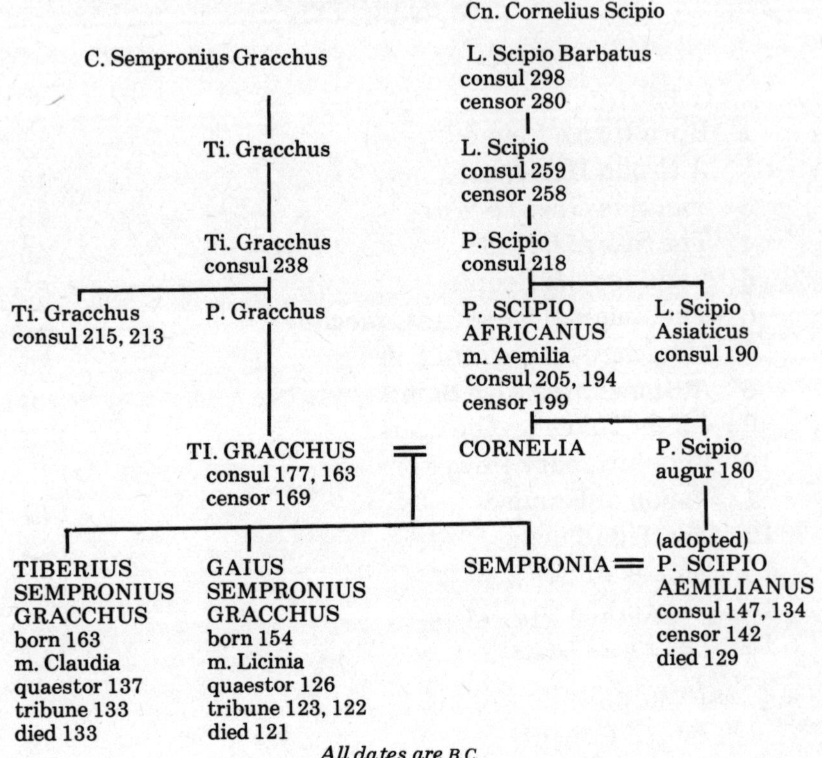

All dates are B.C.

More family ramifications. pp. 234-6.

This book is about political revolution, and the men and women who made it happen, who built a great society and then fought to change it or to preserve it.

TIBERIUS SEMPRONIUS GRACCHUS, soldier and statesman, tribune of the Roman people, murdered in 133 B.C.

GAIUS GRACCHUS, his younger brother, twice tribune, hunted to death in 121.

SEMPRONIA, their sister, married to Scipio Aemilianus in a loveless match.

TIBERIUS GRACCHUS, their father, a great censor and pillar of the state.

CORNELIA, their mother, daughter of Scipio Africanus and the wisest woman of the age.

SCIPIO AFRICANUS, their grandfather, whose defeat of Hannibal laid the foundations of an empire. A commander of mystic genius, who yet died in exile.

SCIPIO AEMILIANUS, their cousin, who tried and failed to solve new problems in the old way. Adopted into the family of his uncle, Scipio Africanus, he married Sempronia.

 Every Roman had two or more names. First comes the personal forename: for example Gaius, Publius or Marcus. These are usually abbreviated. Second comes the name of the main family or clan: Sempronius, Cornelius or Claudius. Third may be a family subdivision: Gracchus, Scipio or Pulcher. Fourth may be a nickname such as Frugi ('honest') or Dives ('rich'); or an honorific such as Africanus ('conqueror of Africa'); or a mark of adoption such as Aemilianus ('born in the Aemilius family'). Sons frequently have names identical to those of their fathers, which is simply a nuisance. In the text names are given in their most convenient form, they appear in full in the index.

 Sums of money are normally quoted in terms of the silver *denarius*, abbreviated to *d.* A day's wage for a labourer would be around $\frac{1}{2}d$. A Roman foot-soldier was paid 120*d.* a year, a centurion 240*d.* and a cavalryman 360*d.*[1]

The everyday bronze coin was the *as*, reckoning at first 10 and later 16 asses equal to 1*d.* The smallest silver coin was the sesterce, equal to $\frac{1}{4}d$. The Athenian drachma was regarded as equivalent to 1*d.* Large sums were sometimes reckoned in terms of the talent of 6000*d.*

INTRODUCTION

Tiberius Gracchus was beaten to death in the streets of Rome, the capital city of the Western world, and his body flung into the yellow River Tiber, two thousand one hundred and eight years ago.

For the first time blood had been spilt in the city to settle a political dispute. While holding public office that made his person sacred, Tiberius was killed by the most respectable men in the state, led by the high priest in person, because of the political cause he was championing. It was the cause of reform, of the right of the Roman people to change the world they lived in. But it looked like the cause of revolution and it was to claim many more victims.

Twelve years later his brother Gaius was killed after travelling farther on the same road. Tiberius was not yet thirty when he died, and Gaius only a little older.

From their deaths the history of Rome, and so of Europe, took a new turn. After such savage treatment the reform movement itself became more violent and more bound up with the struggle of ambitious individuals for personal power. In the end it destroyed the free republic. After decades of turbulence and strife Julius Caesar finally overthrew the constitutional government in the name of the Gracchan movement, and it was at the hands of their enemies that he died. Not until after ferocious civil wars did the last of the revolutionary line, Caesar's heir Octavian, manage to bring peace and stability to a battered world.

Caesar had claimed that his justification was 'to free myself and the Roman people from oppression at the hands of a minority clique', and Octavian chose similar words to describe his own achievements: 'At the age of nineteen I raised an army on my own initiative and at my own expense and with it restored to freedom the state which had been oppressed by one dominant clique.'[1] The clique in each case was the same selfish narrow-minded oligarchy that had crushed the Gracchus brothers. Yet the end result of a century of struggle and revolution was that the revolutionary champion Octavian became an emperor and in the name of freedom banished the very idea of popular government, the idea that major political decisions should be influenced by the votes of common men.

The Gracchan story is a story of revolution. Their lives began the chain of events that ended with Octavian founding an absolute monarchy. Yet while Tiberius and Gaius Gracchus lived the idea of popular government had not been a total sham, for the people had important political rights under the complex Roman constitution. In their lives can be seen all the classic tensions of revolution: the interplay between personal ambition, the letter of the law, and the political needs of each moment. What were they really trying to achieve? In what sense were they justified? Why did they have to die so wretchedly? Rome was in a crisis to which nobody else seemed to be offering an answer. But in their zeal to put right all the problems of the day, did the brothers go too far?

Their revolution was not an attack on a clear and identifiable enemy, as those in France or Russia were to be. Rather it was the gradual but overpowering expression of general discontent with a whole political and social system. Their apparently stable and prosperous world failed to cope with the accelerating pace of change and simply shook itself apart. But it is this aspect which makes their story so fascinating to a modern reader. Their age was closer to ours than much of what lay between. The Mediterranean world had transformed itself in two generations. An onrush of prosperity had brought strange new economic and social problems. Slowly changing institutions were unfitted to deal with the new world, but men disagreed as to whose fault this was and where the remedy lay.

A sudden opening of cultural horizons to new influences from the east was accompanied by a crumbling of moral standards. Corruption and brutality could be seen among the rich, while the poor would no longer accept suffering and injustice with the stoical resignation of earlier generations. Rome's conquest of the world had brought luxury to too few and discontent to too many. Rome found its own Vietnam in the corrosive effect of the long and terrible Spanish wars. The problems and the grievances needed an answer. It fell to the Gracchus brothers to make the attempt.

*

Their story is also a romantic tale in its own right, for the young men were both talented and well born, and they could effortlessly have attained the highest honours Rome had to offer if they had chosen to side with the established order. Instead they died in the streets, leaving behind the memory of the noblest of heroes—or the most dangerous of revolutionaries.

Yet strangely their story has not often been told at length in the English language. The brothers are tucked away into cursory chapters introducing too many lives of Julius Caesar and too many potted histories of the republic. Part of the trouble is that Roman history is still too much like a great endless jigsaw puzzle with most of the pieces missing. The known facts are too few and it has taken the lifetimes of many great scholars to fit them into their proper context. We understand far more about the Gracchan period today than we did fifty years ago, but there are still serious gaps in the picture. To write the story of the brothers is to launch into a complex detective story, and clues have to be picked up and examined wherever we can find them.

This factor is reflected in the shape of this book. It begins by placing the young boys in the context of their family in an aristocratic world, pauses to consider the mechanics of the political system against which they were to do battle, then looks more closely at the two great families from which they were descended. Their father and grandfather had done much to shape the new Rome, and their lives, by the force of heredity and example, must give some clue to the hopes and personalities of the brothers themselves.

The early life of Tiberius Gracchus shows the build-up of the crisis, the storm about to break, for revolutionary forces of such magnitude did not develop overnight. Then comes Tiberius' own year of history, the backlash, and his brother's more determined attempt to change the world. The issues involved are discussed as and when they become important, with the actual words of the ancient authors quoted in translation as frequently as possible. A note on these authors will be found in the bibliography together with a list of some important modern works. The list and the references in the footnotes are meant to be helpful rather than complete. No background knowledge of Roman history is needed to read this book, which is intended for the general reader as much as for the specialist. Its subject is the universal one of political change and the men who make it happen.

The Roman revolution cannot be explained simply in terms of economic pressures, military needs, or family politics. The revolution came because there were too many of these interlocking problems. Too many for the old order to solve and, as it turned out, too many for the Gracchus brothers too. Their glory is that after their deaths it was their cause that in the end triumphed. Their tragedy is that their cause was distorted almost out of all recognition by the memory of their deaths. Europe was united by the Romans under an absolute monarchy, a militarist autocracy that carried within it the seeds of its own decline long before it fell. Had the Gracchan revolution succeeded it might all have been very different.

1 Born into a Legend

Tiberius Gracchus was born towards the end of the year 163 B.C., since we know that he was 'not yet thirty' when he died in 133. His brother Gaius was born nine years later.[1] They were well born in a society where noble birth could unlock every privilege.

Their father, the elder Gracchus, had been one of the great men of the state, equally distinguished as a civil magistrate and as a commander in the field. Yet even more famous was their grandfather, Scipio Africanus, the brilliant general who had defeated Hannibal and destroyed the power of Rome's greatest enemy, Carthage.

In contrast to what we know of their father, able and hard-driving in the classic Roman style, Scipio was a strange and mystical figure, an enigma to his contemporaries, a romantic legend to later generations, a man of great personal magnetism who yet died in inglorious exile. His talented young daughter Cornelia married the ambitious and energetic Gracchus in a sensational match whose consequences fascinated the ancient world.

Later it became a common school exercise to discuss this theme: 'If Scipio had not given his daughter to Gracchus, so through her creating the two Gracchus brothers, then those great seditions would never have happened—so it should all be blamed on Scipio.'[2]

Rome was a superstitious city and in such a household there had to be a miracle. When Gracchus one day found two snakes in his bedroom, according to the story told by Gaius, the priests warned that he must kill one of them but if he chose the male he himself would die, while to kill the female would mean the death of his wife. As an old man with a still young and attractive wife, he killed the former and dutifully passed away a few days later.[3]

Cornelia took charge of the children and estate, quickly showing herself to be so wise and affectionate a mother that people thought Gracchus had done nothing unreasonable in choosing to die for her sake. She even refused the crown of Egypt, when one king Ptolemy offered to marry her, no doubt to win Roman support against his brother and rival. Instead she chose to devote herself to her surviving daughter and two sons, and the education she gave them became a byword. She brought them up with such care that the most talented young men of their time seemed to owe even more to their education than to their natural gifts.

Like some great lady of eighteenth-century France, Cornelia kept a salon where she entertained her many friends and visitors. Greeks and intellectuals were always around her, and she exchanged gifts with every foreign king. Her letters were published and still read a century later as evidence that she had the wit to instruct as well as the love to cherish her children.[4]

Coming from a cultivated and philhellene family, Cornelia sought out Greek tutors for the boys. Diophanes of Mytilene taught them the valued skills of public speaking, while the Stoic philosopher Blossius of Cumae acquainted them with those radical political ideas that had already disturbed the peace of conservative southern Greece.[5]

In a male-dominated society Cornelia's strong personality played a father's role, and the Roman people later showed their esteem by erecting a bronze statue of her, seated and wearing strapless sandals. It was placed by the portico of Metellus, near the great popular meeting-ground of the Flaminian Circus, where her sons must have held many a political gathering. The legend on the base of the statue, *Cornelia mother of the Gracchi*, would have pleased her, for she had often teased her children that the Romans still referred to her as her father's daughter rather than as their mother.[6]

The title was to become hers soon enough, though.

*

The lives of the old Greek and Roman heroes that Plutarch wrote down during the golden age of the empire were romantic and picturesque. He was interested in personality and anecdote, and preferred moralizing about the rewards of vice and virtue to analysing cause and effect. Yet his character studies of Tiberius and Gaius Gracchus, and the contrast he draws between them, are vivid and convincing.

They were like each other, he says, in their bravery and self-discipline, in their generosity, eloquence, and grandeur of spirit. But Tiberius was gentle and composed in looks and manner while Gaius was earnest and vehement.

In public Tiberius spoke in a quiet, orderly fashion, standing in one place, but Gaius paced up and down and was the first Roman habitually to tear the gown from his shoulders in the excitement of his speech. Tiberius' speeches were cool and persuasive, playing on his audience's more tender emotions with a careful and correct choice of words. But his younger brother spoke with fire and fury, hammering home every point with a rich and colourful vocabulary.

In their manner of life they also differed. Tiberius was frugal and plain at home, whereas Gaius, without approaching the luxury typical of the day, was fond of new fashions and rare objects and once had to defend his reputation against the charge of squandering money on costly silver dolphins. Gaius' rough and passionate temper was such a contrast to his brother's mildness that sometimes it ran away with him, turning his eloquence into shrill abuse. So he trained a servant, Licinius, to stand near and play a soft note on his pipe whenever his master became angry to steady both his voice and his temper.

Such were the differences between the two. But their valour against the enemy, their justice in government, their care and industry in office and their self-control in private life, these qualities they shared equally.[7]

*

Birth, talents and education gave the boys a brilliant start to life in a world where youthful ability had every opportunity to display itself, for those whose fathers bore the right names. It was a world dominated by a tight, almost incestuous network of noble families. Tiberius Gracchus, for example, was the grandson of one Scipio, fought at Carthage under the command of a second, and died at the instigation of a third.

It was also a proud world. Rome was a city of unshakable confidence, living and thriving on its own legends, and now was a great moment to be born into it, for the long Roman history of hard work, civic virtue and military discipline had suddenly been rewarded with the mastery of the world. To be a Roman noble in the second century was to be the equal of kings, as one vivid story shows.

Popillius Laenas was sent in 168 on an urgent mission to help Egypt, then being overrun by the Syrian king Antiochus, a matter which was arguably none of Rome's business. Near the mouth of the Nile he met the king, refused the royal handshake, and brusquely told him to read the Roman senate's decree first.

> But when the king then said he would like to consult his friends, Popillius acted in a way which was thought to be offensive and very arrogant. He was carrying a stick cut from a vine, and with this he drew a circle in the sand round Antiochus and ordered him not to step outside it until he had answered the decree. The king was astonished at this high-handed approach, but after hesitating said he would do everything the Romans asked. Whereupon Popillius and his staff all shook the king's hand and greeted him warmly.[8]

By a mere gesture Popillius had humbled a proud conqueror and disposed of a great kingdom. Was it any wonder that such men began to show a touch of arrogance at home, too?

Yet Rome's success was still something new, for the foundations of her power had been laid slowly and carefully. The city which had grown up on seven low hills by the bank of the Tiber became a free republic in 510. After a century of desultory local wars and political squabbles it was destroyed by wild Celtic invaders in 390 and everything had to begin again. Another hundred years of patient fighting brought the mastery of central Italy. The Greek cities farther south came into the net after a bloody struggle against Alexander the Great's kinsman Pyrrhus. A first war against Carthage, the African city which for centuries had dominated the western Mediterranean, brought control of Sicily as well.

A pause, and in 218 the death struggle began. Hannibal led the Carthaginian army across the Alps and descended into Italy like a thunderbolt. One Roman army was smashed on the snowy banks of the Trebia, a second was swept bodily into the waters of Lake Trasimene, and a third was annihilated on the open plains of Cannae in one of the most devastating military victories of all time. With not an army in the field Rome was on its knees. Its fields were wasted, its allies deserted, and yet its spirit held out. Stubbornly the Romans fought on, and when they finally invaded Africa themselves Hannibal was recalled to defend his mother city. At the battle of Zama in 202 Scipio beat him once and for all.

The long stormy night was over. In a new dawn Rome emerged as the strongest power in the Mediterranean. Never again would an outside enemy put the republic in danger of its life. Yet the war had been a shattering experience. The panic of those dreadful days after Cannae was never forgotten. Generations were moulded by the lessons of victory.

Why had Rome survived the terrible ordeal? A legend was needed, and one grew up. It was the valour and obedience of the people, and the wisdom of their hereditary ruling classes, that had brought them to safety. And it was on the foundations of this legend that the arrogance and self-satisfaction of the Roman nobility was erected. It was from this moment of victory that the Gracchan revolution began to be inevitable.

*

Self-glorification was an old Roman tradition. The praises of famous men were sung, most loudly by their descendants, for in this way the leading families kept green the memory of their own ancestors. The war with Hannibal gave the families a fine tale to tell, so that the reputation of Fabius the prudent general could be established for ever by the work of Fabius the loyal historian. In memorable verses the poet Ennius captured the dignified and selfless face which Rome wanted to present to the world, the face of Fabius 'who by delaying saved the state', of Curius 'who could not be mastered by either steel or gold'. Rome herself 'stands supported by her ancient customs and her men', and 'the Romans are as brave as the sky is profound'.[9]

This Roman legend was most vividly expressed by the historian Livy, who wrote much later, after a generation of civil war and with a longing for a golden age long past. He aimed to tell his readers what kind of men had founded their country's greatness, 'for I honestly believe that no country has ever been greater or purer than ours, or richer in good citizens and noble deeds. None has so long been free from avarice and luxury, and nowhere else have thrift and plain living been so highly valued'.[10]

So Livy hammered home his theme, that everything had gone well when people clung to the old virtues of loyalty and obedience, but badly when these rules of behaviour were broken, and disastrously when power was entrusted to ill bred men of the people like the wretched Varro, who commanded the army defeated at Cannae. Countless dramatic stories enshrined the solid Roman virtues, and gave Scipio the confidence to tell mutineers that 'Rome will survive though a thousand generals perish'.[11]

To look beyond the pretty tales, and give the Roman legend its most elaborate expression, needed a Greek mind, however. Polybius, whose life spanned from the defeat of Hannibal to the Gracchan revolution, was active in the politics of southern Greece during its last days of freedom, was taken captive to

Rome after the great battle of Pydna but there won the friendship of the victorious Aemilius Paullus. He became tutor and close companion to Paullus' two sons, who had been adopted into the families of Scipio and Fabius.

So he observed events from inside the very heart of the Roman nobility, and his history can be read partly as propaganda for the Roman way of life as lived by his friends. But his purpose went deeper, for the monumental task he set himself was to explain this great 'paradox' to the people of the world.

'For who is so worthless or idle,' he asked, 'as not to want to know how and by what kind of government the Romans, in less than fifty-three years, have brought under their own control almost the entire inhabited world—a thing without precedent in history?'[12]

He was impressed by Roman integrity. He marvelled at their determination, 'to carry out their projects in the face of any obstacles, thinking that nothing is impossible once they have decided on it'.[13] But the real cause of their success, he believed, lay in the way they had governed themselves for so long, and so he devoted his sixth volume to describing the Roman constitution, 'at the moment when it was at its best and nearest to perfection, at the time of the war against Hannibal'.[14] But his judgments must largely reflect political life at the time he was writing, only a decade or so before the Gracchan revolution.

Plato had brilliantly shown how governments could be classified into rule by one man, by the few or by the many, and how all three types carried the seeds of their own deterioration. To Polybius, the scientific historian, the lesson was clear: 'The best constitution must be the one which combines all these three varieties.'[15] And he believed he had found that durable ideal, the 'mixed constitution', in Rome and that there lay the secret of Roman success.

'So fairly and properly was everything arranged that not even a Roman could state with confidence whether the whole system was aristocratic, democratic, or monarchic.' Carefully he analysed the checks and balances between the three great elements in the state, the people in their assemblies, the nobles in the senate, and the consuls wielding the power of kings, and reached this rousing conclusion.

Since each element has the power to restrain or support the others, their union can cope with any emergency and so it is impossible to find any better form of government than this. For whenever some common menace forces them to act together the state becomes so strong that nothing that needs doing is neglected. Everyone eagerly competes to meet the crisis and nothing is delayed; they all help in public and in private to fulfil the tasks they have set themselves; and so this constitution possesses an irresistible power of securing every object on which it sets its heart.[16]

And yet it was against this near-perfect constitution that the Gracchus brothers rebelled, only a few years after Polybius penned those very words. During his last years even Polybius began to lose confidence, after witnessing the savage outburst of 146 when the Romans utterly destroyed the historic cities of Corinth and Carthage. But the decline was more dramatically summed up by the historian Sallust, for a time an active partisan of Julius Caesar.

> Down to the destruction of Carthage the people and senate shared the government peacefully and with proper restraint, nor did the citizens compete for glory or power. Fear of its enemies preserved the good morals of the state.
>
> But when the people were relieved of this fear [*i.e., after 146*] then those vices of licence and pride, which always accompany prosperity, naturally followed.
>
> So the peace and quiet which people had hoped for when times were hard proved to be even more painful and bitter. For the nobles began to exploit their position, and the people their liberty, all to gratify their selfish passions, and each man snatched what he could for himself. So the whole community became divided into two parties and between them the state was torn to pieces.
>
> One small group of nobles had everything under their control in both peace and war—the treasury, the provinces, public offices, all honours and triumphs. Military service and poverty were the burdens of the people, while the spoils of war were seized by the generals to share with a few friends. Yet the parents or the young children of the soldiers might be driven from their own homes by powerful neighbours.
>
> So the possession of power gave endless scope to cruel greed, which violated and plundered everything, respecting nothing and holding nothing sacred, until in the end it brought its own downfall.
>
> For the day came when noblemen rose to power who preferred true glory to unjust dominion. . . .
>
> [*In other words the Gracchus brothers.*]

> . . . Then the state was shaken to its foundations by civil strife, as if by an earthquake.[17]

*

The speed of its collapse revealed the true instability of the Roman political system. The harmony between classes had been a sham. It was a mixed constitution in this sense only, that the people were sovereign in theory but powerless in practice. Polybius' account is so evidently the work of a retired aristocrat, the friend and confidant of other aristocrats. Its intellectual basis can be traced straight back to those paternalist doctrines of Plato, who had said that 'the greatest principle of all is that nobody should be without a leader'. When drawing up his ideal constitution Plato had pointed out that 'in it you will find the desires of the mass of the people, the rabble, controlled by the desires and wisdom of the more worthy minority'.[18] And this was precisely how things were managed at Rome.

When politics had become more sharply polarized Cicero drew this distinction between the two groups in the state, 'those who want their words and deeds to please the mass of the people, and those who so behave that their policies win the approval of all the best men'. And he held that this political distinction had always existed.[19] What Polybius was applauding was that during the war against Hannibal the second group of 'the best men', the sons and friends of the leading families, had established their ascendancy. He also noted how the people were persuaded to accept the leadership of their betters, especially by the use of religion, 'which in my opinion is the biggest single advantage that their constitution provides'.

Almost every move in public life was subject to religious formalities, which could be used to influence the most important decisions. 'My opinion,' ventured the cynical Greek, 'is that they adopted all these to cope with the common people. The rituals would not be necessary if a state could be made up only of wise men, but since the common people are fickle and full of lawless desires, of unreasoning anger and violent passions, they must be held back by invisible terrors and empty play-acting.'[20]

For centuries the Roman people had struggled for political rights. A series of great reforms, culminating in 287, had brought them access to the highest offices of state and the power to make laws. And yet in practice the ruling families, with their prestige and self-confidence raised to new heights by the victory over Hannibal, could still preserve a constitutional machinery that gave them an apparently total control over the Roman state.

*

In the Gracchan period over 300,000 adult male citizens lived in the city or on Roman land. The rest of Italy was bound to Rome by a system of perpetual alliances. Six overseas provinces were governed directly by Rome and a looser pattern of alliances and friendships covered most of the Mediterranean world.

The executive officers of the republic were a small number of magistrates elected each year. Chief among these were the two consuls and then the six praetors.

The senate was in principle an advisory body. But its prestige was immense, and consuls holding supreme office for one year only would rarely think it wise to oppose the declared wishes of the senate, of which they themselves were now senior members, especially since all their hopes of future political influence lay in the senate's hands. This was even more true of junior magistrates. The senate's rulings on policy, especially on diplomatic and financial matters, went almost unquestioned.

In practice, therefore, by the weight of its unwritten authority the senate governed Rome and so the world. Though three times rebuilt, the lofty senate house with its cool and dignified interior is still one of the principal monuments of the Roman forum.

The senate comprised the 300 most experienced men in public life. Senior magistrates normally became members for life.[21] In addition two censors were specially elected every five years from among the most distinguished ex-consuls, and they had powers to remove members and to enroll new senators from the ranks of the junior magistrates.

Election to office was thus a pre-requisite for entry to the senate and for any political career, and election lay in the hands of the people. For electing junior magistrates the people were divided into 35 tribes. Not all votes were of equal value, for a candidate had to win a majority of the tribes and these were of unequal size. Most of the city's inhabitants belonged to the four crowded urban tribes, where one vote counted for little. A vote in one of the 31 rural tribes was more valuable simply because fewer people from the countryside turned up to use their votes. Being landowners, most rich men were registered in the rural tribes and so had an advantage unless crowds of farmers came to town to outvote them. But for all that the assembly of tribes was the nearest thing to a fair and democratic vote at Rome, and a young man's first step towards the senate-house lay under its control.

But entry to the senate was itself only a preliminary step, for its affairs were conducted on the basis of seniority. The first say on any subject went in turn to men who had been censors, consuls and praetors. They were the men who counted and they were elected by the people voting in the assembly of centuries, which was not democratic at all and never intended to be.

Cicero was honest enough to make this clear. 'Servius,' the king traditionally supposed to have founded this assembly, 'organized it in such a way as to place voting power in the hands of the rich, not the common people, and so put into effect the principle that should always apply in politics, that the greatest number should not have the greatest power.'[22]

So voters owning property worth over 10,000*d.* (representing prosperity rather than great wealth) controlled probably 89 centuries out of 193. Poorer voters were allocated into other centuries, while the poorest of all, with less than 400*d.* to their names, were lumped into one huge century.[23] Each century counted equally in the voting. Moreover the propertied classes voted first and the lead given by the first century was customarily followed by the others.

Seniority in the senate was thus controlled by the wishes of the propertied classes.

Actual entry to the senate was restricted even further. It was open 'to the industry and virtue of any citizen'. But such a citizen had first to acquire wealth if he had not been born to it, for only the richest, 'those highest ranks of men to whom the senate-house is open', were eligible for office.[24]

A property qualification of 100,000*d.* gave entry to the all-important officer class of knights, and only knights could be voted into those offices which took men into the senate.

Before standing for office a candidate had also to have completed ten years of military service.[25]

*

Political advancement was thus reserved for well-to-do young men who successfully lobbied for the votes, first of the tribes and then of the centuries. Power inevitably gravitated towards a limited number of rich and well known families. Elections could be hard fought, for any ambitious young man from a politically conscious family, whose ancestors had held office before, regarded it as his right and duty to do likewise, if possible in the first year he was old enough to qualify. To achieve this the families developed elaborate techniques for bringing in the votes, which were delivered as a mark of personal loyalty, and in return for favours received or expected, more than for reasons of policy.[26]

'The glory of men's ancestors is like a light shining on their descendants,' said Sallust, and a family name made famous by the constantly repeated stories of past heroes was the first and almost essential step in bringing a candidate to the attention of the electors.[27] The great families which bore these names repeatedly held office and political power, until their patronage and influence penetrated every corner of the land. Often a great family helped talented outsiders to junior office, but it was rare for such 'new men', without senatorial ancestors of their own, to become consuls.[28] To be consul was what counted above all, and those families that had held that office at least once were distinguished by the epithet 'noble'. The consular families were the Roman nobility and, said Sallust, 'they passed the consulate around from hand to hand among themselves'.[29]

So by inherited patronage, traditional friendships, marriage alliances and the sheer familiarity of their names, as well as by the lavish use of money to impress the electorate and finance their carefully organized election campaigns, a few families came to hold the highest offices in their grip. A score of powerful clans, bearing such historic names as Claudius or Cornelius, Fabius or Fulvius, carried off more than half the consulates, dominated the senate, and moulded the careers of young men who sought their aid.

The system gave them continuity of office so that collectively they built up an unsurpassed reserve of administrative experience. It also gave the families a position of immense privilege. Kings treated the sons of Roman senators like brothers.[30] Repeated office added still further to the families' fame, their patronage and their wealth. Well might their grip seem unshakable.

And yet the people were still sovereign. The assembly of tribes had the right to pass binding laws. Each year it elected the people's own champions, the ten tribunes. The senate's prestige might well shape the laws; the hope of advancement and favour might well keep unruly tribunes in check. But there lay the opportunity, within the legal framework of the state, that bold and influential men could exploit.

Open that tiny crack, and the whole elaborately structured dam might burst.

2 A Proud Heritage

In a quiet suburb beside the Appian Way, just within the old walls of Rome and now hemmed in by a shady children's park, lies a dark and gloomy burial vault. It is the tomb of the Scipio family. Until its discovery in 1780 here lay buried, surrounded by five generations of his descendants, the great-great-great grandfather of the Gracchus brothers, L. Cornelius Scipio Barbatus.

Copies of the tombstones still lie in the murky passages of the vault, and tell of the pride of one of the republic's greatest families. Of Barbatus himself, consul in 298, 'a brave man and wise, whose handsome appearance matched his virtues, who took two towns from the Samnites and reduced the whole of Lucania'. Or of his son, consul in 259, 'by general consent the best of the good men at Rome—who captured Corsica and the city of Aleria'.[1]

But one tomb is missing from the collection, that of the family's brightest star. Scipio Africanus, grandfather of the Gracchus brothers and the real founder of Rome's Mediterranean empire, died and was buried in exile. His life had been a paradox. A great noble, he had built his career on popular support in the teeth of constitutional precedent. An imaginative general, an enlightened diplomat, a lover of Greek civilization, he cultivated a mystical personal image that cast a spell over the ancient world and touched the heart of the Renaissance. The character and career of this remarkable man must cast some light on those of his revolutionary grandsons.

*

Young Scipio became a man of destiny at a crucial moment in history. In the war that would decide the fate of the world, Hannibal was sweeping all before him. Yet prominent among those grim Roman commanders whose determination slowly turned the scale were Scipio's father and uncle. They were sent to attack the Carthaginian empire in Spain, and their victories in that remote and unknown country brought them the title of 'the thunderbolts of war'. Then suddenly they were separately surrounded and killed. It was this dangerous set-back that gave Scipio his chance.[2]

At the age of seventeen he had fought well under his father's command in Rome's first clash with Hannibal, at the Ticinus.[3] Two years later he distinguished himself again, after the disaster at Cannae. The survivors chose Scipio and Appius Claudius to command them. Seeing signs of defeatism in the camp, the 'destined leader of the war' ran to the house where the plotters were proposing to abandon their country to Hannibal, shook his sword over their heads, and swore 'never to desert my country nor to permit any other Roman to do so.' The mutineers gave in and honour was saved.[4]

In beleaguered Rome a noble of strong personality could make his mark quickly. Two years later Scipio stood for the office of aedile. No matter that the tribunes denounced him for being too young. 'If all the Romans want me, than I am old enough,' he cried, and so many people rushed to register their votes that the tribunes withdrew. Once elected, Scipio showed his thanks by holding magnificent public games and distributing oil to the people.[5]

In 211 came the calamity in Spain and the experienced C. Claudius Nero was rushed out to hold the north of the country. This he seems to have done, and yet a year later he was replaced by the twenty-four-year-old Scipio, who demanded as his inherited right the command where his father and uncle had fought and died.

What we are told seems incredible, that 'nobody else dared accept the Spanish command'. But when Scipio offered to go then 'all eyes turned on him and amid roars of approval every century and every individual voter supported him for the job'. Yet such a command, with its consular authority, was quite unprecedented for one so young, holding no official position at all.[6]

So Scipio went to Spain, and in three sparkling campaigns drove the Carthaginians clean out of the country, paved the way for ultimate victory, and laid the foundations of the Scipionic legend.

As a general he showed such dash and enterprise that no less a critic than Basil Liddell Hart has called him 'greater than Napoleon'. First he marched his men through shallow lagoons to surprise the fortress of New Carthage. Then in a complicated uphill battle at Baecula he handled the traditionally stolid Roman army with a skill and flexibility it had never known before. He changed the organization of the army, equipped it with longer Spanish cutting swords, and trained it to fight in looser, more manoeuvrable formations. Early in 206 this superb fighting force won him total success at Ilipa.

The same open mental attitude showed in his dealings with the Spanish tribesmen fighting for the enemy. His generosity quickly won them over, and perhaps this was what persuaded the Carthaginians to cut their losses and quit. Scipio's deliberate personality cult reminded people of Alexander the Great, and Livy calls him remarkable, 'not only because of his talents but also because from youth he had been careful to show them off in a special way.

'He would present his public actions as though they were inspired by dreams and divine warnings, and never performed any public or private business without first meditating, silent and alone, in the temple on the Capitol hill. This confirmed the widespread belief, perhaps deliberately spread, that he was of divine birth.'[7]

No wonder the wild Spaniards were so impressed by this magnanimous stranger that they hailed him as a king. This, Scipio calmly explained, was not an appropriate title for a Roman but he would be happy if they would call him 'kingly'.[8]

Yet the famous charm was not wasted on mutinous soldiers, whose leaders he brutally executed. And for all his cultured airs his idea of how to celebrate final victory in Spain was to hold spectacular gladiatorial fights.[9] Similarly, even his military achievements may have been exaggerated. The overriding reason for fighting in Spain was to prevent the enemy sending more troops overland to Italy.[10] Unfortunately while seeking tactical success at Baecula he had left an open road for the Carthaginian army to slip away and follow Hannibal, to the Alps and into Italy.

For a moment Rome was terrified, and then overjoyed when this new invader was caught and destroyed at the Metaurus, thanks to the energy and boldness of the consul C. Claudius Nero, the man whom Scipio had displaced in Spain.

The rivalry between the houses of Claudius and Scipio, which was to be so prominent a feature of the Gracchan revolution, was underlined. And of Scipio himself the same question could be asked as of his grandsons. Did his personal glory count for more than the welfare of the state? Was his war principally just a means to serve his ambition, as his final speech in Spain might suggest?

'It is my wish,' he told his troops, 'to take you back home with me, to share the triumph we have earned together. Then I hope you will support me when I stand for election as consul, as if it were an honour that belongs to us all.'[11]

Every century voted for the glamorous hero, with his long hair and soldierly good looks.[12] But the great nobles of the senate were less enthusiastic about his plans for taking the war to the gates of Carthage. Fabius insisted that 'we raise armies to defend Rome and Italy, not for arrogant consuls who fancy themselves kings to whisk away to whatever part of the world they fancy'. Scipio countered that he would take an army to Africa by the people's authority alone if the senate opposed him. Finally he was sent to Sicily, with permission to go on to Africa if he wished, but given no troops or ships. Volunteers and cash lent by his friends had to make do.[13]

In 204 his armada sailed for Africa, and after a difficult first year Scipio broke out and won two crushing victories. At last the Carthaginians recalled Hannibal. That prince of generals, who had held his motley army together in Italy for so long and against such overwhelming odds, inspired his people to one last effort, and finally met Scipio face to face at Zama in 202.

The decisive battle was uncertain for most of the day. Hannibal did everything a good general could have done, as Polybius admits. But Scipio neutralized the first charge of his elephants and at the end of the day eluded Hannibal's last trap. The cunning enemy had put his best troops in the reserve line of battle but Scipio managed to steady his own men just in time. The battle was won and the war was over.

Scipio quickly signed a generous peace, leaving Carthage disarmed but independent. He was in a hurry, it was said, because the senate had already nominated a replacement commander, Ti. Claudius Nero, cousin of the victor of the Metaurus.[14] But Nero never turned up. The people voted Scipio the honour of ratifying the peace and bringing home the army. He entered Rome in a magnificent triumphal procession, deposited 120,000 pounds of silver booty in the treasury, and took the extra surname of Africanus, the first such title in Roman history.[15]

*

After arranging for land to be distributed to his veteran

soldiers, Scipio was elected censor and became leader of the senate until his death. Yet his political influence waned almost immediately. A new war had sprung up, embroiling Rome in the Greek world of the eastern Mediterranean. This was governed by the successor kingdoms of Alexander the Great's generals and a scattering of free cities. Philip V of Macedon had troubled Rome before and was menacing again. After some hesitation an army was sent east, with little success at first.

Suddenly another brilliant young man flared on to the scene. T. Flamininus was not yet thirty when elected consul, but in the Greek cities of southern Italy he had learned to understand their language and their people. Now clever diplomacy rallied Greece to his side, and with the flexible Roman army created by Scipio he smashed the heavy Macedonian phalanx with which Alexander had once conquered the world. But did this mean a new Roman empire in the east? Not at all. Before the anxious crowds assembled for the Isthmian Games of 196 Flamininus brought off a dazzling theatrical coup, when his herald proclaimed 'the freedom of the Greeks'. Two years later the Roman armies were gone.

None of this pleased Scipio, who won a second consulate in 194 but not the Macedonian command he wanted. Instead the senate brought the troops home, while Scipio lost further popularity with his proposal to give the senators separate seats at the public games from those of the common people. An arrogant interference with 558 years of tradition, said the man in the street.[16] Where stood the people's darling now?

Yet his sun had not yet set, for a new war was brewing in the east, this time against Antiochus the Great, the formidable Syrian king whose dominions spread to the Hindu Kush. And the dreaded Hannibal was in the king's service. Scipio may even have met him on an embassy, when Hannibal told him that the three greatest generals in history were 'Alexander first, then Pyrrhus, then myself: but if I had beaten you, Scipio, I would place myself first above all'.[17]

Antiochus invaded Greece and was quickly driven back again, but Rome wanted a decisive victory and in 190 Scipio at last sailed east, with the consul, his brother Lucius. His grand style of diplomacy won the friendship of kings on both sides of the Hellespont, and for the first time in history a Roman army crossed into Asia. He warned Antiochus to surrender rather than fight, but while Scipio lay sick his brother forced the issue and at Magnesia destroyed the king's oriental horde of elephants and camels, mailed horsemen and scythed chariots.

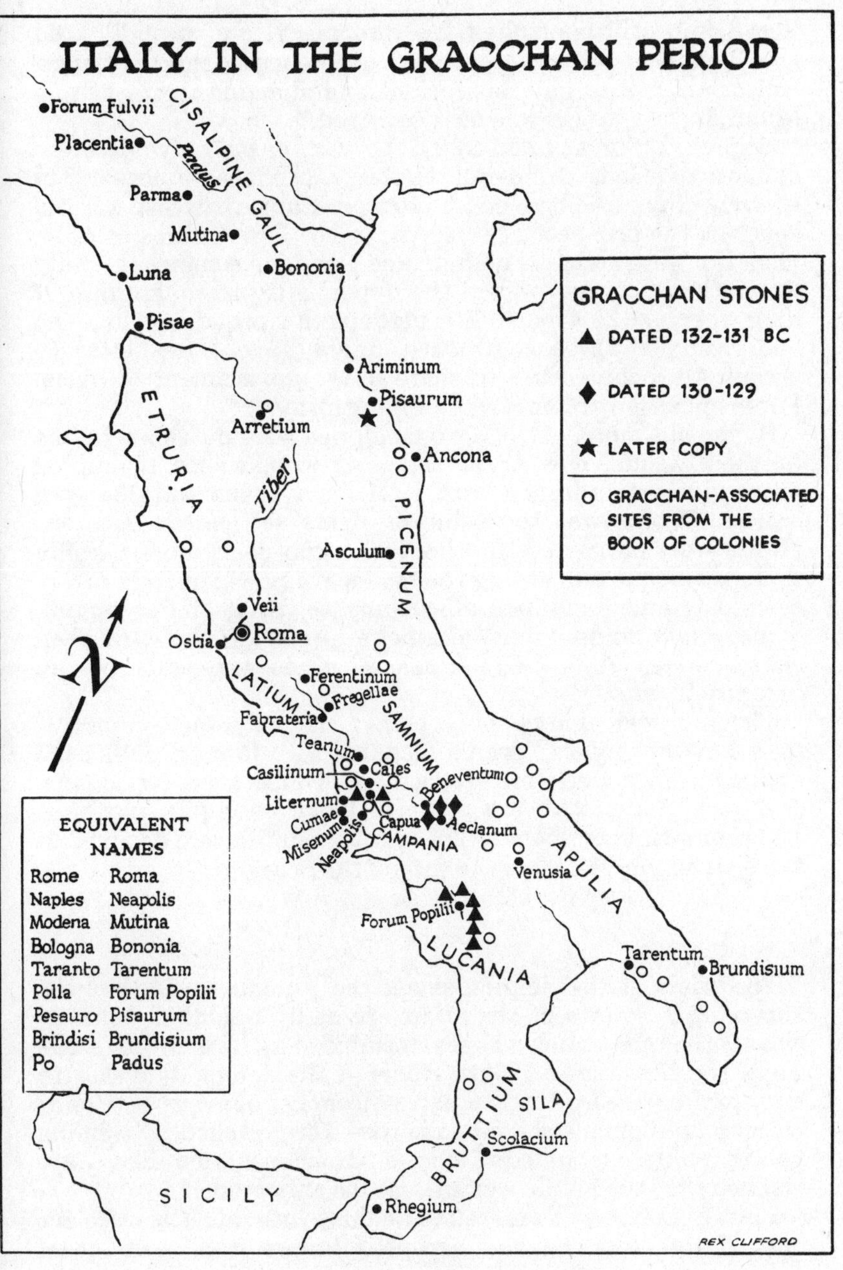

ITALY IN THE GRACCHAN PERIOD
Forum Fulvii
Placentia
Parma
Mutina
Luna
Bononia
Pisae
CISALPINE GAUL
Padus
Ariminum
Pisaurum
Arretium
Ancona
ETRURIA
Tiber
PICENUM
Asculum
Veii
Roma
Ostia
LATIUM
Ferentinum
Fregellae
Fabrateria
SAMNIUM
Teanum
Casilinum
Cales
Beneventum
Liternum
Cumae
Aeclanum
Misenum
Capua
Neapolis
CAMPANIA
APULIA
Venusia
Forum Popilii
LUCANIA
Tarentum
Brundisium
BRUTTIUM
SILA
Scolacium
SICILY
Rhegium
REX CLIFFORD

GRACCHAN STONES
DATED 132-131 BC
DATED 130-129
LATER COPY
GRACCHAN-ASSOCIATED SITES FROM THE BOOK OF COLONIES

EQUIVALENT NAMES
Rome   Roma
Naples   Neapolis
Modena   Mutina
Bologna   Bononia
Taranto   Tarentum
Polla   Forum Popilii
Pesauro   Pisaurum
Brindisi   Brundisium
Po   Padus

Yet Scipio still controlled the diplomacy, and proudly told the king that victory made no difference to his demands. Antiochus had to pay reparations and abandon western Asia Minor, but his power was not destroyed.[18]

Scipio's diplomacy had ended the war in a year, avoiding the dangers of a long campaign. He had established a network of friendly kings who had learned to treat Rome with respect, and held out the prospect of freedom for the Greek cities of Asia. Honours were lavished on him, and Polybius somewhat wildly wrote that Scipio now had the opportunity to make himself king wherever he wished. But perhaps this proud Roman, who had reshaped three continents, might have done better to accept Antiochus' offer to share in the government of Syria. For his position at home was slipping away.[19]

It was not merely that his own glories were outshone by his brother Lucius, now surnamed Asiaticus, whose triumphal procession was adorned with 1231 ivory tusks and 234 gold crowns. Worse was the collapse of his settlement. Eastern affairs were entrusted to other men, who dealt more harshly with Antiochus and swung the balance of power in Asia firmly towards Rome's staunch ally Eumenes, King of Pergamum, whose rich lands later became a pivot of the Gracchan controversies. A few Greek coastal cities were left only an insecure freedom.[20]

The political change only paved the way for a massive personal onslaught. Furious disputes tore Roman public life apart. Leading men were accused of incompetence, corruption, and vice. Attempts were made to block triumphs, elections and provincial commands. The highest names were dragged in the dirt, and in 187 came the turn of the Scipios.

*

The trials of the Scipios shook the Roman world, but the surviving accounts of the affair are badly muddled. What is clear is that the attack was masterminded by the cantankerous Cato, the first man to warn Rome of the danger that wealth and empire were leading her astray from her old virtues. But at the crucial moment the fallen heroes were rescued by a rising young politician called Tiberius Gracchus, who like Cato claimed that the public welfare was his only guide.

First L. Scipio was ordered to be flung into jail. The effective charge was that he had accepted bribes from Antiochus. Whereupon Gracchus exercised his right as tribune to veto the deed. He would not permit the man who had extended the

Roman empire to the limits of the world to lie in prison. And yet as a known enemy of the Scipios he swore that this did not mean he had become their friend. Moreover he sharply reproved the great Scipio Africanus for trying to cut across the law and use his own authority to protect his brother.[21]

Then Africanus himself was formally accused of accepting bribes and assuming too much authority. Old innuendoes of luxury and Greek manners were thrown in. In reply Scipio simply pointed out that it was the anniversary of his victory over Hannibal, and led the people out of the assembly to the Capitol hill to give thanks in the temple of Jupiter Best and Greatest.

The trial broke up, but 'it was the last day of glory for Scipio'. He withdrew to his country estate at Liternum, and when an attempt was made to recall him for trial it was again Tiberius Gracchus who stood in the way, asking if there was no service to the state that could entitle a man to a safe old age. The senators thanked Gracchus for placing the public good above his private quarrels, but Scipio never returned to Rome. When he lay dying he asked to be buried on his estate rather than in his ungrateful native city.[22]

Livy felt Scipio's career had been memorable, but more for the arts of war than for those of peace, and that in his latter years he had found no opportunity worthy of his talents. His friend, the poet Ennius, claimed that to Scipio alone the great gate of heaven stood open. Polybius called him 'almost the greatest man of all time', while Cicero spoke of the empire 'whose proud and glorious fame is due to Scipio'.[23] His personality, his achievements, and the awful drama of his fall gave a magic to his memory. He was a second Alexander, a second Hercules, a son of Jupiter.

When Cicero wanted an artistic vehicle for his highest political ideals he chose Scipio, appearing in a dream to warn his adopted grandson Aemilianus of his country's needs.[24] That idealized picture of the Roman virtues, tinged with Neoplatonist philosophy through the commentaries of Macrobius, was handed down as 'the Dream of Scipio' and became one of the most influential of all classical works.

Petrarch glorified Scipio as a more than human hero. Dante saw the hand of God in his victory over Hannibal. Yet Cicero's dream sequence had its ironic side. For Scipio was also the grandfather of the Gracchus brothers, and so the parent of revolution.

*

High on the Aventine hill, in a crowded working-class district overlooking the Tiber, the Gracchus family had its own monument. It was a temple which the earliest Gracchus known to history had built and dedicated to Liberty in 246. It was paid for out of fines imposed on the arrogant Claudia, who had publicly wished for a Roman naval defeat to keep down the size of the mob.[25]

The Gracchus family was of lesser fame than the Scipios, with whom it was to be so fatally linked. But it was still old and respectable, a branch of the Sempronius clan which held three censorships and nine consulates in the third century.

Gracchus the temple builder became consul in 238, and led an expedition to seize Sardinia, later a regular scene for the family's exploits. Of his two sons Publius, the grandfather of the revolutionary brothers, is almost unknown to us, but the other, also named Tiberius Gracchus, was one of the heroes who leaped into history after the disaster at Cannae.

Chosen master of cavalry in the emergency, he helped rake together a force of 24,000 men by arming boys of sixteen and even slaves. Gracchus inflicted one of the first setbacks on Hannibal at Casilinum, and in gratitude was elected consul for 215. With a rousing speech he rallied the senate after another disaster in north Italy. Then he took over the army of slaves, whom he carefully treated as the equals of citizens. Fighting with great care he won several minor engagements and avoided Hannibal's traps.

The next year he won a great victory at Beneventum, after promising his loyal slaves that 'any man who brings an enemy's head from the field will be given his freedom'. After a hard fight he did even better.

'By my orders every one of you is a free man,' he told his slaves. 'May it bring blessings, prosperity and happiness upon our country and yourselves.' The citizens of Beneventum then held a great feast for the soldiers, who proudly sported white woollen headbands as caps of liberty. So moving was the scene that Gracchus had a picture painted of it and set it up, appropriately enough, in his father's temple of Liberty.[26]

Consul again in the following year, Gracchus succumbed only to treachery. Trapped and surrounded in a narrow canyon he struggled with such ferocity that the enemy could not take him alive. Hannibal gave him a hero's funeral, but Rome's loss was doubled. So personal was the bond between him and the former slaves that on his death they all promptly deserted.[27]

Gracchus was one of the most attractive of the broad-shouldered heroes who brought Rome through the war. His life is also important because it marks the first point at which we can trace faint but undeniable evidence of political links between the families which supported the Gracchan revolution—the great houses of Claudius, Fulvius, Mucius and Licinius.

When Gracchus was chosen consul in 215 on a wave of popular enthusiasm, three of the praetors elected with him bore the names of Claudius, Fulvius and Mucius. The fourth, Valerius, may also have been an associate for he had already held joint office with Mucius, and married the widow of another Fulvius.

In 213 Gracchus was consul again. To hold the elections he nominated a Claudius as dictator, who in turn appointed a Fulvius as master of cavalry. Fulvius and another Claudius were elected consuls. Yet another Claudius and another Fulvius were elected praetors. Under the influence of this new team, apparently chosen to speed up the war, the senate changed every command in Italy—except that of Gracchus.

The precise significance of these links is the subject of some debate, but in the light of later events their existence cannot reasonably be denied. In the next three years the names of Sempronius, Fulvius, Licinius and Valerius turn up again in high office. A more aggressive policy in the east, where the Fulvian family had traditional interests, was led by Valerius and a Sulpicius, whose name was also to reappear in the Gracchan movement. So was the theme of involvement in the east.[28]

*

The next Gracchus to become consul, the nephew of the dashing war hero, is a difficult man to evaluate. His personality has been almost submerged by adulatory comment, mainly designed to highlight the depravity of his sons. What is clear is that he was one of the city's leading men, able, patriotic, and fiercely ambitious.

This Tiberius Gracchus was born about 220. In 204, 'while still a young man', he became an augur, lifelong member of an influential priestly college.[29] He next appears on military service in Greece as 'by far the most energetic of the young men', sent by Scipio to make overtures to Philip of Macedon. Gracchus galloped 200 miles in three days, made sure of the royal friendship, and came back as fast as he had gone.[30]

Perhaps Scipio gave him that important job for his merit alone, for the enmity between the two is repeatedly attested when Gracchus intervened in the trials of the Scipios. Yet a little later Gracchus married Scipio's daughter, the talented Cornelia. Many stories were invented to embellish the occasion. One is that during an official dinner on the Capitol the senators rose and begged Scipio to present his daughter to Gracchus there and then. But more probably we should believe Polybius, who tells that it was after Scipio's death in 183 that the family chose Gracchus for his daughter. She brought with her the very handome dowry of 300,000d.[31]

Cornelia was much younger than her husband, for she was still of child-bearing age when he died in mid-century.[32] So she may have been born in perhaps 195 and betrothed at thirteen or soon after. In selecting Gracchus for her, Scipio's family must have noticed not only his talents but also the signs that he was attuned to the rather different political climate now emerging.

The consuls for 189, Manlius Vulso and Fulvius Nobilior, set the new style. Having blocked an extension to Scipio's eastern command they fought controversial and almost private wars in Asia and Greece, but despite furious opposition they each secured the honour of a triumph on their return. Prominent in support of Fulvius in 187 were the tribune Gracchus and the praetor Sulpicius Galba.[33]

Gracchus's evident interest in the east brought him membership of an embassy, which managed to offend Philip of Macedon and favoured Eumenes of Pergamum. The bonds with Pergamum, already befriended by Manlius, were tightening, and they were to be fruitful beyond belief.[34]

After helping to found a colony in Etruria, Gracchus next made his mark as aedile in 182, when he drew ruthlessly on his connections in Italy and the provinces to finance the customary public games. This caused so much annoyance that the senate felt obliged to set a limit on such spending in future.[35]

In 180 Gracchus went off as praetor to take over the important command in northern Spain from Fulvius Flaccus, son of his uncle's old ally. They amicably arranged for Fulvius to take home the battle-weary veterans who had been out there for six years or more, and whose support he wanted at the coming elections.[36] Then with fresher troops Gracchus fought a famous campaign.

Victory followed victory in the difficult Spanish mountains, but what counted even more was that he finished the war with a peace that was to last for twenty-five years. He gave land to the Spanish poor, and fixed fair tribute, and when war flared up again it was to the Gracchan treaties that men looked back with regret. When his son was defeated in those same mountains his father's name was enough to secure his freedom.[37] After founding the city of Gracchuris on the Ebro Gracchus returned home in triumph, to find the political tide again running in favour of the families that were to support his sons.

Fulvius Flaccus had already been elected consul for 179, together with his own brother, who had been adopted into the Manlius family. Another Fulvius had been consul in 180, a third was censor in 179, and another Manlius was consul in 178.

The links back to 215 when Gracchus' uncle had been consul are unmistakable. Directly descended from the praetors of that memorable year were: both the consuls of 179; three praetors of 179 (P. and Q. Mucius Scaevola and C. Valerius Laevinus, half-brother to Fulvius the censor); and C. Claudius Pulcher, praetor in 180 with Gracchus.

So are the links forward to the next generation and the four most prominent of the Gracchan supporters: C. Claudius was the father of one of them, P. Scaevola of two more, and Fulvius Flaccus was the uncle of the fourth.

Not surprisingly Gracchus and C. Claudius secured election as consuls for 177. Laevinus followed in 176 and then the Scaevola brothers. Fulvius Flaccus became censor in 174. Yet we know these elections were bitterly contested and men of good family were passed over year after year.

As consul Gracchus again served his country well, crushing a serious rebellion in his grandfather's old province of Sardinia. After a string of victories he sold so many of the rough tribesmen into slavery as to create a famous proverb about 'Sardinians for sale'—a pun on their reputation for accepting bribes. So valuable were his services that the senate voted him two days of public thanksgiving. When he finally returned, no doubt remembering the painting commissioned by his uncle, he set up his own tablet in the temple of the mother goddess, down by the crowded Cattle Market. The tablet was shaped like the island of Sardinia, covered with battle pictures, and carried these words.

Under the command of the consul Tiberius Sempronius Gracchus the army of the Roman people conquered Sardinia. More than 80,000 of the enemy were slain or captured in this province. After a successful administration, in which he freed Rome's allies and restored her revenues, he brought his

*army home safe and laden with plunder. For the second time
he entered the city in triumph. In commemoration of which
he dedicated this tablet to Jupiter.*[38]

*

Yet another monument had been set up to inspire this stern
commander's impressionable sons. At the next opportunity
Gracchus was elected censor for 169, along with his old colleague C. Claudius. It was to be the peak of his career, for
the Rome which had only just learned the taste of empire was
beginning to lose its way.

The most serious crisis since Hannibal had suddenly broken
out. Perseus, the new King of Macedon, was determined to
shake off Roman influence in the east. War began in 171 and
went badly for Rome. The first general sent out was from
another Gracchan family, P. Licinius Crassus, with the same
familiar names, Claudius and Manlius, Scaevola and Laevinus,
among his lieutenants. Yet the clique, which it was beginning
to look like, was defeated in the field and so was the next team,
Hostilius Mancinus and Claudius Centho.

Panic struck Rome. Every senator was summoned to the
city. Morale in the army of the east was reported to be
appalling. New consuls found it difficult to raise fresh troops.
In this black moment Gracchus and Claudius were elected
censors, by tradition the guardians of Rome's moral purpose.
They were equal to the task. They made every eligible citizen
offer himself for military service, while soldiers who had
drifted back to Italy on leave or even discharge were rounded
up and sent off east again.[39]

Yet Romans were beginning to wonder whether military
problems were only part of a wider deterioration. Was empire
sapping the moral roots of the republic? The censors seem to
have thought so. They expelled at least seven senators, and
struck more names from the list of knights than had ever been
done before. This they could do for the broadest moral
reasons, and it was said that when Gracchus went home after
supper citizens put their lights out so that he would not
suspect them of late-night drinking.[40]

The knights were the wealthiest of the non-senators, and
included the leaders of the rising class of businessmen and
public contractors, with whom the censors tangled next. The
previous censors had let out building contracts on an
unprecedented scale and something must have gone wrong,
for Gracchus and Claudius announced they would give no work

to the firms that had taken jobs then.

The furious contractors found a friendly tribune, who managed to outmanoeuvre the censors and put them on trial for treason. Claudius, hot-tempered in his family tradition, bore the brunt of the attack. The votes of the knights and the prosperous first class told against him. Senators pleaded for his acquittal, while Gracchus swore that if his colleague was condemned he would go into exile with him. Even so Claudius was released by only eight votes. For the first time business interests had revealed their political muscle—another lesson for the Gracchan revolution.[41]

There was one more task, which Cicero was to call Gracchus' greatest service to the state. For ten years political life had been in turmoil. Consuls had flaunted the senate's authority. Allies and neutrals had been badly mistreated. For the first time two plebeians were elected consuls in 172. Electoral considerations were even hampering military discipline. Perhaps part of the reason lay in the changed voting procedure introduced by the censors of 179, and Gracchus determined to turn the clock back.

To this end he severely limited the voting powers of the freedmen by restricting them to one of the thirty-five tribes. These former slaves, originally the booty of war, were rising in numbers and could be dangerous, for they clearly owed their votes to the rich men who had set them free. Many were clerks and skilled workers, who must have been involved in business affairs and may have played a part in the row about contracts.

The senate praised Gracchus for persisting in so good a cause despite some hesitation from his colleague. When writing in the later republic, when the freedmen had become a major problem, Cicero went so far as to say that if Gracchus had not acted 'the republic would not have been preserved for us'.[42]

In his census Gracchus counted a record number of Roman citizens, over 310,000 adult men, and celebrated by buying the house of Scipio for the state with some stalls that all lay behind the Old Shops on the south side of the forum. In their place he built the great Sempronian Hall for business and legal meetings, and as rebuilt by Julius Caesar its foundations can be seen today. No doubt it was in front of this hall that his statue was erected, while opposite it stood the Aemilian Fulvian Hall, built by the censors of 179. Rome was beginning to look like an imperial capital, for the censors of 174 had been the first to pave its streets.[43]

Meanwhile Scipio's brother-in-law, Aemilius Paullus, took

the war in hand. With its discipline restored the legion crushed the phalanx at the decisive battle of Pydna, the kingdom of Macedon was removed from the map, and in 167 Paullus returned home to the most splendid triumph that the streets of Rome had ever seen. It took 3000 men to carry the coined silver, and 250 wagons to bear the statues and pictures looted from the palace of Perseus. In all the booty was worth 30,000,000*d.* and from that moment on the Roman people were relieved of all direct taxation. Paullus in the field, like Gracchus in the forum, had indeed saved the state, and the rewards were beginning to flow in a torrent of gold.[44]

*

Gracchus played a major role in the settlement of the east, heading a grand embassy in 165 and establishing close friendship with the kings of Pergamum, Syria and Cappadocia.[45] In 163 he was consul again, now a rare honour, and once more served in Sardinia, to put down a Corsican rebellion. Also in a rather curious incident he declared void the election of the consuls for 162 (one of whom was his brother-in-law Scipio Nasica), because as presiding officer he felt he had not performed the rituals properly. Cicero regarded this as an outstanding example of Gracchus' integrity and respect for the state religion.[46]

Next year he was back in the east. The Syrians had killed Octavius, leader of a mission sent by the senate 'to cripple the royal power', by burning Syria's warships and hamstringing its elephants. Yet even this delicate situation yielded before the Gracchan charm: he quickly made friends with the young new king and then repeated his grand tour. Peace blossomed in his footsteps, just as it had done in Spain.[47]

It was in 163 that his son Tiberius was born, probably his eldest since he took his father's first name. Gaius was born nine years later. Of Gracchus' twelve children the only other known to us is his daughter Sempronia. She may have been the eldest child, for perhaps as early as 152 she was splendidly married to her cousin, the son of the victorious Aemilius Paullus. During these last years of his life we know of no further official action by Gracchus, though no doubt his views continued to command respect. And sometime between 154 and 147 the great man died.[48]

To his children he left the most talented and devoted mother in Rome. He left monuments of family glory, his own hall and statue in the forum and his Sardinian memorial, to add to the temple of Liberty on the Aventine and the tombs of the Scipios down by the Appian Way. He left overseas connections of inestimable value. Spanish tribes, Sardinian townships and eastern kings would all reward the sons for the father's sake. He left a network of political links with some of Rome's greatest families, even though he had had the self-confidence to take an independent line, disagreeing with his friend Claudius or helping his enemy Scipio, when he chose.

Above all he left a glowing memory of one of the great servants of Rome. Cicero came back again and again to Gracchus as a paradigm of the great Roman virtues.

Gracchus was 'eloquent as well as statesmanlike, as his speech in Greek to the Rhodians showed'. He was 'a helmsman of the state and a leader of public policy', and again 'a supreme augur, a wise man and an outstanding citizen'. Even more, he was 'a man of the greatest wisdom and almost unrivalled excellence'. It was the people's 'love for Gracchus' that saved the unpopular Claudius.[49]

In particular Cicero idealized the memory of Gracchus as a glowing contrast to his unspeakable sons.

So much praise was heaped on Gracchus—would that his sons had never degenerated from his statesmanship.

Gracchus will be praised for as long as Rome is remembered; but his sons when alive were detested by the good men, and dead they are numbered among those who have been justly killed.

While the sons were the most eloquent of men, their father was prudent and sage but not particularly fluent. Yet he was often the salvation of the state, above all as censor. It was with a mere nod and a word, not any fancy flow of rhetoric, that he moved the freedmen into the city tribes, without which the republic which we are now struggling to maintain would not have been preserved for us. But his talented sons, equipped for public speaking by every gift of nature or upbringing, took over a state which had been brought to the very pinnacle of prosperity by the arms of their grandfather and the wise policies of their father, and then used their eloquence to destroy it.

By seeking fame and honour Gracchus reached a high point of virtue . . . . And surely you would agree that he was happier than his son, for he devoted himself to serving the state, but his son to overthrowing it.[50]

3 Tiberius Goes to War

Tiberius Gracchus, son of the great censor, was born in what was still recognizably the old Rome. The virtues that had conquered Hannibal had triumphed again on the battlefield of Pydna. The nobility was in command and the old image barely tarnished. Yet when Tiberius died at the age of twenty-nine, his head beaten in with the leg of a stool, he had shattered that image for ever.

Yet the sudden crisis which Tiberius precipitated did not come unawares. Through his short lifetime, even when as a boy he sat by his wonderful mother listening to the talk of the chief men of the city and the world, both the city and the world were already changing fast and, from many points of view, not for the better.

As soon as he was old enough, at fifteen or sixteen, to put on a man's toga Tiberius was honoured by election to the priestly college of augurs, as his father had been at a similar age.[1] The college was small, with membership for life, and it is even possible that he 'inherited' the seat directly on his father's death. Or perhaps the influence of Cornelia can be traced. To a young man born with such family connections every door was open.

At the same age, in 147, he must have begun the ten years' military service that were compulsory before a Roman could offer himself for political office. The next year he won his first taste of glory. Once again a Roman army was battering at the walls of Carthage where his grandfather had won undying fame. Tiberius, 'already foremost among the young men in discipline and bravery', was the first man to scale the enemy's walls, along with the historian Fannius. For this he will have received a military decoration, the mural crown. He was much liked in the army, and greatly missed when he left.[2] But his position in it was no ordinary one, for he was a member of the personal staff, 'sharing the same tent', of the commanding officer. And the commander was his kinsman and brother-in-law Scipio Aemilianus, the man who came to dominate the Rome in which Tiberius grew up and who, in a tragic repetition of the love-hate relationship between an earlier Gracchus and an earlier Scipio, became his great enemy.

Scipio Aemilianus was as closely enmeshed into the tight Roman aristocracy as anyone could be. His father was Aemilius Paullus, the victor of Pydna, and his grandfather had fallen at Cannae. His aunt Aemilia had married Scipio Africanus; he had been adopted by his own cousin, their intellectual but infirm son, P. Scipio the augur; and another of his cousins was their daughter Cornelia, widowed mother of the Gracchus brothers. To close the net still further, some time between 152 and 147 he married the unlovely Sempronia, but unhappily for Rome it was a childless and a loveless marriage.[3]

This Scipio, like his great namesake, shone in an age of wars, but he too had tragically little to contribute to the problems of peace. Born probably in 185, he first distinguished himself at Pydna, the victory which for a decade calmed the Mediterranean world while ambassadors like Gracchus reorganized whole kingdoms by simple diplomacy. Yet around 154 trouble broke out in all directions.

First the long peace of Gracchus collapsed in Spain. It was the beginning of twenty years of bloody war, stained by Roman treachery and cruelty, and by a continuous loss of life that cost the republic dearly. As early as 151 it was becoming hard to raise troops for the hated war until Scipio set the example by volunteering for it. Again he did well, beating a Spanish chieftain in single combat and leading a successful assault on a town. But the Spaniards found a heroic leader, Viriathus, and the war blazed on.[4]

The Macedonians found their own hero in the pathetic figure of Andriscus, finally crushed by the praetor Metellus in 148. Unrest spread south into Greece—but now Africa was in turmoil too. Through fear or envy the Romans had found an excuse to attack the old enemy Carthage, but even with 84,000 men at their backs the consuls of 149 had little success. The only Roman to distinguish himself in the fighting was again Scipio. In 148 he came back home to stand for aedile, but the people were so worried about the war, and so excited by the name and spectacular achievements of Scipio, that they chose him consul on the spot.[5]

It was an extraordinary move, flatly contravening the laws which now laid down minimum age limits and a proper sequence in which offices should be held. But the people cried out that it was their right to elect whoever they wished, and the objections of senate and consuls were set aside. The sovereignty of the people (at least of those middle classes who controlled the consular elections) was triumphant, a crucial precedent for the Gracchus brothers. But the senate had the wit to give in with a good grace and have the relevant laws suspended for one year only, so as to preserve the constitution intact.

Scipio returned to Carthage, now in command of the army, and with young Tiberius Gracchus in his camp. After an initial row with the naval commander, L. Hostilius Mancinus, he tightened up discipline and settled down to a hard siege. Carthage fell amid scenes of horror in 146; the site was razed to the ground and a curse pronounced on anyone who settled there, a curse of which Gaius Gracchus was to fall foul.[6]

In the same year the final solution was applied to another problem. Reckless Greeks thought that Rome was too preoccupied to keep them under control, but Roman patience at last gave way. After a crushing victory the consul Mummius destroyed the ancient city of Corinth, sold its people into slavery, and shipped its priceless artistic treasures back to Rome.

An era was over, and the Romans knew it.

*

Scipio certainly knew it, as he stood amid the smoking ruins of mighty Carthage and wept and quoted Homer, and told the historian Polybius of how he feared for the future of his own country when faced with this stark evidence of the uncertainty of fate. And the observant Greek caught the mood perfectly, the doubts and worries that were beginning to disturb the more reflective Romans as they saw their city steeped in the blood and gold of empire. At one point he had even traced 'the beginning of the demoralization of the people' back to the popular leader Flaminius, who in 232 had distributed newly conquered land in North Italy to the Roman poor, anticipating the Gracchan reforms by a hundred years.[7]

More seriously he pointed to the changes that followed the great victory of Pydna, the end-point of those fifty-three years of conquest which had been the subject of his history. As the luxurious and corrupt manners of the Greeks took hold of Rome, he quoted with approval the puritanical Cato's complaint that 'you can tell that the state is going to the dogs when pretty boys are sold for more than farms and jars of caviar for more than ploughmen'. From the aggressive wars of 146, and the sack of Carthage and Corinth, he drew a moral of Roman deceit and arrogance, 'a lust for dominion over others such as Athens and Sparta once had', that had certainly not been in his mind when he began to write.[8]

So disturbed was he that he decided to change the balance of his great book. After describing those fifty-three years, he explained, 'I shall now have to add an account of the subsequent policy of the conquerors, so that people can see whether Roman rule is desirable or not,' and he promised to extend the book right up to the upheavals of 146.[9]

He was echoing the thoughts of many Romans. In 157 the senate was believed to have started a Dalmatian war deliberately just to prevent the Italians becoming effeminate in the long peace.[10] But the great debate was whether or not to launch a final war against Carthage. Cato, worried about weakness and luxury at home, called for the destruction of the enemy because he thought it wisest 'to remove all outward dangers when we have so many inner ones at home'. Yet against him Scipio Nasica argued that the Romans were becoming insolent and only fear of Carthage would keep the mob in check, a line of thought praised by Saint Augustine 600 years later in a curious example of the continuity of Roman ideas.[11]

Part of the problem was the vast wealth now flowing into Rome. The spoils won by Manlius Vulso in Asia were used to repay the national debt outstanding from the war against Hannibal. Direct taxation of citizens was abandoned after Pydna. In 157 the Roman treasury contained the equivalent of 25,000,000d. in gold and silver bullion and coin.[12]

Later writers picked out 'the lust for money and so for empire' as the cancers which now began to destroy the ancient virtues. The elder Scipio, it was said, showed the way to power, the younger to luxury. 'Luxury was born when Carthage was destroyed, for the fates had conspired to make the Romans both eager and able to turn to a life of corruption.' Bribery became a serious problem.[13]

The money that flooded in, along with slaves and works of art, from Carthage and the east, financed development in Italian agriculture and in banking and trading across the whole Mediterranean world. It paid for rebuilding and decorating the new capital of the world, and for roads to link it to its subjects. The public spending boom of the 170s was repeated after 146, when Metellus, conqueror of Macedon, built Rome's first two marble temples. Mummius 'filled Rome with statues' after his sack of Corinth. Marcius Rex spent a colossal 45,000,000*d.* on his great high-level aqueduct, the wonder of the age, to relieve the thirst of the fast-growing city.[14]

Polybius refers to the 'almost innumerable' contracts for public works, which brought jobs and business 'for almost everybody'. Much plunder also went straight into private hands. Generals and provincial governors could make fortunes, and even private soldiers might earn the best part of a year's pay as bonus after a good war, as well as the loot they carried off in their knapsacks. Soldiers who fought against Philip or Antiochus became rich, and their example inspired young men to volunteer for the war against Perseus. The spending of all this money helped finance small-scale industry of every kind, providing steady jobs for urban workers as well as the skilled slaves from the east, and bringing growth to Italy's rural cities as well as Rome itself.[15]

To the traditionally frugal Romans such wealth naturally seemed a bad influence. Accusations of avarice, corruption and extravagance became more common. Ineffectual laws were passed to prevent bribery and to curtail private spending on banquets and entertainment. Along with eastern luxuries the rich cultural heritage of Greek art and literature was pouring over Italy, but this brought its own problems too. Teachers of philosophy were twice expelled from the city, and in 155 old men were as shocked as the young ones were entranced by the subtle arguments of the great philosopher Carneades who had come as head of an embassy from Athens. Roman play-writing began to ape Greek: the Adelphi of Terence was performed at the funeral games of Aemilius Paullus in 160. But when the censors of 154 decided to build the city's first permanent theatre the senate had it torn down on a motion by Scipio Nasica, arguing that it could only do harm to public morals.

Coarser Roman tastes were also developing. At the funeral of Flamininus thirty-seven pairs of gladiators had fought to entertain the people. Even Scipio, patron of the new cultural movement, thought fit to celebrate the sack of Carthage by throwing captured deserters and fugitive slaves to the wild beasts.[16]

A more selfish note in foreign policy was becoming apparent, too. The Italian allies received a less than generous share in the fruits of empire and fell into a more subordinate status, piling up another problem for the Gracchans. Roman commanders forced cash out of neutral powers, made unjustified attacks on peaceful tribesmen, and sold whole nations into slavery.[17] In the decades after Pydna Roman commissioners disposed of the fates of free cities and ancient kingdoms, fomented dissension even within their old allies such as Rhodes and Pergamum, and, suspicious of any sign of strength in any quarter of the world, arrogantly interpreted constitutions and treaties according to what suited themselves.

'For this is now the typical pattern of Roman diplomacy,' wrote Polybius. 'They exploit the mistakes of others and in practice increase and consolidate their own power while at the same time conferring favours and apparent benefits on their dupes.'[18] The destruction of Carthage and Corinth showed the intolerance, even though Rome did not seek annexation for its own sake. After 146 Rome still had only six organized provinces under her direct rule: Sicily, Sardinia-Corsica, Macedonia, Africa (Carthage), and northern and southern Spain. The rest of the world was left to stew in the unsatisfactory dependent role of 'client states', which seemed to give Rome whatever rights she chose but none of the responsibilities of government.

*

In the east, where wars were infrequent, short and profitable, such attitudes were merely corrupting. In the rugged mountains of Spain they were almost disastrous and it was the Spanish war that most directly created the tensions that exploded into the Gracchan revolution.

Greed and stubbornness kept Rome in Spain, which had been the economic pivot of the later Carthaginian empire, with its corn and iron and salt, and the vast silver mines near New Carthage where Polybius saw 40,000 miners at work yielding the Roman people a revenue of 8,000,000d. a year. If this was indeed clear profit it meant the silver mines alone would pay the complete wage bill for the 45,000 or so citizen soldiers that Rome mobilized in the average year.[19]

But the Spaniards were reluctant to yield either wealth or freedom, and their obstinacy brought out the worst in the Romans. As early as 171 a special law court had had to be set up to investigate Spanish complaints that Roman officials had broken the rules laid down by Gracchus. Nobody was convicted but the rules were re-emphasized for the future.

But when war broke out again in 154 standards fell rapidly, and this was the turning point picked out by the historian Calpurnius Piso Frugi, 'Piso the Honest', as the moment from which 'all morality was overthrown'.[20]

The war began with two years of disasters, in which Rome

lost 25,000 troops. In northern Spain the great soldier Marcellus fought successfully and agreed with the tribes to restore the peace of Gracchus, but the senate insisted on total surrender. Lucullus brought out a further army (including Scipio), broke the peace, and treacherously massacred 20,000 Spaniards who had already agreed to surrender to him, a deed which 'brought infamy on the Roman name'.

In the south, Sulpicius Galba lost 7,000 men, signed a truce with the Lusitanian army, and when they laid down their arms, butchered them on the spot. Few escaped, but one who did became the national hero Viriathus. The revolt flared up again, costing the Romans 8,000 more men in two years, and it took Scipio's natural brother Fabius Aemilianus to steady the situation for a moment in 144.[21]

But only for a moment. Fabius was succeeded in the south by his adoptive brother Fabius Servilianus, who ran into further trouble, until, trapped against a mountain wall by Viriathus, he was compelled to sign a treaty of peace and alliance, as between equals. Although ratified by the Roman people, the treaty was considered disgraceful. Q. Servilius Caepio, the natural brother of Servilianus, won the senate's permission to reopen the war in the south and found the only practicable solution, in 139, by bribing three of Viriathus' friends to slit his throat as he slept fully armed. Caepio's successor in the south settled Viriathus' followers, probably in the town of Valencia, and peace, such as it was, was restored.[22]

Northern Spain was still in turmoil, though. Metellus, the conqueror of Macedon, managed to limit the resistance to the area round the hill-town of Numantia, near the headwaters of the Douro. His successor, Pompeius, fought with some difficulty but at last persuaded the Numantines to agree a peace and even pay over some money. Yet this too was denounced in Rome as a disgraceful peace. Nothing less than total victory would do, and M. Popillius Laenas, the consul for 139, was sent out to start up the war yet again. Rome's word had been broken over and over again, but the greatest disgrace was still to come.[23]

*

At home the war had already produced terrible political strains, to be examined in the next chapter. Disputes about recruitment, the rights of magistrates, and the responsibility for broken faith, tore the city apart. And now the stormy issue of peace or war was to break about the head of young Tiberius Gracchus.

In summer 138 the Roman people, voting in their assembly of tribes, in the fields of the Campus Martius outside the walls of the city, elected Tiberius to the office of quaestor. On 5 December he entered the position which was to hurl him into public controversy. He was just twenty-five years old, though already an experienced soldier.

The quaestor's job was originally financial. By now twelve were elected every year, and it was the custom for a senior commander overseas to take a quaestor with him. The command in northern Spain was given to the consul C. Hostilius Mancinus, and who better to take with him than the man whose father and grandfather had successfully made both war and peace in this most difficult of countries?

But the new Spanish expedition was ill-omened from the start. When the consul was offering the initial sacrifice the sacred chickens escaped and flew out of their cage. When boarding his ship in the harbour of Hercules (possibly at Monaco) he heard a mysterious cry, 'Remain, Mancinus'. Shaken, he disembarked and took ship at Genoa, to meet another bad sign. A snake was found on the ship, and escaped from capture.[24]

Mancinus, says Plutarch, was not a bad man, but the unluckiest of generals. Frequently he was beaten in the field, although always the good sense and bravery of Tiberius shone out in the middle of disaster. It was just as noticeable that the talented young quaestor persisted in showing all due respect and deference to a commander who had soon reached his wits' end, floundering in difficult country against a cunning enemy.

One terrible night a rumour reached the consul that the Numantines who already hemmed in his camp were about to receive massive reinforcements from friendly tribes. Rashly he tried one of the most difficult manoeuvres of war, to shift his camp secretly at night in hostile country. His move was discovered, and in the confusion of the night the Spaniards pressed on him from all sides, cut down stragglers and forced the Romans into even worse country. Mancinus brought his army to an old Roman campsite, which was not fortified nor prepared in any way. Dawn broke. The enemy was all around, and there was no way of escape.

At least 20,000 Romans were trapped—one account says 40,000—ensnared by only 4,000 Spaniards. Terrified at the thought that the whole army would perish, the consul sent heralds to sue for peace, but after years of broken treaties the

Spaniards insisted that the only man in the army that they would deal with was young Tiberius Gracchus. They respected what they had seen of him in the war, but above all they remembered his great father who had fought them so well and then personally made sure that his peace was fairly and justly maintained.

Tiberius crossed into the enemy lines, negotiated terms, and signed the truce. The formal terms acknowledged full equality between the two sides. The Romans kept their lives but all their equipment was carried off by the Spaniards. To double the insurance, they insisted that the consul back up the peace with a solemn personal oath.[25]

By his own efforts Tiberius had saved a large Roman army. Once it was safely departed, he went back to the city of Numantia to ask as a personal favour for the return of his official account books, without which he would not be able to give a proper account of his tenure of office and so might expose himself to personal attack in Rome. The Numantines could not have been more affable. They asked him always to treat them and trust them as friends, feasted him royally inside the city, gave him his account books and offered him his personal belongings as well. Of these he was careful to take nothing but some incense used for public sacrifices; then, exchanging every promise of friendship, he rejoined the army.[26]

It was not surprising that he returned home in a state of exaltation, hoping for some recognition of his services to the state. His reception was shockingly different. If other treaties in Spain had been disgraceful, what was this but an unthinkable act of surrender, the most ignominious of all?[27] The point at issue seems to have been that the Numantines were rebels and must be forced to surrender, and Rome would accept nothing else. This was the stubbornness that had won an empire, and in this equation the jeopardized lives of Mancinus and 20,000 soldiers were of no account.

A furious debate now raged. Mancinus was put on trial. He and his friends argued that he could have done nothing else in such a situation. The defeat was not his fault because of the appalling state in which Pompeius had left the army, the very dregs of the levy, inexperienced and badly trained. The bad omens were remembered and blamed on the illegality of the war itself, which had been started in breach of the peace of Pompeius. Numantine ambassadors came to the walls of Rome and pleaded their own good faith to Rome in the past, pointed out the injustices they had suffered and the perfidy of

Pompeius, and begged for kind treatment now in return for sparing Mancinus and the army.

All was in vain. Even the friends and relatives of the rescued soldiers, while flocking to thank Tiberius for saving them, insisted that the consul was to blame for the disgrace. The senate refused to accept the treaty and the peace was torn up. But now the state had to be absolved from the religious guilt involved in Mancinus' broken oath. And so, in accordance with a decree of the senate, the people voted to ship the wretched man back to Spain and hand him over naked and bound to the Numantines in expiation. The proud Spaniards refused to accept this miserable offering, when they had had 20,000 Romans at their mercy, and Mancinus returned in ignominy to Rome.

But where now stood Tiberius Gracchus? He came within an ace of condemnation himself, and according to Plutarch it was only for his sake that the people voted to spare the other officers and staff. But the hand of Scipio can be seen plainly in the affair. The official inquiry during 136 was conducted by Scipio's close friend, the consul Furius Philus, with Scipio and another friend Laelius as advisers. It was also Philus who actually took Mancinus to Spain to hand him over.

Mancinus' cousin Lucius had already had a row with Scipio at Carthage (and won enough popular support to be elected consul for 145 while Scipio was still fighting), but this family counted for little in Rome. A Sempronius Gracchus was in a very different category. Scipio was credited with helping to save Tiberius and the other officers but blamed for not supporting either the commander or the peace that his kinsman had signed.[28]

The conclusion seems clear, that it was the unbending Scipio, wrapped up in his dreams of his invincible ancestors, who was determined that Rome should not compromise but force the Spaniards into surrender, cost what it might. For a year later, with ultimate victory in Spain apparently further away than ever, Scipio achieved what may have been a long-planned goal. The Roman people, weary beyond measure of the appalling war, at last gave the job to the only man who looked capable of winning it, Scipio himself.[29]

Senate and tribunes co-operated to release Scipio from the laws which now forbade anyone to be twice a consul. Elected consul for 134, he took out to Spain a whole troop of friends, clients and volunteers from foreign kingdoms. He besieged and in 133 finally destroyed the city of Numantia, bringing a savage and merciless end to the Spanish war that had so tortured the Roman people.

It was while Scipio was far away overseas and busy with war that Tiberius Gracchus took his revenge.

Tiberius had suffered a terrible humiliation, and this was the spark that turned his ambitions into something so far beyond the normal aims of public life. About this the ancients were agreed.

Cicero was in no doubt, for instance. 'It was his humiliation over the Numantine treaty that enraged Tiberius Gracchus against the good men of the state and determined him on his riotous tribunate.' Or again, 'Tiberius Gracchus was filled with resentment and apprehension by the unpopularity of the Numantine treaty and the harshness of the senate in rejecting it: and that was what drove so brave and distinguished a man to break away from the honourable policies of his fathers.'

Dio spelled it out in more detail.

All Tiberius' advantages of birth and upbringing only drove him farther along the path of ambition, and once he had turned away from the respectable cause he found himself dragged into the very opposite camp.

For when his treaty with the Numantines had been voted down, and so far from receiving any rewards he came near to being handed over himself, then he made up his mind that deeds were valued not according to their worth or genuineness but by mere chance. So this road to fame he abandoned as insecure, and since he was eager to become a leader in one way or another, he attached himself to the cause of the common people rather than the senate because the prospects looked better.

Plutarch softened the point a little. 'The disagreement between Scipio and Tiberius arose mainly from Tiberius' ambition and the friends and intellectuals who urged him on. But this brought no irreparable damage, for my view is that Tiberius would never have suffered as he did if only Scipio had been in Rome during his tribunate.'[30]

The reliability of these judgements, seeking as they do to show how so good a man came to such a bad end, can only be tested against the events of the next few chapters. But the effect of the whole affair on a proud young Roman noble cannot be minimized. The clients that such a man inherited from his father were a major part of his political power. Gracchus the censor had put tribes of Spain and Sardinia as well as eastern kings under such a personal obligation, and the family honour had been staked at Numantia. It had been treated as worthless by Scipio and the other Romans. Gracchus' dignity had been trampled on, his trustworthiness impugned, while the tribesmen who had sworn friendship with him were annihilated. There could be no greater justification than this for personal revenge in aristocratic Rome.

The anger fell on fertile ground. For there was a cause and there were allies ready to hand, and a crisis on a scale that could now justify the most extreme measures in the interests of the Roman people.

In the late summer of the year 134 Tiberius Gracchus was elected tribune of the people for 133. The revolution was about to begin.

4 The Storm Breaks

The motives that drove Tiberius Gracchus to the edge of revolution have been long a subject of heated debate. Was it a bitter personal grievance, a true sympathy with the sufferings of the poor, or just a cynical bid for power by a close-knit group of families? But this is an artificial debate. What made it a revolutionary situation was the fact that so many problems came to a head simultaneously, at a time when feelings on both sides had become so strong that men would not withdraw until blood had been shed. For this the Spanish War must bear the principal share of the blame.

The war was the midwife of revolution. It was the stresses of the war that made all Rome's problems so much worse, and took them beyond the apparent ability of the existing political system to solve. The war built up the sense of popular grievance and the pressure for constitutional change. It brought together a group of distinguished men, whose dissatisfaction with what was being done made them determined for change. And it produced a brilliant leader in Tiberius Gracchus, to whom the Mancinus affair gave a furious impetus that took the whole political movement a long way farther than anyone can have originally expected. Such is the genesis of revolution.

Tiberius was crushed and killed by the nobles, and afterwards execrated as the wildest of revolutionaries. Yet he was as noble as any of them, and supported by others of the highest rank. Merely listing his principal known supporters, those who reached consular rank, shows what a powerful political group this was. It did not come together by chance or overnight, though, for its four leading men came from those very four families whose co-operation during two previous generations has already been noted.

Chief among the group was Appius Claudius Pulcher, after Scipio the most important man in Rome, consul in 143, censor, and leader of the senate. He was the son of the C. Claudius whose career had been intertwined with that of the elder Gracchus, and his daughter married young Tiberius Gracchus.

The eminent lawyer P. Mucius Scaevola was actually consul during 133. He was son of the consul of 175, and a future high priest.

Another future high priest and consul was P. Licinius Crassus Dives Mucianus, Scaevola's natural brother, adopted into the wealthy Crassus family. His daughter married Gaius Gracchus and Crassus himself. may have married into the Claudian family.[1]

Fourth of these family allies was M. Fulvius Flaccus, nephew of the consuls of 179, and himself consul in 125, from when he became Gaius Gracchus' leading supporter.

In addition to these four attested supporters, another Claudius was consul in 130 and four other Fulvii held that office in 159, 153, 135 and 134. One of these was censor with Appius in 136. Tribunes named Claudius and Licinius are also to be found supporting the group at various moments.

Closely linked with them was Ser. Sulpicius Galba, consul in 144, an old enemy of Aemilius Paullus and one of the most persuasive speakers of the day. His son Gaius also married a daughter of Crassus.

Two other known supporters were young men who became consuls much later, C. Papirius Carbo in 120 and Scipio's own nephew C. Porcius Cato in 114. There was also an ex-consul, 'Mallius', who in view of that family's known historical links with the Fulvii may have been one of the Manlius Torquatus brothers who held that office back in the 160s.

Some of these men will become more solid figures as the story develops, while others are little more than names. The nearest we have to a group portrait can be drawn from Cicero's account of the great public speakers who had dominated Roman life up to his own day.

Galba was noted by Cicero as 'beyond any doubt the pre-eminent public speaker of the day', and the first to develop an elaborate and highly emotional manner of speaking. Crassus was a hard-working and accomplished speaker who, as a Mucius by birth, had naturally mastered the study of law and was much in demand as a counsel or advocate. Scaevola was a man of great wisdom and a penetrating mind. Appius was eloquent though perhaps too forceful. Fulvius and the young Cato are dismissed as mediocre speakers only. But as for Tiberius Gracchus and his brilliant contemporary Carbo, 'Would that their statesmanship had been comparable to their eloquence, for then nobody would have surpassed them in glory. Whereas in the end Gracchus was killed by the state itself, and after a lifetime of rabble-rousing Carbo only saved himself from the courts by taking his own life.'[2]

Like Tiberius Gracchus, these were men whose ancestors had built and governed Rome over the centuries. Only a great crisis could have brought them to support the tribunate of 133. The Spanish War precipitated such a crisis in almost every aspect of Roman life, military, economic, social and political.

*

One result of the war persists to this day. From 153 onwards consuls took up their year of office on 1 January instead of the traditional 15 March, to permit them to reach their provincial commands in good time to start the spring campaigning.[3] But the next development was more serious in tone.

The indomitable citizen soldiers who had built Rome's empire were already becoming hard to find and harder to discipline. Determined generals like Paullus, Metellus or Scipio found they had to make a special effort to bring their troops under control. The disastrous opening of the Spanish War led to a near panic in 151. Citizens complained at the draft procedure, no doubt because the consuls were trying to pick out the most experienced men for the war. The tribunes tried to secure exemption for the aggrieved men; the consuls refused to listen; and so the tribunes threw the consuls into jail.

For a tightly disciplined military state this was an incredible step, to imprison the heads of state. Certainly the tribunes had a duty to help ill-treated citizens, for whom they kept their doors open night and day during their year of office, and traditionally this included protection against unfair recruiting. But earlier in the century a basis had always been found for compromise: this time a sense of real injustice compounded the fears of the unpleasant war, and the senate had to back down. It ruled that from now on the troops would be selected in the only fair way, by drawing lots. And it took the example of Scipio to bring forward volunteers for positions as officers.[4]

In the development of the tribunes' powers an important milestone had been passed, unleashing a flurry of activity to which the evidence gives us scattered clues. The use of the lot may have been part of a series of laws, forced through by these or allied tribunes, which possibly included a reduction in the period of overseas service to a maximum of six years at a stretch, the extension to soldiers in the field of a citizen's normal right of appeal against severe punishment, and a lowering of the property qualification for serving in the army. Military service was still regarded as a duty of the propertied classes only, but the lower limit was brought down to only 400*d.*, less than half in face value and much less in real terms than it had once been. Rome was having to scrape the barrel for her troops for the gravest of reasons: her total manpower was falling.[5]

The census figures collected every five years were now declining from the peak of 337,000 reached in 164. Whether this figure included all adult male citizens or only those qualified for military service is not clear, though probably the latter in practice if not in theory. The birth-rate itself was slipping, but what mattered more, and became a central theme of the reform programme, was that under economic change more of the citizens were drifting into landless status. Veterans who came home from long service to find their land overgrown and unusable were almost as direct a loss to the effective manpower reserves as the thousands who actually fell in battle. And so the army desperately needed access to as many of the citizens as possible even if it was still unthinkable to recruit the very poorest.[6]

The unpopular burden imposed on Rome's limited manpower by the endless fighting of the 140s brought concern over recruiting to fever heat. This was why tribunes insisted in 148 that Scipio be elected consul and given the Carthaginian command, despite the senate's reluctance to flout precedent, for if the war had to be fought it needed to be fought properly. It explains the special exemptions given in 145 to all who had fought in Macedon, Greece or Africa, so that instead of hardened veterans Fabius had to take young men to Spain who had never seen war before, and precious little use they were until they had spent an entire year training.[7]

This surge of popular and tribunician pressure must have led to a reaction for which we have only indirect evidence. Probably in the early 140s the Aelian and Fufian laws were passed, which made it easier to obstruct legislation on religious grounds, by scanning the sky for unfavourable omens. They forbade legislation altogether in the weeks before elections, when the temptation to pass partisan laws might be at its greatest. Cicero afterwards described these laws as 'our surest defence against the furies of the tribunes' and Asconius explained that they were meant to block 'pernicious legislation'. Legislation by tribunes to interfere with the recruiting procedures is precisely what they would have regarded as pernicious, and it can only be assumed that this was what those two famous laws, not repealed until Julius Caesar's time, were designed to counteract.[8]

Yet these new laws were themselves attacked in 145, when the tribune C. Crassus, cousin to Mucianus, proposed to make the priestly colleges open to popular election rather than co-opted membership. This would have established popular control over the new powers of religious obstruction, but in a brilliant speech Scipio's close friend Laelius persuaded the superstitious Romans to stick to their old ways. Yet Crassus found another way to strengthen the voice of the people, by arranging that the votes of the tribes be taken in the wider spaces of the central forum instead of the original assembly area, cramped in front of the senate house.[9]

The people's judiciary powers were also under pressure. A legal battle broke out over the head of Galba, for his alleged massacre or enslavement of Spaniards who had surrendered to him. Even Cicero seems unsure of his guilt, and Rome's most histrionic politician escaped by appealing to the people and parading his young sons before them with tears in his eyes. The affair reeked of political intrigue, for Galba was a close friend to Mucianus (whose political career he had assisted and into whose family his son married) and his leading supporter in the lawsuit was the ex-consul Q. Fulvius Nobilior. While who were Galba's prosecutors? Aemilius Paullus, whose harsh disciplinary methods he had denounced twenty years before; the aged Cato, also an old enemy of Fulvius; and Scipio himself.

Galba escaped, but as a result of the dispute the tribune Piso Frugi managed to pass a law establishing the first permanent law court, to deal with all cases of misbehaviour or extortion in the provinces on the lines of the special court in 171. The new court was manned by senators and from it there was no appeal to the people, who might always be ready to acquit a popular figure such as Galba. Control of an important part of the legal system had changed hands and it was to take Gaius Gracchus to reverse the new bias—Gaius Gracchus, kinsman to Crassus and so to Galba, and a bitter opponent of Piso.[10]

*

The problems that were to dominate the Gracchan era were now crowding in on the harassed city; and Tiberius Gracchus was growing up. But before the storm broke, Scipio had his own try at resolving the darkening situation. Much might have been expected from this compelling figure, who in some ways seemed a throwback to the heroes of the past—self-controlled, a harsh disciplinarian, brave and desperately ambitious, his record made him arrogant but also popular, as his electoral successes showed. But he had also been exposed to the widest of the new cultural influences. Brought up among Greek schoolmasters and sportsmen, he was a close friend of the historian Polybius and the Stoic philosopher Panaetius, a patron of the playwright Terence and the satirical poet Lucilius. Cicero revered the memory of Scipio and portrayed him as the most selfless of heroes, and as leader of a brilliant intellectual circle hunting for the solutions to the problems of the age. In real life, unhappily, Scipio never found them.

In fact his political support was never as widely based or secure as his personal popularity might suggest. Even as he triumphed over Carthage one of his opponents, L. Hostilius Mancinus, won a consular election by claiming that Scipio had done him out of his fair share of the credit for the victory.[11] The following year Galba became consul, along with another hostile figure, Aurelius Cotta, later prosecuted by Scipio for extortion. At least Scipio was influential enough to prevent either of them from taking over the Spanish command from his brother Fabius.[12]

In 143 Scipio's greatest rival became consul, Appius Claudius, father-in-law of Tiberius Gracchus. Appius was the head of Rome's proudest family, one which finally claimed no less than twenty-eight consulates as well as four out of the first five emperors. They traced their ancestry back to the Sabine leader Attius Clausus, who had fled to Rome in 504, but despite an early record of harshness towards the people the family owed its greatness to the blind censor Claudius Caecus who in 312 had won popular support by reforming the voting procedure and bringing low-born citizens into the senate.[13]

The Claudian had always been a maverick family, impatient of the pretensions of other noble houses, and Appius was no exception. After a mixed year's campaigning in the Alps he was greeted with the humiliating news that the senate refused him the funds to celebrate a triumph. This was not enough to check a Claudius. He promptly held a private triumph on his own account, with his daughter beside him in the triumphal car. As a Vestal Virgin her person was sacred, so that not even a hostile tribune dared to interfere with his progress.[14]

A year later Appius and Scipio fought a great electoral battle for the censorship, which each proud noble felt was his due. To counter Scipio's popularity Appius seems to have had more support among the nobles, and Plutarch tells of how he sneered at Scipio for coming into the forum surrounded by men of low rank and birth, charging that his great father would never have stooped so low. On a different tack, Appius claimed to know more citizens by name than Scipio did, to which Scipio grandly replied that his own ambition was not to know many people but to be unknown to nobody. Once again the propertied electors, voting in their centuries, gave Scipio their support and his chance to restore the city's moral tone—the traditional duty of a censor in times of crisis.[15]

The result fell sadly short. After a stern and solemn opening speech Scipio tried to expel certain senators and deprived some knights of their status, for perjury, extravagance or homosexuality, but his mild and easy-going colleague Mummius stopped him. The censorship fizzled out. While Mummius adorned the city with his Greek plunder Scipio's only permanent achievement was to build the stone arches for the Aemilian bridge, one of which can still be seen precariously standing in the Tiber as the Ponte Rotto.[16]

During this unhappy year Scipio lost an important supporter, the low-born Q. Pompeius, who suddenly decided to try for consul himself in opposition to Scipio's closest friend Laelius. Despite Scipio's sneers it was Pompeius who won the election, by the well tried technique of walking about and cordially shaking the hands of as many voters as possible.[17] This probably wrecked Scipio's last attempt at reform, for on finally becoming consul in 140 Laelius proposed measures for tackling the drift from the land, but quickly dropped them when they produced uproar in the senate. But if he had brought them in the previous year, as intended, with the moral support of Scipio still censor, then he might well have pressed the matter further. As it was, his withdrawal earned him the surname of Sapiens, the Prudent, and the problem was left to Tiberius Gracchus.[18]

Scipio lost further support. To this period must be dated Tiberius Gracchus' marriage to the daughter of Appius, marking a final break with his kinsman Scipio, while Metellus the conqueror of Macedon also fell out with Scipio over some question of public policy. And now, since the bickering at home had still done nothing to ease the burden of the war, the issue of peace came into the forefront of politics.[19]

*

After further Roman defeats Sevilianus had made peace in

southern Spain in 140, as we have seen, and Pompeius did the same in the north in the following year. Both of these treaties were labelled disgraceful and torn up by the senate, which insisted on carrying on the war. Both times Q. Servilius Caepio figured as a leader of the war party, as consul in 140 renewing the war in the south and then on his return to Rome joining in a rancorous though unsuccessful prosecution of Pompeius.[20]

But Caepio was not unopposed. Appius Claudius secured a senatorial decree to prevent more than one levy a year, so obstructing Caepio's attempt to reopen the war, while the tribune Claudius Asellus actually tried to veto Caepio's departure. The impatient Caepio had the way cleared at sword's point, another infringement of the tribune's inviolability and a display of arrogance that was repeated in Spain, where apart from the murder of Viriathus his tenure of command was most notable for disciplinary methods so harsh that his troops tried to burn him alive in his tent.[21] Like Pompeius and Appius, Asellus was a bitter personal enemy of Scipio, who as censor had charged him with extravagance and wickedness and in return was prosecuted by him on religious grounds, escaping only with some difficulty.[22] There seems clearly to have been a concerted attempt by the two Claudii to prevent Caepio restarting the war, and it is not too much to believe that the reforming group were beginning to regard peace in Spain as a target in its own right.

In 138 came the last attempt to block the levy by direct action. The consuls involved were Nasica and Brutus, who both turned out be violent enemies of the Gracchan movement. They began by rounding up deserters from the Spanish wars, beating them with rods and selling them into slavery for a penny apiece. They then refused to make any exemptions from the levy, and in retaliation the tribunes Licinius and Curiatus followed the example of 151 and flung these consuls too into prison, presumably for trying again to override the tribunician veto.[23]

As arguments raged about the rights of the people and their champions the tribunes, the whole system of government was coming into question, and other far-reaching changes followed. In 139 the tribune Gabinius, the grandson of a slave, passed a law to introduce secret written ballots into elections, and two years later the tribune Cassius extended the principle to all trials before the people other than for treason. The secret ballot, which was later extended to all legislative voting by the Gracchan politician Carbo, was regarded as a dangerous and revolutionary innovation. Cicero violently abused these moves, speaking of the mischief they caused and criticizing Cassius for 'standing apart from the good men and always seeking the applause of the mob for his popular policies'.

'Everyone knows,' Cicero argued, 'that the authority of the good men has been destroyed by these voting laws . . . and the people should never have been given such a hiding place in which to conceal a mischievous vote and so keep the good men ignorant of their opinions.' No 'good man' had ever supported such a law, and indeed that of Cassius was passed only with some difficulty, for 'the people thought their liberty was at stake but the leaders of the state disagreed, fearing that the rashness of the mob and the freedom of the secret votes would be a danger to the good men'.[24]

What happened was that the consul Lepidus and another tribune, Briso, tried to block Cassius' proposal, and curiously it was Cicero's hero Scipio who persuaded Briso to let it through, to the annoyance of some other nobles. This helps to explain why latterday popular leaders sometimes claimed Scipio himself, as well as Cassius, Pompeius and the Gracchans, as their own political ancestors. The point at issue seems to have been that the tribune's right of veto was intended to protect individuals, and if instead Briso was using it to prevent the people from passing whatever law they wished then he was breaking with precedent and Scipio was wise to caution him.

The rights of tribunes had already been under pressure, but the principle of the Roman constitution was that the people were sovereign and the tribunes were their champions and now was not the time to breach it. For it was the breach of this very principle in 133, in the absence of Scipio overseas, that turned an argument about Gracchan farm reform into a blazing and bloody constitutional battle.[25]

The issue of peace or war in Spain was now drawing to its climax. Brutus and Popillius (cousin of another Gracchan enemy) pressed ahead with the war. Peace terms were signed by Tiberius Gracchus and Hostilius Mancinus, cousin to Scipio's old enemy. Lepidus reopened hostilities, unprovoked and unsuccessful, for which he was recalled and fined. Scipio's friend Furius Philus headed the Mancinus inquiry and then carried on the war, followed by Q. Piso, probably cousin to the conservative Piso Frugi.

Finally in 134 Scipio took the war in hand, and brought it to a successful conclusion in 133—too late to prevent the Gracchan explosion which the war had done so much to bring about. And yet so reduced was Rome's power that when Scipio set off for Spain the senate refused to give him either ready cash or the right to levy fresh troops.[26]

*

The Spaniards were beaten; yet the Spaniards had split Rome irretrievably into two. It was the Spanish War that first revealed how the Roman government was ceasing to cope. It was now that the charge of incompetence in the ruling families, as well as of greed and cruelty, began to be justified. The evidence shows plainly what some modern scholars have been curiously reluctant to admit, that it was under the stresses of this war that Roman politics began to polarize into the two great factions of the late republic.

On the one hand a conservative group had inherited the mantle of Cato and Aemilius Paullus. Men like the brutal Q. Caepio and the honest Piso Frugi, like Nasica, Brutus and Lepidus, like Scipio (despite his exceptional personal position) and his friend Laelius and his brother Fabius, these men clung to their belief in the old military virtues and the subordination of the people to the senate's leadership.

Against them was a group that was pressing for change. It was focused on the Gracchan families of Claudius, Fulvius, Mucius Scaevola and Licinius Crassus, but also included Galba, Cassius, Carbo, and perhaps even Metellus and Pompeius for a time. Members of the ruling nobility themselves, these men were not content with the achievements of their peers, they showed more understanding of the problems facing Rome, and by their birth claimed as much say as the conservatives in solving them.

Perhaps some of them felt real sympathy with the interests of the common citizens, perhaps some just saw the popular vote as an alternative source of power. Certainly it would be a mistake to credit either side with a monopoly of altruism or selfishness. Galba may have been as unscrupulous as Q. Caepio, and the high priest Nasica as principled as his successor Scaevola. But the fact remains that there had grown up in Rome, not anything that could be called a united political party, but one loose grouping of nobles that was prepared to stand up for the interests of the people, and another that was prepared to resist them. They tended to split the same way over such issues as corn supply, tribunes' rights, fair recruitment, and peace itself.

According to Cicero, the 'slanderers and enemies of Scipio' were led originally by Crassus and Appius Claudius, and later by Metellus and Scaevola, who kept half the senate opposed to him.[27] And it was into this grouping that Tiberius Gracchus was drawn by his marriage, perhaps by his inclinations and the memory of his independent-minded ancestors, and certainly by his smouldering indignation over the Mancinus affair.

*

During the 140s the Spanish War had imposed the stresses which were to make Rome break out into violence. It had also distracted the city from other problems now yawning, for the 130s brought economic crisis to Rome and open warfare to Italy itself.

There is evidence to suggest that the latter part of the second century saw a general economic decline across the Mediterranean world, as Roman conquests disrupted the complicated trading structure that the Greeks had built up in the wake of Alexander the Great. Prices collapsed, living standards fell, trade declined, up to 140 or 138, from when prices suddenly rose again. During these violent fluctuations social unrest and nationalist revolts can be traced in almost every country of which we have records.[28]

It was in 138 that trouble first struck in Italy, down in the pine forests of Sila in Bruttium, where slaves working on pitch production were charged with the murder of several well known men, an affair serious enough to warrant a special investigation by the consuls.[29] A year or two later slaves broke out in wholesale rebellion, beginning in Italy, where they were quickly put down,[30] but then on a far larger scale on the rich and fruitful island of Sicily. Ill treated and brutalized slaves, many of them employed as herdsmen and long accustomed to sporadic violence, seized control of half the island. Said to have numbered 200,000 they defeated Roman armies and tried to establish an independent state, choosing their own king who even issued his own coins.

Their successes stimulated a tiny outbreak by 150 slaves in Rome, and more serious troubles in Greece and elsewhere. It needed three successive consuls, C. Fulvius Flaccus in 134 followed by Piso Frugi and then Rupilius to bring Sicily back to peace. In 133 there was a more serious rebellion in Italy, involving many thousands of slaves in the region north of Naples, and two senior ex-consuls, Metellus and Cn. Caepio, had to be given a special command to put them down.[31]

The sheer military burden of these frightening wars, so near to home, on top of the Spanish War and the more routine fighting on the other imperial frontiers,[32] was severe enough. Perhaps it fully justified the senate's refusal of troops to Scipio on the grounds that 'Italy would be left deserted'—in other words undefended.[33] But the slave wars served another function. They at last brought attention to bear on the changes that were taking place in the Italian countryside, with the decline of the free peasant farmer and his gradual replacement by hordes of slaves. It was from this theme that the great debate of 133 was to begin.

But the long developing problem of the land was matched in the 130s by a sudden and very pressing crisis in the city of Rome itself. Rome had become a great commercial and manufacturing centre, into which slaves and freemen alike had been drawn, from Italy and the provinces, to produce clothing and armaments and furniture, to man the docks and shops and the houses of the rich, and to build the temples and aqueducts and crowded tenement buildings.

The opportunities for employment in the capital city of the world were enormous, particularly after the great inflow of foreign money after 167 and 146. A drift to the city helped accelerate the depopulation of the land, and the pattern of agriculture shifted, at least in the areas near to Rome, towards the more profitable vines, olives and livestock. The swollen city had to buy half of its grain from overseas, from Africa, Egypt, and above all from Sicily, Cato's 'storehouse of the nation, the nurse who feeds the Roman people'.[34]

But in the 130s this urban prosperity seems to have taken a sharp turn for the worse. The wars of the moment were costly and unprofitable. The outburst of new public building seems to have slowed down, with no major construction between 138 and 125. Because slaves were cheaper, as well as more skilled, the burden of unemployment must have fallen on the citizen poor, who were also badly hurt by the steady depreciation of the bronze coins of everyday use in relation to the silver coinage now rising in economic importance. Around 140 the silver denarius was officially revalued to equal 16 instead of 10 bronze asses, a move which may have been forced on the state but can only have helped people who owned silver or were paid in it.[35]

At this worst possible time the slave war broke out in Sicily. As soon as grain prices began to rise in 138, the tribune Curiatus urged that the state take steps to buy corn for the city, but this novel proposal was apparently quashed by

Nasica, one of the consuls who also fell foul of Curiatus over the recruiting dispute. But the shortage of corn quickly grew worse. There is evidence to suggest that grain prices doubled and doubled again in the Mediterranean world during the 130s, and the speculative habits of Roman capitalists could have compounded the local problem.[36]

By 133, with the Spanish and Sicilian wars both unsettled, with the treasury empty, unemployment rife and prices soaring, the Roman poor must have been at starvation point. And still the established government did nothing to help. But votes were now swinging behind the reformist group. In 136 Appius Claudius reached the office of censor which had escaped him in 142, and like Scipio he entered office with high hopes, planning to do harsh and unprecedented things. Unfortunately for him his colleague, the much older Q. Fulvius Nobilior, while undoubtedly a political ally who had helped to defend Galba a decade before, was a milder character, trained by his father to the study of literature and the patronage of poets. Fulvius had no stomach for aggressive politics and seems to have prevented Appius from doing anything startling. But he did establish Appius in the influential position of leader of the senate, and ominously the two recorded the lowest census figure for over thirty years, of just under 318,000.[37]

Next year a Fulvius Flaccus was consul, and in 134 another, perhaps his brother. And while one of the consuls elected for the fateful year of 133 was Piso Frugi, the virtuous and conservative historian, his colleague was the reformist leader Scaevola. With Scipio out of the country and Scaevola consul; with Appius leader of the senate and Rome's richest and most celebrated lawyer Crassus ready to draw up the legislation; and with the brilliant young tribune Tiberius Gracchus to force it through, the moment for reform had arrived at last.

5 Land for the People

'The nourishing grain runs short, and there is no bread for the people.'

So wrote the satirist Lucilius, who actually lived through the Gracchan period, and who is a surer guide than that romantic imagination which inspired Cicero to write that 'it was in the best of all republics that Tiberius Gracchus sprang up to disturb the tranquillity'.[1]

It was in fact against a background of unemployment, misery and starvation; of popular unrest and dissension in the senate; and of two unfinished wars in Sicily and Spain, that Tiberius Gracchus took office as tribune, on 10 December 134, with less than nine months yet to live.

Early in the new year Tiberius brought forward his land reform bill, proposing to redistribute to the poor much of the publicly owned land that had, over the years, fallen into the occupation of wealthy investors over and above the maximum limits permitted to them by law. The proposal offered a cure for unemployment, for poverty, for the hunger of the overcrowded city; it would restore the countryside of Italy and rebuild the peasant population on which Rome's military greatness had been founded. It offered something for almost every social and economic problem of the age. Only the opposition of those wealthy squatters had to be feared.

*

For a continuous account of the troubles that followed we depend on two books written long after the events, Plutarch's life of Tiberius Gracchus and the first volume of Appian's history of the Civil Wars. Unhappily they differ frequently in detail and emphasis, and where convenient their accounts will be distinguished in this book with a (P) and an (A) respectively.

But both writers agree that land was already a serious problem at Rome.

As the Roman conquests had spread across Italy they regularly seized land and took it into public ownership. This they allocated for cultivation by the poor and landless in return for a small rent (P), or let anyone who wanted work it in return for a payment in kind (A).

Unfortunately the rich began to offer higher rents and drive out the poor (P); acquiring the greater part of the land that had not been distributed they then gradually took over the narrow allotments of the poor either by purchase or by force (A).

The results of the process were disastrous. Once ejected from the land, the poor no longer cared about serving in the army or bringing up children, so that soon the whole of Italy seemed to be empty of free men and filled only with the foreign slaves used to till the land of the rich (P). For cultivating their great tracts of land, instead of single estates, the rich preferred to use slaves because free men might be drawn off into the army. And so the powerful men became wealthy, the slaves filled the countryside, and the Italians dwindled in numbers because of poverty, taxes, and the demands of military service. What escape they had from these evils could only be into idleness because the land was in the hands of the rich and their slave workers (A).

To redress these evils a law was passed forbidding anybody to hold more than 500 Roman acres of land, and for a while this stemmed the greed and helped the poor to remain and cultivate their holdings (P). This law was passed by tribunes, against some opposition, and also forbade one man to pasture more than 100 cattle or 500 sheep on the public land (A). But all in vain, for the rich clung to their land, at first fraudulently, using false names or the names of their relatives, and then in open defiance of the law. And this was the situation which first Laelius and then Tiberius Gracchus attempted to correct.[2]

The picture is a dramatic one, but other evidence suggests that it is largely true. The spread of state-owned land was a regular accompaniment to the long wars of conquest. Friendly communities were welcomed as allies or even absorbed into the citizen body, but others had to surrender as much as a third of their land to the victorious Romans. This public land was much extended after the defeat of Hannibal, at the expense of those Italians who had gone over to the enemy, mainly in Campania and farther south in Bruttium and Lucania, towards the very toe of Italy. Much of this land was used for colonial settlements, in small towns often with a military purpose such as Parma and Bologna, guarding the newly won lands of the fertile Po valley. But especially in the south a great deal of the land was of poorer quality, naturally and because of frequent devastation in war.[3]

This inferior land was not at all suited to traditional small-scale mixed farming, and new forms of agriculture were bound to develop. Indeed, perhaps much of it never passed into the hands of smallholders at all, but quickly found its more profitable use (and one needing far less labour) as pasture land.[4] It was the spread of public land to the south that gave the real boost to stockbreeding in Italy, for there the ranchers found easy access to cool hills in summer and rich low valleys in winter, where they could graze without any regard to the interests of farmers on the spot. On this expropriated rebel territory the cowman was free to displace the ploughman.[5]

Evidence about this land is uncertain, but apart from particular colonization schemes it seems as though a good deal of it was merely left vacant for any citizen to use. The people who could best exploit this situation were plainly the rich, for large-scale pasturing, as well as the new cash crops such as vines and olives, needed heavy investment first before producing their reward later. The rich could most easily find the funds and the slave-labour to develop this neglected and almost depopulated land.[6] It was the rich and well organized creditors of the state who took up allotments of public land in 200 in place of a part-repayment of their loans.[7] But the real financial base came from the vast inflow of money from the east during the wars of the second century—which also brought huge numbers of slaves to Italy, where the slave population may have grown to over half a million.[8]

These slaves were the ideal workers for the big farms, not that they were always much cheaper than free labour, but because the master had them under his firm control without their constantly being taken off to the wars. And so it was on the broad swathes of state-owned land that there began to develop this new phenomenon of large-scale capitalist farming, owned by absentee landlords, managed by skilled slaves and worked by unskilled ones, and providing less and less scope for the free man.

Yet even by mid-century the picture was still varied. Cato wrote that the ideal farm was a hundred acres of mixed soil, but then considered more specialized projects such as a 240-acre olive grove that could be run with only 13 slaves including the overseer, or a 100-acre vineyard requiring 16. But these were run on the assumption that free labourers were within reach and could be hired at harvest-time, and that small free farmers existed to buy second-hand slaves and equipment from the big farmer.[9]

Cato was writing about the west of Italy, and his picture is confirmed by the finds of pottery that have been dug up round the rich Tuscan city of Veii, showing that the land was still occupied by many homesteads rather than a few giant plantations.[10] Of course a rich investor might hold many small farms, each under its own bailiff, but it was probably only in the south that the huge ranch and plantation came into their own and had so great an impact on the life of the community. Much of Italy was still self-sufficient in grain, and the standard Latin word for big farm does not seem to have been used in the Gracchan period.[11]

If the scale of the problem is sometimes exaggerated, though, it is clear that economic forces were running strongly in the capitalist farmer's favour. Perhaps up to 50,000 small farms were created for Romans and their Latin allies in the early part of the second century,[12] but even given a fair run they would not have found it easy to compete with the capital resources, the broad acres and numerous slaves of their wealthy rivals, nor with the cheap Sicilian and other imported grain that was taking over the Roman market.

Bad harvests would throw the small man into debt, recruiting could tear him from his land, and he might understandably prefer to throw in his lot and go off to the plentiful jobs in the big city.[13] By changing his status to that of a landless urban worker he may even have lost his liability to military service too. And so just as crofters from the Scottish Highlands to this day grow tired of eking out with casual labour the inadequate subsistence provided by their wretched plots of land, and drift off to the building sites of Glasgow and the south, so the Roman drifted to Rome. And if he would not drift he could be pushed.

Sallust and Florus tell of free men driven from their land, Seneca speaks of men adding one farm to another by either buying out or forcing out their neighbours, and Frontinus describes how they would extend their land by gradually taking over any neighbouring strips that lay empty. In 173 the consul had to investigate reports that even in the rich Campanian land private citizens were claiming public land as if it were their own, 'so that private greed had an open field in which to spread itself',[14] and the following year a law was passed to bring this back under the control of the censors. By 167 Cato was speaking of the law that restricted holdings of

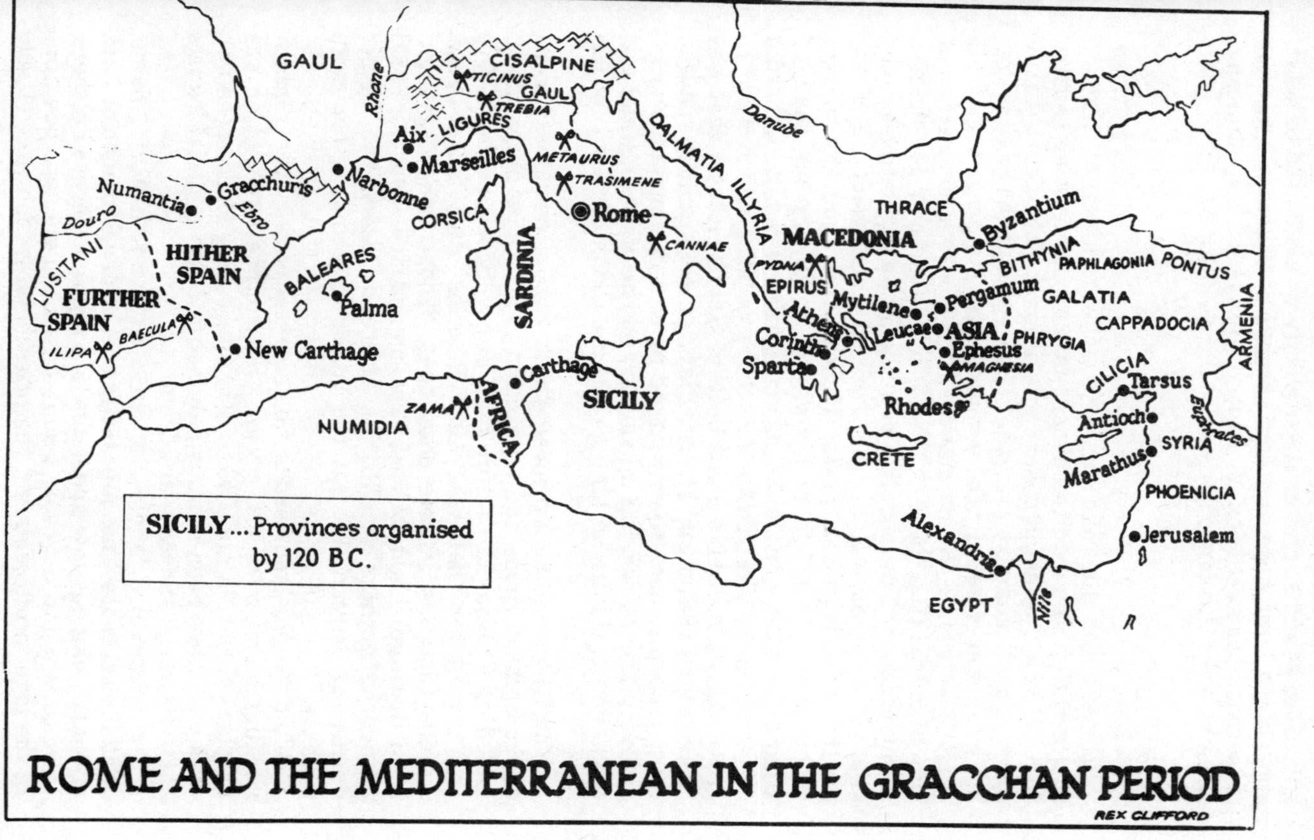

ROME AND THE MEDITERRANEAN IN THE GRACCHAN PERIOD

public land to 500 acres as if everybody would like to break it, and Cicero later observed how the bill of Tiberius Gracchus threatened the expulsion of the rich from their 'long-standing' occupation of this land.[15]

*

So with all due allowance for the touches of literary exaggeration, the traditional account can be accepted as true. Economically the small farmer was becoming obsolete in many parts of the Italian countryside. The wealth of the empire that he had won created the resources to support large-scale capitalist farming, which may well have been a more efficient way of cultivating the land. But it left little room for the free countryman, and more or less voluntarily he began to leave the land. The emptying of the Italian countryside, like the Scottish, had begun. It was as Tiberius Gracchus was passing through Etruria in 137, on his way to Spain, and saw the land almost deserted, and the farms and herds tended by barbarian slaves, that he first conceived those policies which were to prove fatal to himself and his brother Gaius. At least that was the story as Gaius told it, but Plutarch adds that it was the Roman people themselves who did most to inflame his energy and ambition by writing up slogans on the porches, walls and monuments, calling on him 'to recover the public land for the poor'.[16]

'But Tiberius did not draw up the law on his own, for citizens of the highest virtue and reputation joined in its preparation, including Crassus the future high priest, Scaevola the lawyer and consul for that year, and Tiberius' own father-in-law Appius Claudius.' Cicero adds that, 'Those two wisest and most distinguished brothers, Crassus and Scaevola, were said to be the authors of Tiberius Gracchus' laws, the former openly, as we can see, but the latter, it seems, rather more secretly.'[17]

While Appius, as leader of the senate, was the highest ranking member of the group, the emphasis placed on the brothers Scaevola and Crassus is interesting since these two may well have been more widely accepted as political leaders than the tough and arrogant Claudius.

The Scaevola family, of ancient and historic name, contributed more than any other to the development of both civil and religious law under the late republic. These brothers, their cousin and Scaevola's son all reached eminent positions in the legal profession and the priesthood (which were closely intertwined at Rome) and Scaevola was to make his own period as high priest notable for the publication of an 80-volume record of Roman history. Such men were guardians of Rome's past, not revolutionaries, even though their family also patronized the radical Stoic philosopher Blossius of Cumae, another advisor to Tiberius.[18]

The prudent Scaevola was the cooler of the two, as Cicero's comment and later events make clear, but his brother on adoption into the Licinius Crassus family had taken on a rather different tradition. Crassus was to become known as the richest and noblest man in Rome, the best speaker and the best lawyer, as well as high priest. He appears as elegant and accomplished, carefully mastering the law before handling cases himself, yet advising his quieter brother to develop a more forceful manner.[19] He was a cultivated man who could speak Greek in five dialects, and now inherited the immense wealth of the Crassus family which passed on the surname Dives, 'The Rich', from father to son. He may have died worth the huge sum of 6,000,000*d*.[20]

Yet for all its wealth it was a family well known to the Roman people. A Licinius had been one of the very first tribunes elected in 493 to protect the people. Licinius Stolo had been one of the tribunes who led the great constitutional struggle of the fourth century. Within recent years a Licinius Crassus had tried to open the priesthood to popular election in 145 and the tribune S. Licinius had helped throw the harsh consuls of 138 into prison.[21] While, most striking of all these links with the popular cause, it was a Licinian law that had forbidden the holding of more than 500 acres of land and that Tiberius Gracchus was now trying to defend.

When had this law been passed? Appian and Plutarch write as though it had been recent, after the conquest of Italy had been well advanced. But Livy refers it back to the great reforms of Licinius Stolo and Sextius in 367. Cato is reported as speaking familiarly of it in 195, 'what provoked the Licinian law about 500 acres except our limitless greed for extending our estates?' But in 167 he spoke as though it were a fresh source of resentment, 'Surely nobody is punished by the law merely for *wanting* to occupy more than 500 acres or *wanting* to pasture more animals than are allowed.'[22]

It is hard to believe that so large a limit was set as far back as 367, when Roman territory was much smaller and social conditions quite different from those so vividly described by Appian and Plutarch. More probably a land law was passed then (since we know of people prosecuted for breaking it in 298) but tightened up in the early part of the second century, perhaps by yet another member of the Crassus family like the man who was high priest for thirty years or either of the two brothers who became consuls in 171 or 168. In the latter case it could plausibly have been associated with the other political tensions that we have noted in the 170s, and perhaps preceded the special efforts made to drive illegal occupiers off the Campanian land in 173 and 172.[23]

Crassus Mucianus had therefore a close family interest, perhaps a very recent one, in sustaining the law now being so flagrantly broken, and a conscientious lawyer like his brother Scaevola must have tended to the same view. And so once again the extraordinary range of motives that could be brought to the support of the land bill is illustrated. The sanctity of past laws was at stake as well as the sufferings of the poor, the security of Rome's corn supplies as well as the recruiting base for her armies. Here was a chance to ease the disquieting sight of so many unemployed citizens in the town and so many slaves controlling great swathes of countryside. Votes could be won, and a way cleared for a more realistic and forward-looking approach to other Roman problems.

This is the broad base from which any great political movement must always draw its support, from a mixture of motives both immediate and far-sighted, the partial and the disinterested, the sympathetic and the cynical, the urgency of the moment and the stirring memory of struggles long past. How Tiberius' attitudes developed will be seen, but there is no reason to believe that when he embarked on this path he saw all that was to follow, or that not all his ideas were equally shared by all who supported the bill. But it was to promote the land bill that the group had come together, and Tiberius Gracchus was commissioned with the task of pushing it through.

It would have been possible for the consul Scaevola to promote a bill through the assembly of centuries, but that was a rarer and less appropriate procedure, and a consul could more easily fall foul of opposition in the senate, such as had recently defeated Laelius. The assembly of tribes had the real claim to be the voice of the Roman people on an issue as controversial as this; presenting such a law to the assembly of tribes was a tribune's job and Tiberius, with his popularity, his talent, and his ambition, was the ideal tribune. The consul, the leader of the senate, and the galaxy of supporting nobles would add prestige and the votes of their own supporters. Religious problems could be guarded against, for Appius and Tiberius were both augurs while Crassus and Scaevola must already have been priests of some seniority. These two could also provide any legal help needed. With such backing, how could the land bill and the whole reform movement possibly fail?

*

So, 'Tiberius Gracchus proposed his land law, and very welcome it was to the people. The poorer classes thought their fortunes were made.'[24]

The essence of the bill was to renew the old law, that nobody should occupy more than 500 acres of public land. Another 250 acres were allowed for each child. The remainder of the public land was to be divided among the poor by three specially elected commissioners. Plutarch emphasizes the moderation of the proposal, considering that it was directed against injustice and greed. At first it may even have been suggested that those men who deserved to be punished and fined for their illegal occupation of the land should instead be compensated for what they gave up, but this idea, if it was ever serious, was later dropped (P). The real compensation lay in the legal and indisputable title that they now received, without any charge, to the land they were allowed to retain (A).[25]

The allotments of land were to be inalienable, so that the poor could not find themselves selling them back to the rich and so recreating the whole problem all over again. (A) This safeguarding clause, which was to be copied in other land reforms right down to Julius Caesar, shows clearly how the law had a serious social purpose over and above the simple transfer of wealth.

The size of the allotments no doubt varied with the quality of the land. A maximum limit of 30 acres appears on a rather later land law, of which a few bronze fragments have survived, but on the other hand we know that in attractive colonial settlements like Parma and Modena eight or even five acres had been regarded as a fair allotment. Whether the new tenants had to pay rent to the state is quite unknown, although such a rent was imposed under the land law of Gaius Gracchus, in rather different circumstances.[26]

Another inscription that has survived from this period is a milestone from Polla in southern Italy, containing the following graphic message, 'I was the first man to make the herdsmen on public land give way to the farmers'. The Gracchan law may not have insisted that grassland be ploughed up, but some switch to more labour-intensive types of farming must have been the expected result.[27]

The final uncertainty is whether the land was to be distributed to Roman citizens only. Appian throughout refers to the 'Italians', which ought to mean Rome's allies and not the Romans themselves. Yet to make non-citizens the prime beneficiaries would seem unlikely and at variance with the whole political situation. They may have been written into the law but in practice they must have come second.

The long debate on the bill was off to a vigorous start, as Appian records.

> Tiberius Gracchus, a brilliant and ambitious man, a powerful speaker and a well known public figure, became tribune and made a stirring speech about the Italian people. They were closely related to the Romans, he said, and they were valiant in war. But now they were slowly sinking into poverty and declining in numbers without any hope of recovery. Then he bitterly complained about all the slaves, unreliable and useless for purposes of war. He warned of the outrages that the slaves of Sicily, imported for the same agricultural purposes, had inflicted on their own masters and the long, hard and dangerous war the Romans had had to wage against them.

The military problem, together with this notion that all Italy was embraced by the reform, dominates Appian's account and colours his own analysis. The Romans had first begun to make public land available to those who wanted to work it, 'in order to increase the Italian race, which they regarded as the toughest of all, so as to provide allies close to hand'. It was 'the Italians' who suffered when the rich took over the land, at which point 'the people became anxious that they would not have enough Italian allies and that perhaps even their own empire would be put at risk by the masses of slaves'.[28]

Quickly the poor people of Rome took up the cry, that they were being dragged down from a decent livelihood to the extremes of poverty, so that they could not even afford to raise any children. They told of all the military campaigns that they had fought to win this land; they grumbled at being deprived of a share in what was common property; and they attacked the rich for giving jobs to surly and untrustworthy slaves instead of free citizens and soldiers.[29]

More men, rather than more money, was the true object of the bill, according to Appian's famous judgement, and he felt that it was because Tiberius was carried away by the practical value of the project, than which he believed nothing greater or more glorious had ever been done for Italy, that he ignored all the political difficulties.

As the day for voting on the bill approached, Tiberius made one great speech after another, emphasizing four questions above all.

'Isn't it fair that common property be divided in common?'

'Isn't a citizen more valuable than a slave?'

'Isn't a soldier more useful than a man who cannot fight?'

'Won't a man given his own share in the state become more devoted to the public good?'

Then he would raise his arguments to a higher plane, and spell out his hopes and fears for their country. They had conquered so much land in war that they had hopes of securing the rest of the inhabited world. But now they had put everything at risk: with plenty of brave men they could win the rest, or else by their own weakness and jealousies they could lose even what they had to their enemies.

Tiberius emphasized the glory and riches that could be won, and the dangers and terrors that otherwise awaited them; then he turned to the rich and called on them in their own interests to give this land away as a free gift to men who would raise families on it. They should not neglect their greater interests while arguing about the lesser. And it was with words like these that Tiberius rallied support among the poor and among all those thinking citizens who were not just motivated by private gain.[30]

Such is the account of the imperial civil servant and military historian Appian. By contrast, the philosophical moralist Plutarch is less conscious of the military problem, and quite unaware of any pan-Italian approach, but gives us an even better speech. Tiberius, he tells us, fought for a fine and just cause with an eloquence that would have adorned a meaner one. When he stood on the platform, with the people surging round him, and pleaded the · cause of the poor, he was irresistible—and Plutarch has preserved for us a passage from a speech which, judging from its vividness and forcefulness, must reflect the very words that Tiberius used.

Even the savage beasts in Italy have their dens and lairs in which to lay their heads. But those men who fight and die for Italy have no share of it, except for the fresh air and the sunshine. Without homes or shelters they are left to wander about with their wives and children.

The generals tell them lies when they call on the soldiers in battle to defend their temples and their tombs from the enemy. For not one of all these Romans has a family altar, nor an ancestral grave. Instead they fight and they die to support the wealth and luxury of other men.

They are called the masters of the world, but they do not have a clod of earth to call their own.

It was from a noble spirit and a sincere emotion that these words were spoken, and when they fell on the ears of the enthusiastic people then none of the other side could stand against them.[31]

The popularity of the bill was unquestioned. Even Cicero, normally an unreserved critic of the Gracchan movement, found it wise to speak vigorously in its favour when he himself was on his feet before the Roman people attacking a far more radical land bill seventy years later.

'I can recall,' he said, 'those ablest and most talented of men, those most devoted friends of the Roman people, Tiberius and Gaius Gracchus, who settled the people in the public land that had previously been occupied by private individuals. I am not one of those who think it a crime to praise the Gracchi, by whose wise policies and laws many features of our present republic were established.' Cicero compared the new bill most unfavourably with the legal and democratic procedures of the Gracchan law, just as its author was 'far behind the fairness and modesty of Tiberius Gracchus'. He referred to the 'liberality' of the Gracchus brothers, 'who vigorously planned for the welfare of the Roman people'. That was the way the people remembered the land bill.[32]

From the start of the debate, however, other Romans took a different view. The rich were worried because they would be able neither to ignore the law as before, because of the commissioners appointed to enforce it, nor to buy the land back. So they grouped together to oppose it. 'It is our own crops and buildings and the work of our own hands that the poor will acquire', they complained. 'Some of us paid for this land—shall we lose land and money as well? Some of us have our fathers' graves on the land, which we received as our inheritance. Some bought the land with our wedding dowries, or gave it as dowries to our own daughters. Some of us have even borrowed money using this land as security.' And such indignant complaints were heard everywhere (A).

It was greed that made the men of wealth and substance hate the law, and their anger and malice brought them to hate its proposer. So they tried to turn the people against the bill, by charging that Tiberius was using the redistribution of land as a means to throw the whole state into confusion and stir up a general revolution. But they achieved nothing (P).

Once again Plutarch shows himself less fascinated by the land question as such than Appian, but far more sensitive to the explosive political implications.[33]

As the argument raged between the landed and the landless, crowds of other citizens anxiously flocked into Rome, from the colonies and smaller towns, and whoever else had an interest in the public land to join one side or the other.

Made bold by their numbers they came into conflict and caused endless disturbances as they waited for voting day, some determined to block the new law by every means possible, others to push it through at all costs. A keen rivalry grew up and spurred them on, as well as the consideration of personal interest, and so against each other they laid their plans for the appointed day (A).

Another historian, writing nearer the event than Appian, gives the same vivid picture. 'The crowds poured from the countryside into Rome like rivers flowing into the sea, open to receive them all. For the people were excited by the prospect of saving themselves; they had the bill as their leader and their ally; while their champion was a man who was a slave to neither fear nor favour. For the sake of restoring the land to the people he had determined to endure any labour, and any danger, right to his very last breath.'[34]

The tension in Rome must have been almost unbearable. This was by far the most heated political dispute since the city had reached its grand new status of capital of the world. Into its already crowded streets had come thousands of rough peasants, some eager for their own land, others loyal to the service of local proprietors. Country gentlemen, small town magistrates, family retainers, landless labourers and hungry veterans had come from every corner of Italy for a political tussle that promised to affect the livelihood of every one of them. Brawling and drunkenness no doubt accompanied the incessant speeches, with crowds of supporters already following Tiberius about wherever he went.

Yet, although there were two sides to the argument, the passage of the bill must have seemed a foregone conclusion. The rich who wanted to hang on to their excessive and illegal holdings can have had no hopes at all of voting the bill down in the assembly of tribes, when it met in the forum some time in early spring of 133.

For all that, the opponents of the bill found a way. They spoke to another of the tribunes, Marcus Octavius, and enlisted his support. When the tribes met to vote on the bill, Tiberius asked the clerk of the assembly to read it out. Whereupon, Octavius, tribune and in law the champion of the Roman people just as much as Tiberius was, stepped forward to interpose his veto, and ordered the clerk to keep silent. In Rome the tribune's veto was an unassailable weapon.[35]

The land bill had been blocked.

6 The Reign of Tiberius Gracchus

In every revolution there comes a moment of discontinuity, a break with the past, an hour when those stored-up rules and precedents, by which any political system normally functions, cease to hold good.

At that moment, one group will classically argue that the rules stand in the way of change and should be obeyed, while the other will maintain that the need for change is so great that if necessary the rules made for other days should be broken. What is more, the rules themselves, now coming under such close scrutiny, will invariably be found to be dubious and uncertain.

Then the debate rages on two levels, about the validity and meaning of the rules as well as about the underlying issue of the moment. It is in the course of this double debate that the smouldering heat of political unrest can burst out into the naked flame of revolution.

So it was when Octavius vetoed the land bill of Tiberius Gracchus. Tiberius could, and on one view should, have respected the authority of the veto and permitted his bill to lapse. By drawing his year of office to a tranquil close he could have prepared the way for the respectable and distinguished political career to which his name and talents entitled him. But that was not how he chose to play it. And indeed, the legal authority of Octavius' veto is arguable today and must have been so even then. The question whether this was a proper use of the tribune's right of veto permits of no unqualified answer.

The rights and privileges of the tribune dated back to the beginnings of the republic. But at Rome there were two views about their office. Cicero described the tribunate as 'pestilential, born in and for sedition', yet the tradition recorded by Livy was that they had been established as 'the people's own magistrates, sacrosanct, with the right to give help against the authority of the consuls'.[1] Their fundamental right and duty was to help citizens with a grievance and it was from this that the right of veto derived. Frequently tribunes intervened to help citizens against the pressures of recruitment. They fended off the attacks on Scipio in 187. A tribune vetoed a bill which would have terminated the command of the consul Manlius Vulso in 178 (although there was some argument before the veto prevailed). Tribunes vetoed a war proposal in 167 (although it was argued that they had no right to do so without a general discussion first).[2]

The use of the veto in fact always led to arguments. In 294 no fewer than seven tribunes, 'the slaves of the nobility', had vetoed the attempt of the consul Postumius Megellus to hold an unofficial triumph, but the other three had come to his aid and amid popular acclamation he finally held it. Four tribunes vetoed a bill extending the Roman citizenship in 188, on the grounds that the senate had not given prior approval, but withdrew when it was pointed out that it was the people's right, not the senate's, to give the vote to whoever they wished. Briso's resistance to the bill of Cassius in 137 may not have been a formal veto and was in any case withdrawn. In fact there was no recent precedent for what Octavius was trying to do, to use the veto to block a bill of general application. Tribunes clearly had powers to veto bills, and yet if the right of any tribune to veto any bill had been accepted as part of the normal constitutional machinery it is difficult to see how any of the more controversial bills had ever come to be passed at all.[3]

It is difficult to conclude other than that the veto was a permissible tool, but that the use Octavius made of it was quite unexpected. This was an attempt to prevent the people from disposing as they wished of their own property. It was a new move in the game of politics, but Tiberius was not the man to give way as easily as that.

Octavius himself came from a reputable family, the junior branch of which was later to produce Octavian, the emperor Augustus. His father had accumulated enough wealth to build a large and dignified house on the Palatine hill. The prestige this brought had helped him to become the family's first consul in 165, after which he had been killed on a famous embassy to Syria, in memory of which a statue had been raised to him at public expense.[4] No doubt it was because Tiberius' father, on his own rather grand eastern mission in 161, had so signally failed to avenge the elder Octavius that some coolness grew up between the two sons. For the young Octavius, apparently a sober and dour character, was a close acquaintance of Tiberius and yet clearly less than a friend. Dio says that because of family jealousy he willingly joined in the attack, Plutarch that at first he was reluctant until the persistent urging of so many influential men finally persuaded him. They certainly chose the right man, for once he moved Octavius proved just as stubborn as his opponent.[5]

Now what was to be done? The arguments about the bill itself were nothing to the uproar that now burst out. Every day the two tribunes were on their feet, arguing their causes and rallying their supporters (even though Plutarch paints a pretty but not very credible picture of passionate arguments which never degenerated into vulgar abuse, thanks to the Roman virtue of self-control). It was a serious situation. As a first move (P) Tiberius toughened up the law by withdrawing any prospect of compensation for the re-claimed land.

Then he offered money from his own pocket to compensate Octavius for the land that he would lose under the law, a theatrical gesture that served both to insult his opponent and to remind the people of the selfish nature of the opposition. With still no sign of withdrawal, Tiberius went on to use his own powers of veto to obstruct all forms of public business until the law should be decided on. He sealed up the public treasury in the temple of Saturn, so that money could not be paid in or out. He brought the lawcourts to a halt. There were brawls and bitter abuse in the streets, in the forum, and even in the senate house, so that the whole city, in Dio's words, began to look more like an armed camp. In public many of the landholders put on mourning costumes and the appearance of misery and despair, but in private they began to utter threats. Murder was spoken of. In self-defence Tiberius began to wear a dagger hidden under his clothing.[6]

For a second time the bill was brought to the assembly for the tribes to vote on. This time Tiberius had an armed bodyguard standing by (A), and yet once again when the clerk began to read, Octavius silenced him with a veto. Again uproar broke out, and Diodorus describes the rival passions surging across the crowded thousands of voters like waves in the sea. Then it was discovered that the voting urns had been stolen (P), apparently by the party of the rich, and at this many of Tiberius' indignant supporters threatened to force the issue and insist on a vote.[7]

But the forces of moderation were not yet lost. At this moment two former consuls, Manlius and Fulvius, intervened. They were probably both among Tiberius' supporters, and had no doubt been standing close by during the preliminaries, until they began to feel it was all getting out of hand. Now they fell on their knees before Tiberius and appealed to him with tears in their eyes. What should he do? he respectfully asked them. They urged him to consult the senate and he agreed to do so, even though he had so far carefully avoided taking the reform issue before the senators. Unhappily his reception there was just as he had always feared; the landholders were in the majority and shouted him down, despite the support of the consul and the leader of the senate. Indeed perhaps Tiberius had expected this, but at least he had demonstrated his own willingness to meet his opponents half-way.[8]

So immediately he hurried back to the tribes, and revealed his next move. Since the senate had not been able to resolve the unprecedented constitutional impasse, then the people would do it for them. It was now Tiberius' turn to stand constitutional precedent on its head. If Octavius would not withdraw his veto then Octavius must be removed.

*

After announcing this historic proposal, and speaking eloquently in its defence, he again implored Octavius not to make such a drastic step necessary and then dismissed the tribes until the following day.

Next morning the people assembled again. It was a momentous occasion. To the best of our knowledge the eviction of a tribune, or any elected magistrate, from office was without precedent. Plutarch explicitly describes the proposal as illegal as well as undesirable, while accepting that there was no other way of bringing the land bill to the vote. So now, for the third time, the land bill was formally introduced. For the third time Octavius vetoed it. Then Tiberius introduced his resolution to deprive Octavius of office and put it immediately to the vote.

Of the thirty-five tribes, the first seventeen to vote gave it enthusiastic and overwhelming support. Only one more vote was needed—but Tiberius held back the eighteenth tribe, to give Octavius one last chance.

Brief reports of Tiberius' speeches on both this and the previous day have come down to us, and they make it clear that he leaned over backwards to avoid the last step. He begged and entreated Octavius to drop the veto, taking his hands and with soft words urging him to give in to the people, who were only asking for their just rights and who still stood to gain only moderate rewards in return for all their great dangers and labours (P).

Claiming that his proposal was absolutely fair and of immense value to the whole of Italy, as well as dear to the hearts of the people, he implored Octavius for all these reasons to let it through. It was a tribune's job to support the people's interests, not to put his own office in jeopardy in this way (A).

But even if the dispute continued, Tiberius offered a compromise, and invited his rival first to propose that Tiberius be deposed, promising to accept if the vote went against him (P). But all to no avail. Octavius may have been torn, and Plutarch again stresses the friendship of the two, with Octavius standing silent and on the brink of tears, but still resolute and firm under the eye of his wealthy backers grouped near by.

Once it was clear that Octavius would not yield, Tiberius carried on with the voting and his opponent was removed from office.[9]

Whether at the last stage Tiberius still genuinely hoped for a settlement is difficult to judge, though he cannot have been in any doubt of the grave implications of throwing one of the people's champions out of office. Yet he had powerful arguments ready, and fortunately we have a fuller account of a speech delivered in justification later in the year, when the legality of his move was being questioned.

Why is a tribune sacred and his person protected? It is because he is consecrated to the people as their champion. So if instead he changes his ground and does wrong to the people, by cutting back their power and depriving them of the right to vote, then he must have deprived himself of office by failing to fulfil its basic conditions.

Otherwise what is there to stop him tearing down the Capitol or burning the dockyards? If he were to do that, he would be a villainous tribune. But if he tears down the power of the people then he can be no tribune at all.

We know that a tribune has the right to send even a consul to jail. So how can we deny that the people have the right to take away the tribune's power when he uses it against them? For consul and tribune alike are elected by the people.

Even the king, holding the most powerful and sacred office of all, was expelled by the Romans for wrongful behaviour and his office abolished. The Vestal Virgins now hold the holiest position in Rome and guard the eternal fire—but any one of them who misbehaves is buried alive, for once she breaks the rules of the gods she thereby loses their protection.

In the same way, when a tribune acts against the people, attacking the source of his own power, what claim can he have to retain their protection? If the majority vote of tribes gave him his office, then their unanimous vote must be enough to take it away. The tribunate may be something sacred, but that cannot mean that the people do not have the right to take it from one man and entrust it to another, as with any other sacred object. And the fact that men holding the office have at times resigned from it proves that there is nothing inalienable about it.[10]

If indeed the ultimate sovereignty of the Roman people was the underlying principle of this constitution, that had so slowly evolved over the centuries, then it would be hard to deny their right to find a novel solution to a novel problem, that of a tribune who persisted in vetoing a law that the people wanted to pass. In the same way the people had twice asserted their right to elect Scipio consul even when the rules forbade it. Their right to bestow the franchise had been underlined in 188. Writing around 150 Polybius had given the clearest possible definition of a tribune's duty, 'always to do what the people decree and zealously to pursue their wishes'.[11] And it is noteworthy that none of the other eight tribunes of the year made any move either to veto the deposition or to extend their help to Octavius.

Plutarch's statement that the deposition was illegal should be rejected, therefore. Undoubtedly there was no explicit rule either permitting or forbidding such action, because the situation had never arisen before. But the fact remains that the deposition was just as unprecedented as Octavius' persistent veto. Perhaps it should be compared to the action sometimes threatened by British sovereigns, to create enough new peers to swamp the House of Lords if it made unreasonable use of its legal powers to obstruct the House of Commons. The difference is that Tiberius was forced to carry out his threat, and it was this that escalated the whole dispute to a new and undesirable level.

Here was the crucial stage of the whole affair, and Cicero accurately pinpointed it. 'It was by his patient stubbornness, after being unjustly treated, that Octavius broke Tiberius,' and again, 'A colleague, who had been not merely disregarded but even deposed, still destroyed Tiberius—for what else brought him down but the fact that he had deprived a colleague of office for using his veto?'[12]

In other words, by his persistence Octavius had forced Tiberius on to ground where he could be more easily challenged, and into an action that was bound to arouse indignation. 'What rights did Tiberius' tribunate leave to respectable citizens?' asked Cicero, and commented that 'It was a seditious act of Tiberius to depose his colleague.' Livy describes the deed as an outburst of frenzy; Velleius recalls that Octavius was deposed for upholding the public good; Orosius observes that this was what filled the people with arrogance, and the senate with rage.[13]

Tiberius had begun his year of office with a proposal for land reform that was useful in its own right and fully con-stitutional, in the sense that it was essentially a reinforce-ment of an earlier law. But now he had been outman-oeuvred, into giving the opposition a wider rallying cry than his land bill afforded. He had deposed a tribune, and the manner in which he carried it out was not encouraging.

Once the vote had been taken, Tiberius sent up one of his own freed slaves to drag Octavius away from the platform, a calculated insult, yet the wretched ex-tribune still refused to accept the validity of the deposition. The crowd surged forward, putting him in fear of his life; his wealthy backers ran and held out their arms to protect him, and Octavius slunk away out of sight, but not before one of his own servants trying to shield him had been beaten up and blinded on the spot. Tiberius rushed down from the platform appalled, but was too late to stop the brawl. His cause had again been damaged, and the level of violence was rising.[14]

*

The land bill was passed. A new tribune was elected, probably a Mucius, 'one of Tiberius' personal followers, not a man of any note'.[15] And three commissioners were elected to carry out the great land reforms. They were Tiberius himself; his twenty-one year-old brother Gaius, who was still away fighting in Spain; and his father-in-law, the leader of the senate, Appius Claudius. It was a family party, for otherwise the people feared that the law might still fail to be carried out.[16] The triumphant Tiberius was escorted home by the mob and cheered as the founder, not of one city, but of the whole of Italy (A). But another relative embarked on a different course of action, for it was now that Scipio Nasica, the consul of 138 who had recently succeeded his own father as high priest, emerged as the clear leader of the opposition to his cousin Tiberius Gracchus, in the absence overseas of his other cousin Scipio Aemilianus.

Nasica was one of the largest holders of public land, and since he bitterly resented the prospect of giving it up he abandoned himself to unrestrained hatred of the popular tribune (P). First he initiated a campaign of virulent personal abuse of Tiberius in the senate. Then he persuaded the senate to refuse the tribune's routine request for a tent to be provided at public expense, to use as his headquarters for the land distribution, even though such a tent was normally provided for much smaller tasks. And he had the commission's expenses fixed at the ludicrous level of 1½*d* a day, little more than a labourer's wages.

As well as obstructing the commission's work, these moves added to the ill feeling in the city, so that it was not surprising, when a friend of Tiberius died a little later, that there were immediate and widespread accusations that he had been poisoned. At this Tiberius put on mourning clothes himself, led his children into the forum and begged the people to look after them and his mother, for he was ready to sacrifice his own life.[17]

More to the point, he promoted a further law that gave the commissioners judicial powers to decide which land was public and which private.[18] But how could he overcome the financial obstruction that, by holding up the implementation of the reform, was threatening to undermine the basis of his own popularity? And this in a state where the senate had always controlled the purse-strings.

Suddenly, the most remarkable windfall arrived, in a form that would not only solve the immediate problem, but put the Roman people more than ever in their tribune's debt. It was nothing less than the measureless wealth of the East.

For sixty years the treasures of the East had been flowing into the hands of Rome's generals, traders, bankers and statesmen. Now the people were to have a share. For during this period one of Rome's firmest allies had been the kingdom of Pergamum, which with Roman favour had come to control the western end of Asia Minor. A country naturally rich in corn, vines and silver had been developed by the most enlightened rulers of the age, who had given their patronage and enthusiasm to scientific methods of agriculture and stock-breeding, to a thriving woollen industry, and to the manufacture of such luxury goods as parchment and perfumes. Ephesus became a leading commercial port of the

Mediterranean, while money and care were lavished on building up Pergamum itself into one of the most beautiful of all Greek cities. The kings of Pergamum founded a library second only to Alexandria, they supported arts, philosophy, and science, they created one of the most influential centres of Greek civilization, and they left behind them an example for all time of the benefits that sustained good government can bring to a country.

All this inheritance was bequeathed to the Roman people by King Attalus III, who died in 133, the year when Tiberius Gracchus was tribune at Rome.[19]

It seems too romantic an idea, to think of Attalus, an eccentric gardener, herbalist and brassfounder, consciously trying to hand on his family's trusteeship over all that Greece was to mean to the world, to the nation whose military power best qualified it for the role. Yet more than a thousand years later his territory endured as a pillar of the Byzantine empire that was still preserving Greek civilization long after Rome had fallen. Perhaps he was also troubled by the social unrest already seething in his state, which must have been very seriously affected by the Mediterranean world's general economic crisis. But in any case, what mattered was that Pergamum was the most prosperous and highly developed economy yet to come under Roman control. It matched what India was to mean to the British empire. As Cicero told the Romans, 'The revenues of our other provinces are hardly sufficient to justify the cost of defending them; but Asia (as the province became officially called) is so rich and fruitful as to excel all other states in the productivity of her fields, the variety of her crops, the extent of her pastures and the volume of her exports.'[20]

While this golden bequest laid down that the city of Pergamum itself, its surrounding territory and perhaps some other cities were to be left self-governing, under Roman suzerainty, it was clear that the revenues and the private fortune of the monarch changed hands. It was the immediate cash sum that met Tiberius' needs, while his brother was later to exploit the revenues.[21]

Hearing of the death and the bequest before anyone else at Rome, Tiberius immediately brought forward the sensational proposal that the whole of these funds would be taken over and distributed along with the land allotments so as to pay for the new farmers' equipment and initial supplies. It is even alleged that he wanted to go further, and distribute some of the money to other citizens instead of land, or hand it out to the people at large. True or not, here to suspicious minds there was scope for bribery on a scale never seen before. To Orosius, Tiberius was 'trying to win popular favour by paying for it'.[22]

Indeed, the grounds for suspicion were now multiplying fast, for by his latest move Tiberius was undermining that basic principle of the Roman constitution, the allocation of jobs between senate and people. Above all other tasks the senate had reserved to itself, as Polybius had clearly seen, the control of foreign and financial policy. These were the levers by which it moved the state. But now Tiberius was claiming the right of the people to allocate large sums of badly needed money just as they thought fit (only a year after Scipio had had to be refused funds for the vital Spanish war), and he was also intervening in foreign policy decisions of great moment. His decision to accept the bequest brought an administrative burden which the senate might not have welcomed, since it was generally reluctant to make overseas acquisitions except in pressing need. Tiberius had declared his intention to bring forward proposals about the cities of Pergamum, saying they were no concern of the senate's, even though they had apparently been excluded from the bequest. This could sound like a claim to expand still further his rights of patronage.

A still more serious worry was that he would involve Rome in another war, for at this very moment Attalus' half-brother Aristonicus was stirring up a revolt against the bequest. His ambitions may have been known in Rome already, or they may reflect Pergamene reaction against Tiberius' proposals. Either way Tiberius was playing with fire, and going far outside any conceivable interpretation of a tribune's duties. He was turning the whole constitution upside down—and incidentally setting a precedent for aggressive foreign policies by would-be popular leaders, that was to culminate in Caesar's hard-won but rewarding conquest of Gaul.[23]

There was more than constitutional theory at stake. For now his personal role in the bequest was questioned. Why had Tiberius been able to launch his proposal out of the blue? Because it was to his house that the Pergamene ambassador Eudemus had brought the royal testament. The reason for this lay back in the elder Gracchus' famous eastern mission in 165: for when Attalus' father Eumenes had come under suspicion of treason towards Rome, Gracchus had firmly testified to his loyalty and personally ensured that the charges were dropped and Eumenes restored to favour.[24] No greater service could be conferred on a monarch, who had so become a client or personal ally to Gracchus. a relationship naturally handed down to their respective sons.

So Tiberius' house was the natural place for a Pergamene envoy to stay when in Rome, but this only made the charge of collusion easier. Perhaps Tiberius had already known the contents of the will, perhaps he had even advised on it. Certainly his relations with Pergamum were such that the news was brought to him first, enabling him to use it for his own political aims. His intellectual links with that stimulating country were confirmed after his death, when his adviser Blossius fled to join the revolt of Aristonicus, and his ally Crassus Mucianus went to immense trouble to secure command of the war there. Such associations must already have been well known, and they made it only too easy for upright and respectable citizens to suspect the worst.

*

It was Pompeius who launched the new attack, standing up in the senate to declare that because he lived in a neighbouring house he knew for a fact that Eudemus had given Tiberius the diadem and purple cloak of the kings of Pergamum in the belief that Tiberius was going to be king in Rome.

No more deadly charge could be levied in a proud republic whose noble families had thrown out their royalty almost four hundred years before. And then Pompeius solemnly warned that as soon as Tiberius had laid down the protection of his office then he would prosecute him for what he had done.[25]

Metellus the conqueror of Macedon, one of the great nobles of the age, father of four future consuls and uncle to two more, made almost as damaging a charge, that Tiberius surrounded himself with crowds of penniless ruffians who would light his way home at night. What a sorry contrast this was to the grave and sober standards set by his father![26]

Then an old and harsh-mannered ex-consul, T. Annius Luscus, caused a great stir in the senate by challenging Tiberius to come before the courts to settle whether or not he had broken the law in dishonouring his colleague. While the senators applauded Tiberius rushed outside, summoned the tribal assembly, and ordered Annius to be brought before it to be denounced. Annius had no reputation at all for polished eloquence, but simply asked if he could first put a question of his own to the tribune. When this was agreed, and silence had been established, Annius flung his bombshell.

'Suppose you do insult and abuse me, and suppose I then ask for the support of one of your colleagues. If he comes forward to help me will you fly into a rage and throw him out of office too?'

For all his bold eloquence Tiberius was caught completely off balance by the brutally direct question. Unable to think of a suitable reply he dissolved the assembly. The opposition had gained another point.[27]

The significance of these attacks was that they revealed how widely based the opposition had become. Certainly the friends and relatives of Scipio were conspicuous. Nasica had supported Pompeius' threat of prosecution, and it was probably at this stage that Scipio's nephew Aelius Tubero and one or two other young men broke off their friendship with Tiberius 'for vexing the state'.[28] But the others were not in this group at all. Annius was a man of little background with no clear links to any of the family groupings. Metellus was an attested enemy of Scipio even after 133. Pompeius was a rough-hewn, self-made man, talented and popular, who had successfully challenged Scipio when seeking election for consul. He and Metellus were even opposed to each other, which did not prevent their later holding office together as the first ever pair of plebeian censors.[29]

What had happened, in fact, was that a limited and rather selfish opposition to land reform had widened into a general anxiety about the whole character of Tiberius' actions, particularly his deposition of a colleague and the attempt to exploit the inheritance of Pergamum. Resentful, the opposition began to murmur that Tiberius would be sorry when he became a private citizen again, for having trampled on the holy office of tribune and stirred up so much dissension throughout Italy (A). Suddenly Tiberius realized that the deposition of Octavius had displeased the common people as well as the senators (P).[30]

The impression given is that although he had managed the deposition successfully at the time, his later behaviour antagonized more of the conservative nobles, and they in turn gradually convinced more of the common people that Tiberius had done wrong. Plutarch's repeated references to 'the rich' dominating the senate and opposition seem unconvincing.[31] The point was rather that the powerful men of the state feared the tribune's growing influence, and they resented his freedmen, his villainous-looking bodyguard, and his role in the Pergamum affair—'it was this that most of all antagonized the senate'.[32] Tiberius had got away with lightening their pockets, but when he challenged the very basis of their power, the conventions under which the people's sovereignty had been carefully controlled by the ruling families for generations, then they could no longer stand aside.

A struggle between Gracchan and Scipionic families for office and honours, as it is sometimes described, would have been perfectly manageable within the normal framework of aristocratic politics. But an attempt to make the tribal assembly into the seat of government, using it to fetter tribunes, dispose of the public funds and extend the empire was something else altogether. 'It was after *so many* assaults on its dignity that the senate became seriously disturbed,' explains Livy.[33]

The evidence shows that the opposition to Tiberius steadily gathered strength as the occasions for resentment multiplied, and as people at all levels of society realized what a revolution in the normal way of doing things had taken place. And the charge that headed the list was that brought by Pompeius, that Tiberius Gracchus was aiming to become king.

Later it became a commonplace. Sallust refers to 'the murder of Tiberius Gracchus, whom they said was trying to become king'. Cicero is even more explicit. 'Tiberius Gracchus tried to seize regal power, or rather he really did reign for a few months—when had the Roman people heard or seen such a thing before?'[34]

But the cloak and diadem that Pompeius spoke of could only be the trappings of kingship, and that Tiberius had ambitions to wear them seems inconceivable. It is, however, very plain that his determination to force through land reform and to ride roughshod over any obstacles had brought him close to what today would be called dictatorial power. The charge of seeking such powers had been levelled against his grandfather, the great Scipio Africanus,[35] and were to become common in the disputes of the later republic. By dominating the assembly Tiberius had taken on the functions of chief executive of the state; he had secured great powers for a land commission composed of himself and his relatives; to say that he was seeking and had even secured exceptional personal powers was no more than the truth. The fear that he would hold on to them, and so assume the status if not the garments of a king, is understandable too. The Romans did not need to look back three hundred years into their own dim tales of regal conspiracies: the precedents that mattered were far more recent and came from the Greek world with which Tiberius and his associates were so intimately linked, the Greek world where a strange king's will had just given the latest frightening support to the tribune's ambitions.

*

To begin with, there are grounds for believing that the powerful families which grouped themselves round the Gracchus brothers, together with others that worked with them in earlier generations, had special and long-standing interests in the Greek world. When Rome began to take notice of that world, it is over and over again the families of Fulvius and Manlius, Valerius and Sulpicius, Claudius and Sempronius who provide the crucial ambassadors and commanders. In the second century all politicians have some involvement in Greece, but it is noticeable that Gracchans are consistently hostile to the great kings of Macedon and Syria and favourable towards Pergamum. By now other linked families, such as Licinius, Mucius and Hostilius, appear in the same grouping of interests. The evidence lacks precision, but cumulatively it seems very strong.[36]

Similarly, while most educated Romans were now open to Greek cultural influences, the Gracchus brothers were as much involved as anybody. Their father made a speech in Greek, their uncle P. Scipio wrote a history in Greek, and their friend Crassus Mucianus fluently spoke in all five of its dialects. Tiberius learned Greek from the eloquent Diophanes of Mytilene and his brother Gaius learned it from Menelaus of Marathus. Both of these tutors came from well within the Pergamene sphere of influence.

The most important intellectual in the circle was a certain C. Blossius of Cumae, who was said to have joined with Diophanes in urging Tiberius to his reform programme. So important was his influence that in a famous incident after Tiberius' death he was hauled before the commission of inquiry. Boldly he told them that he thought so highly of Tiberius that he would have obeyed any order given by him.

'What, even if he had told you to burn down the Capitol?' asked an indignant Laelius. 'He never would have done,' came the reply. 'But if he had done so it could only have been because it was in the interests of the people, and so it would still have been my duty to obey him.'

Astonishingly, after such a bold definition of the popular cause, Blossius still managed to get away into exile, but Cicero claimed that 'he had directed, not followed, the wild behaviour of Tiberius; he had been a leader not just a comrade in all that madness'.[37] Such a claim is hard to accept: an intellectual can hardly have 'led' so mighty a group of nobles. And yet that his influence counted for a great deal seems clearly implied.

So who was this Blossius and why did his views matter? He was a protégé of the Mucius Scaevola family, so that Tiberius and Crassus must have known him from an early age. His home, Cumae, was the oldest of all the Greek colonies in Italy, but it has been surmised that he was in fact descended from a prominent family in the neighbouring town of Capua. Twice during the Hannibalic war this family had acted treacherously towards the Romans, which probably implies links with the democratic interests common in most Greek towns and so could make Blossius a radical by family tradition.[38]

But what we know for certain is that he was a close associate of the great Stoic philosopher Antipater of Tarsus, who had even dedicated some of his books to Blossius. Antipater was the sixth man to head the ancient world's most influential school of philosophy, founded by Zeno in the Painted Stoa at Athens. The Stoics had developed a profound system of ethical theory in which virtue was based on true knowledge and consisted of living in harmony with nature and with reason. Many of their moral concepts, of duty and responsibility, of simplicity and self-sufficiency, struck a responsive chord among the more serious Roman nobles, as they were also to do among later philosophers from Augustine to Kant. But this was not a creed for the study. The Stoics took a stand on social questions, and came to believe in the value of man for his own sake, whether rich or poor, noble or slave. They held that the wise man should take part in public life. Many leading Stoics became friends of kings and some wrote books on kingship and its duties.

The previous head of the Stoa, Diogenes of Babylon, had been a member of the famous embassy of philosophers sent by Athens to Rome in 154, when the cynical arguments of Carneades had so shocked the staid Romans. But Cicero quotes a number of disputes which show Antipater trying to reaffirm a more humane view of ethics, arguing that 'you should consider the interests of other men and serve human society . . . and you should remember the bonds that nature has forged between man and man'. This high moral view was in turn passed on to the Roman world through two of Antipater's pupils.

But whereas Blossius gave the ideas a revolutionary interpretation, implying a duty to identify with the interests of the common man, Panaetius of Rhodes moved in the opposite direction to become a close associate of Scipio and his friends, in whose company his views took on a noticeably aristocratic tinge. There was nothing contradictory about this, for profound thinkers have always enjoyed a variety of followers. But the result had to be that the Romans were clearly familiar with Stoic ideas, intimate with all the nuances of theory, and fully aware that Stoicism, however interpreted, was above all a philosophy for the practising politician. In which case they can hardly have been ignorant of the important role played by yet another great Stoic, Sphaerus, as a close associate and adviser to the revolutionary king Cleomenes of Sparta, a king whose sweeping programme of wholesale reform had begun—with the redistribution of land.[39]

Analogies with Sparta, once the greatest military state of classical Greece, had long been dear to the Romans. In Sparta they recognized the Roman virtues of discipline and determination, while both Cato and Polybius carefully compared the constitutions of the two cities (albeit to Rome's advantage).[40] But after Sparta had drifted away from its old ideals, two kings in the third century, Agis and Cleomenes, tried to restore their country to health by reforms of the most radical nature, including distributing land, cancelling debts, and enlarging the citizen body by giving the vote even to foreigners. A later Spartan king, Nabis, boldly defended this tradition against the Roman general Flamininus.

> If you accuse me of having increased the citizen body by freeing slaves and dividing land among the poor, I can only say that such is the original custom of our ancestors. You Romans select your cavalry and infantry according to their wealth, and you are content that a few should own most of the property and keep the common people subservient to them. But our lawgiver laid down that our state should not be in the hands of a few men, such as those you call the senate, nor dominated by any one class. Instead he believed that if he equalized wealth and rank then there would be many men ready to fight for their fatherland.[41]

Here was the complete radical manifesto, expressing a combination of military patriotism and egalitarian reform that precisely matched what Tiberius Gracchus was doing in Rome, and even foreshadowed later Gracchan proposals such as the extension of the franchise. And while Sparta provided the most vivid parallel there were others in Greek history. Land reform was the regular vanguard of revolution. Polybius, whose own political antecedents lay with the bitter enemies of those populist Spartan kings, had graphically warned of the dangers that the common people 'might find an ambitious and daring leader, establish the rule of violence, unite their forces to banish and kill their enemies, redistribute the land, degenerate into complete savagery and end up by finding once again a master and a monarch'.[42]

After the Gracchan revolution had run its course Cicero, too, was deeply impressed by these parallels with Sparta and gave ample vent to his own indignation.

Those who pose as the friends of the people, and aim at either land reform, to expel landholders from their estates, or the cancellation of debts, are undermining the foundations of the republic. . . . For the function of the state is to guarantee to each man the free and undisturbed possession of his own property. . . . How can it be fair to take away land from those who have occupied it for many generations and hand it over to people who have never owned any property at all? It was for just such wrongdoing that the Spartans killed their king Agis, from which moment such violent dissensions arose in their country that tyrants sprang up, nobles were wiped out, and a wonderfully well organized state crumbled away. And then those evils, born in Sparta, spread more widely until they culminated in the ruin of all the rest of Greece. And look at our own Gracchus brothers, sons of the great Tiberius Gracchus, grandsons of Africanus—how they were destroyed by the disputes over land reform.[43]

The analogy with Sparta was thus established long before Plutarch chose to set the Gracchus brothers and kings Agis and Cleomenes side by side in his collection of 'parallel lives'. It must have been present in many Roman minds from the moment Tiberius began to press for land reform. The clause making the new allotments inalienable, for example, was a direct copy of the old Spartan tradition that the two young kings had tried to restore there.[44] His emphasis on the welfare of the poor, their rights to share in the state's success, and the moral and military dividends that reform would bring, were all exact parallels to the Spartan experience. Where would it all end?

The ruthlessness of his onslaught on Octavius reinforced the fears. But then came his sensational dealings with the envoy from Pergamum, his attempt to wrest control of financial and foreign policy from the senate, to wield dictatorial power through the assembly, and to place the mass of the people in his personal debt by distributing the treasures of Pergamum to them. This was the behaviour of an aspiring monarch—how could it look otherwise? It was a blow at the political privileges of the senators. Would their possessions, their freedom, and even their lives be next at risk? What was the true significance of the will of Attalus? Was it some terrible plot, revealed only by the accident of his early death, to link ambitious Romans and visionary Greeks in some sort of condominium of the world?

What frightening rumours must have raced across the city! The charge that Tiberius was trying to make himself king became a perfect rallying cry for all these fears.

The time had come to call a halt to the reign of Tiberius Gracchus.

7 Massacre on Capitol Hill

High summer was beating down on the ripening crops of Italy and the crowded streets of Rome when Tiberius Gracchus began to worry about his future.

For half a year he had dominated public affairs, through his sway over the tribal assembly and the land commission. But he was tribune for only one year, and as the elections for 132 drew near the threats voiced by his enemies grew more alarming. As well as supporting candidates hostile to him, they were talking of prosecution. A trial for the capital charge of treason would be heard by the assembly of centuries, which he could not hope to master as easily as the tribes. And so he had good reason to be anxious, and it was to fend off this impending danger that he announced his last and most radical proposal of all, that he would stand for re-election as tribune. His younger brother Gaius would also stand for tribune, and his father-in-law Appius Claudius would try for a second year as consul.[1]

To his enemies such a move could only confirm their worst fears of his monarchical ambitions. Yet from Tiberius' point of view there was a good deal more to be said. It would protect him against one of those political prosecutions that had become a common feature of city life in recent years, and against any more arbitrary violence that could follow if he once laid down the tribune's cloak of sanctity. But while safety is the aspect emphasized in our sources, continuity of policy must also have played a part.

From the events of 133 Tiberius had learnt an important lesson, that in the politics of reform one thing leads to another. To pass his land bill he had had to depose a tribune; to implement it he had had to seize the treasures of Attalus. What would happen next? The actual work of redistributing land can hardly have begun. To relax the effort at this stage, allowing his enemies to repeal or nullify what he had done, would hardly have been consistent with the stubborn persistence he had shown so far.

Instead, under his proposal all three land commissioners would also be office holders in 132. Gaius would help cement his grip on the tribes, while Appius, already leader of the senate, would be a consul even better equipped than Mucius Scaevola to keep the opposition nobles at bay. The plan went even further, for Crassus Mucianus was meant to follow Appius as consul in 131. Here was continuity politics with a vengeance. This succession of offices would give the great families their reward for building so powerful a combination, while Tiberius obtained a power base stable enough to follow through the action he had begun.

It is even possible that Tiberius was still on the right side of the law. The reforming tribunes Licinius and Sextius were supposed to have held office for ten successive years, from 376 to 367, and although stringent laws were passed in the second century to limit re-election to other offices there is no evidence that they ever applied to the tribunate (which technically was not a normal magistracy). On the other hand, if the legality of the re-election had been unquestioned there would have been no need to propose a law reaffirming the right in 131, nor to find a special loophole in the law to re-elect Gaius Gracchus in 123. Nor would it be easy to make sense of a speech in which Cicero told the senate that, 'We are not today talking of Tiberius Gracchus being brought to trial and the mercy of your judgement for trying to become tribune a second time.'[2] So, even if not strictly illegal, re-election seems to have been without any recent precedent and clearly a sharp breach of what was then thought to be the spirit of the constitution.

Similarly Gaius, only just back in time for the election after fighting the Spaniards with Scipio, was at twenty-one very young for the office of tribune. And Appius, although clear under the ten-year rule (having first been consul in 143), would still have needed special exemption from the law against second consulates. This had been given to his great rival Scipio in 135 and no doubt could have been secured for Appius once Tiberius had been re-elected (for the consular elections normally followed the tribunician). As it was it never came to the test.[3]

But while Tiberius and his friends laid their plans, the result of the election was far from a foregone conclusion. Not only had the opposition gained strength, but his own supporters had begun to weaken.

The question of where Tiberius drew his voting support is

highly controversial, and unfortunately tangled up with the uncertainty about his policy towards those Italians who were not Roman citizens and had no vote. But Appian, who makes so much of the Italian theme, also emphasizes the importance of those Roman voters who lived or worked in the countryside.

During the debate on the land bill, as we have already seen, crowds of other citizens flocked into Rome, from the colonies and smaller towns, and whoever else had an interest in the public land. Once the bill had been passed, 'the victorious party returned to the fields from where they had come to see the proposal through'.

Now once again, as the election neared, 'Tiberius summoned the men from the fields to come and vote. But because it was summer they had no time to spare. So, with very little time now left before the election day, he had to fall back on the mass of people in the city and he went round asking each one of them in turn to vote him back in as tribune, because of the danger he was running on their behalf.'[4]

His anxiety about voting support proved to be well founded, and the sequel shows that Appian has grasped a most important point, going far beyond any crude antithesis between rich and poor; namely that among the citizen poor there were some who cared more than the others about land reform, and it was their support that was missing because the elections were in late July, the busiest time of all on the land. From Cato we know that citizen labourers were available in the countryside to help with temporary work, especially harvesting, and among these will have been those homeless wanderers depicted in Tiberius' own speeches. Landless but still countrymen, they will have been the most enthusiastic of all for land reform.

In the city there will have been many whose links with the land were still close, and who also supported the idea of land reform. But unfortunately these are precisely the men most likely to be away every summer looking for casual work in the fields, just as Londoners used to go hop-picking and Glaswegians gathered potatoes. Dearly might they love Tiberius and his plans, but the fact remains that times were hard and no poor man dared pass by the opportunity for summertime work. The sort of townsman who did not go off to work in the harvests was either a craftsman with a steady job or else a back-street idler. Land distribution would make no appeal to them. Tiberius had done nothing for them, and their support could not be expected to amount to very much.

So Tiberius was to die because his supporters were all away

tattie-howking. At so tense a moment he missed the sheer number of heads and strong right arms, but he missed their votes even more for theirs were the votes that counted most. The tribal assembly was dominated by the thirty-one rural tribes, in which most of his rustic and semi-rustic supporters (including first-generation immigrants into the capital) must have been registered. When they were there those men controlled the assembly. When they were missing the thirty-one tribes were more in the pockets of the landed gentry, who could easily afford to come into the city with their trusted retainers, and of the more influential bourgeoisie who made a point of being registered in them. Many of the deeprooted townsmen, especially the poor, were trapped in the four city tribes where their votes counted for so much less.

In this way the arid technicalities of voting procedure, crucial in so many political crises, caught Tiberius unawares and without the backing that he had had during the spring. We know that he tried hard to strengthen his support by making sweeping promises of further reform if he were returned to power, but the details that we have are hopelessly garbled and confused with the programme of his brother, who set out to build a broadly based political machine in a more systematic fashion.

We are told that he proposed to reduce the length of military service or lighten its burden in some way. This seems possible, although something of the kind had already been done during the Spanish war and his brother was to act in this area too.[5]

He proposed to restore the right of appeal to the people, presumably from those law-courts on provincial extortion which Piso had brought under the senate's control in 149. This might have been important if any of the Gracchans faced prosecution before the senate.[6]

Less plausible is the report that he wanted to give the knights half or even all the seats on the law-courts that were controlled by the senate. Although Pliny says that it was the Gracchus brothers (in the plural) who first gave the knights a distinctive role as jurymen, the idea still seems too close to his brother's schemes. And at this date there was no known dissension between senators and knights, who are twice said to have stood together in opposition to Tiberius.[7]

A final suggestion that he promised to extend citizenship to the whole of Italy is flatly contradicted by Appian, who says that the issue first arose eight years later. In any case it seems monumentally irrelevant to the urgent problem of winning the votes of the city mob.[8]

But we can be sure about none of these proposals. What Gaius Gracchus did later may well have been inspired by lines of thought that his elder brother had laid down, but, true or not, Gaius is bound to have claimed that this was so. Trying to establish a 'Gracchan tradition' was an obvious weapon of propaganda, but it has left the facts deeply unclear. We can only take it all as evidence of feverish electioneering, summed up rather unfairly by Plutarch as 'Trying to curtail the power of the senate in every way he could, from motives of rage and ambition rather than any calculation of justice and the public good'. He was confounding and shaking up all established customs as he grappled for some means of safety, adds Dio, and in his bid for re-election there was nothing that he would not say and promise. Often he even put on mourning and brought his mother and small children before the crowds to help plead for him.[9]

*

The day appointed for the elections arrived at last. A scene which was no doubt unclear and bewildering even to those who took part in it has been doubly confused for us by the contradictions in the surviving accounts. But the bedrock of fact is that things did not go Tiberius' way at all.

The day began well, as the first two of the thirty-five tribes recorded their vote for Tiberius (A). Then the opposition put forward the objection that it was not lawful for the same man to hold office two years in succession. Rubrius, the tribune who had drawn (by lot) the task of presiding over the assembly, was unsure what to do. So Mucius, the tribune who had been elected to replace Octavius, and a known supporter of Tiberius, stood up and asked that the presidency should be turned over to him. Clearly he was in no doubt about how to deal with the objection. Rubrius gave way to Mucius, whereupon the other tribunes leaped to their feet with a new objection: that if Rubrius had withdrawn then lots should be drawn afresh to decide who should take his place.

The scene bears all the marks of a well planned coup, like one of those House of Commons procedural devices which sometimes trip a British government. The opposition had their rule books and precedents ready, and they must have half convinced most of the tribunes that re-election should be opposed, since the implication of the story is that drawing lots again would probably have produced a tribune sympathetic to the objection. Mucius was no longer acceptable to his colleagues.

Here was a change of heart of immense importance, for earlier in the year none of these other tribunes had been ready to oppose Tiberius. Now they were thwarting him. The tide had turned.

Bitter arguments raged, and the friends of Tiberius savagely abused the other tribunes (P), no doubt for changing sides in this way. But all to no avail. Plutarch adds that this was because 'all the people' were not present. Now those harvest workers were missed, for although there was no way of calling a separate vote on the procedural question itself, presumably the other tribunes observed how thin Tiberius' support had become, and it was this that gave them the courage to switch sides. The opposition had seized the upper hand. Amid scenes of general disorder Tiberius managed to get the assembly adjourned to the following day.[10]

Again Tiberius had been caught unawares, by the scantiness of his voting support, which was probably not evident until he saw the assembly actually gathered together, and by the desertion of the other tribunes. No doubt he had won the first two tribes by slender and inadequate margins. Now he was left with one night to rally his supporters, and this time he did his very best.[11]

Down into the forum went the tribune, wrapped in the black clothes of mourning, and until the day faded he walked about, begging for support from one citizen after another. With tears in his eyes he used the humble and desperate language of a frightened man. He asked the people to protect his children and himself, and even had his young son brought from home so that he could show the child to the voters and beg them to look after him.[12]

This wretched self-abasement was the traditional style for a Roman politician in trouble. It had saved Galba in 149 and Scipio had caused a stir by disdaining such methods in 140. The attractive and still popular Tiberius could do as well. And again he went over the arguments, trying to convince the poor that they would end up as slaves to the rich, not citizens equal before the law (A). Then he declared his fear that his enemies would break into his house during the night and assassinate him. This time his words took effect, and in the warm Roman evening a great crowd of supporters rallied to Tiberius' side and escorted him home, many of them spending the night on guard around his house.

*

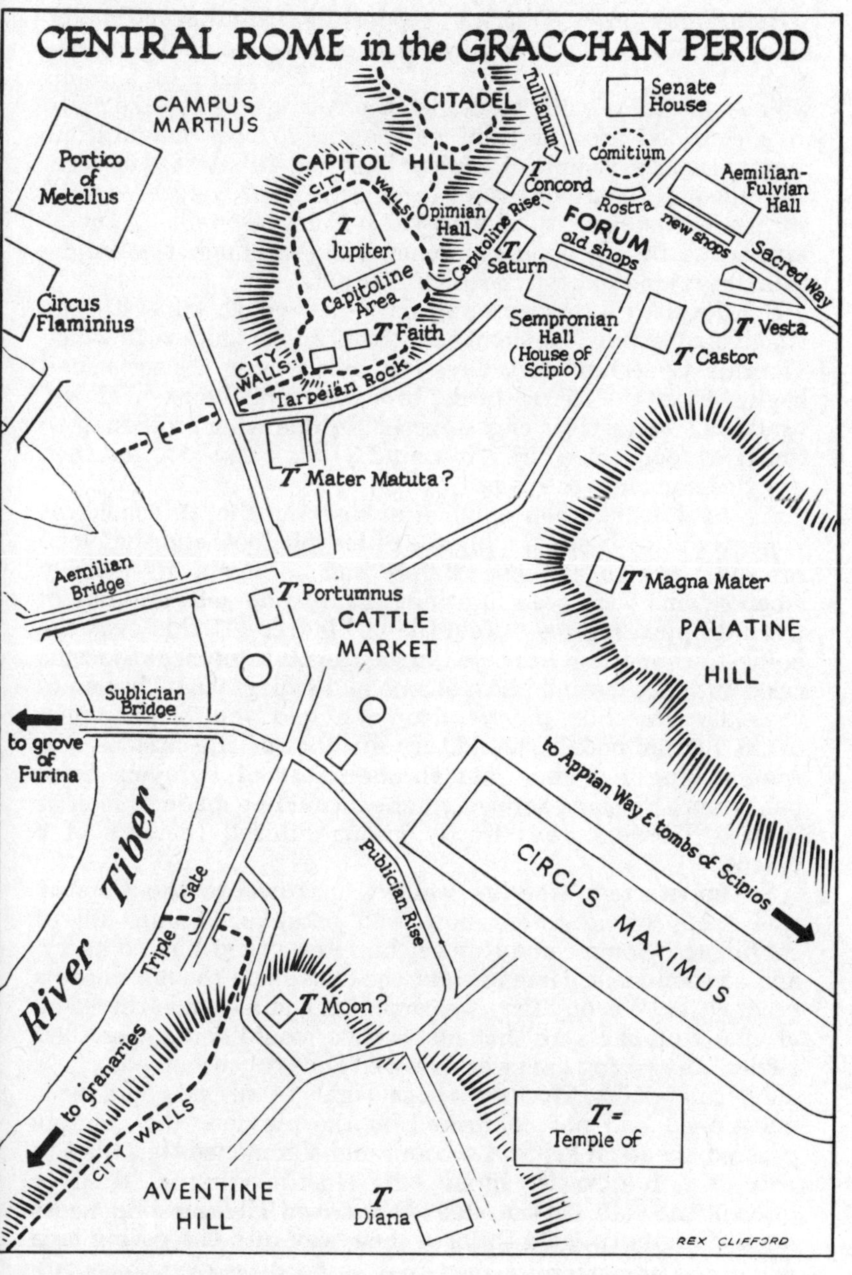

CENTRAL ROME in the GRACCHAN PERIOD
CAMPUS MARTIUS
CITADEL
Senate House
Portico of Metellus
CAPITOL HILL
Comitium
Tullianum
Aemilian-Fulvian Hall
CITY WALLS
T Concord
Opimian Hall
Rostra
T Jupiter
Capitoline Rise
FORUM
new shops
Capitoline Area
T Saturn
old shops
Sacred Way
Circus Flaminius
Sempronian Hall (House of Scipio)
T Vesta
CITY WALLS
T Faith
T Castor
Tarpeian Rock
T Mater Matuta?
Aemilian Bridge
T Magna Mater
T Portumnus
CATTLE MARKET
PALATINE HILL
Sublician Bridge
to grove of Furina
to Appian Way & tombs of Scipios
River Tiber
Publician Rise
CIRCUS MAXIMUS
Triple Gate
T Moon?
to granaries
CITY WALLS
T = Temple of
AVENTINE HILL
T Diana
REX CLIFFORD

Before day broke Tiberius' supporters, including no doubt many who had been called from the near-by fields during the night, began to gather on the Capitol hill. Here, on the hill which was Rome's oldest citadel, the voting was to take place in a confined area in front of the city's most magnificent monument, the temple of Jupiter Best and Greatest. The area, a levelled enclosure of two or three acres, was congested with shrines and statues so that it was not unreasonable to try to secure the best ground beforehand, even though this might look like trying to keep the other side out.

But despite this encouraging show of strength, superstitious Romans afterwards remembered the grim portents with which Tiberius Gracchus' last day, just like Julius Caesar's, had begun. First the sacred birds, brought to his house at dawn, would not leave their cages except for one which, refusing to touch its food, raised its left (unlucky) wing and foot and then scuttled back into the cage.

As he left his house he stumbled on the threshold so violently as to break the big toe of his left foot, and the blood ran out through his shoe. Barely had he begun his journey when ravens were seen fighting, again to his left, and one of them dropped a piece of roof-tile at his feet. At this even the boldest around him hesitated, until the philosophical Blossius cried out that it would be a shame and a disgrace if the son of the elder Gracchus, the grandson of Scipio, and the champion of the Roman people should turn his back on the citizens who were calling for him, just through fear of a raven. Such behaviour, Blossius shrewdly added, could be made to look as though Tiberius was already giving himself the airs of a tyrant.[13]

So undeterred Tiberius walked on towards the Capitol, where his friends were now well established and full of confidence. Some came to meet him and urged him to hurry, and as soon as he came in sight the crowds on the hill raised a great cheer. Warmly they welcomed him, and then gathered all around to make sure that no stranger could come near their leader. The voting area was now well and truly occupied.

At this point Mucius, whose right to preside had been questioned and not confirmed on the previous day, simply pressed ahead on his own account and summoned the tribes to vote. Again disorder broke out. Hostile tribunes tried to prevent the vote. On the edge of the crowd Tiberius' opponents pushed and struggled to force their way into the voting area while his supporters pushed just as hard to keep them out. The din was overwhelming, it was impossible to maintain customary procedures, precedents no longer gave a clear guide. Anything could happen.

Meanwhile in the near-by temple of Public Faith the senate was meeting, with Tiberius' ally the consul Mucius Scaevola in the chair. Should anything be done, they were debating, to prevent Tiberius from being re-elected in such an unruly gathering? Scaevola, an honest lawyer as well as a Gracchan sympathizer, flatly rejected the suggestion that it was the consul's job to interfere with armed force. But at this other senators indignantly began to threaten that they would take the law into their own hands and kill Tiberius themselves, with the help of slaves and retainers already armed and standing by. This was promptly reported to Tiberius by another Gracchan senator, Fulvius Flaccus, who found the Capitoline area so thickly crowded that he had great difficulty in getting through with his message until Tiberius saw him and cleared a way.[14]

As in any riot, the question of how violence began is obscured by the attempts of both sides to disclaim responsibility for it afterwards. Perhaps so far there had been nothing more than jostling and threatening language. Or had the opposition tribunes been forcibly pushed away? Had they tried to veto the election, as Appian seems to suggest, and if so had their veto been overruled or ignored? It is not clear whether even now Tiberius was in the majority, since his partisans are numbered by Plutarch as only 3,000. But these will have been enough to dominate the centre of the voting area, which is why the opponents were so anxious to force their way in. Plutarch, whose account at this stage is distinctly more favourable to Tiberius, argues that he would still have been ready to give way if an attempt had been made at peaceful persuasion. But it was the frightening report by Fulvius that precipitated the next stage.[15]

First thing in the morning Tiberius had agreed with his supporters to give them a signal if he felt his life was threatened. Now he gave it. Immediately his nearest supporters closed ranks tightly round him as a bodyguard. Others girded up their cloaks and seized the rods and staffs carried by the official attendants supposed to be controlling the election, and broke them up into makeshift weapons. Then they drove their opponents out of the assembly with such a show of fury that even the opposition tribunes withdrew in terror, and the priests shut the door of the temple of Jupiter.

This time they had gone too far. The fugitives ran scattering wild stories, that Tiberius had deposed the other tribunes (who were nowhere to be seen) and that he had declared himself tribune for the coming year without an election. But it was the ill chosen signal with which Tiberius had rallied his supporters that did the greatest damage. He had simply stood and raised his hand to his head. But his opponents thought, or claimed, that they had seen him demanding a diadem or crown, to realize that royal ambition that had been rumoured ever since the will of Attalus, and with this terrible news they ran to the senators. This was the last straw.[16]

The hour produced the man. The high priest Scipio Nasica was a pillar of the conservative nobility, descended from five successive consuls on his father's side and from the great Scipio Africanus on his mother's. His tactless canvassing had once made him so unpopular that he lost an election, when he shook the horny palm of a farm labourer and then blandly asked whether the poor fellow walked on his hands. His year as consul had involved him in bitter disputes about the corn supply and the levy, and a spell in jail. 'I know better than you what is good for the state,' he had told the people. Now his estates were threatened by land reform. Suddenly the prospect of revenge on his cousin Tiberius and on the whole disruptive popular movement must have seemed sweet indeed.[17]

Once more Nasica put the question to the consul. Would he rescue the city and put down the tyrant? Scaevola stood firm, calmly stating that he would not begin any violence nor put any citizen to death without a trial. All he would concede was that if Tiberius in fact either persuaded or compelled the people to vote for anything that was unlawful then he would not regard it as binding. In other words anybody who wished to challenge Tiberius should do so within the framework of the law, whose authority the consul would of course maintain.

'But while the consul sticks to the letter of the law,' Nasica angrily retorted, 'he is in fact tearing down the Roman empire and all our laws with it. I may be only a private citizen. But if you wish it I will be your leader. Those men who want to preserve the republic, let them follow me.'[18]

With his dramatic appeal Nasica had cut the Gordian knot. The consul would not act, and his decision bound the other magistrates. But a private citizen could act, and the high priest was the right man to do so, for Romans hated tyrants with a religious fervour. And so as Nasica set off for the centre of the voting area, with the senators behind him, he emphasized this religious element by taking the purple border of his toga and wrapping it about his head as though he were dressed for offering sacrifice.

It is sometimes argued that even now these senators had no wish to kill their enemy, merely to break up what they regarded as an illegal assembly. But Scaevola's refusal to put a citizen to death without trial reveals what was in everybody's mind. By displaying his solemn robes of office and his sacrificial dress, the high priest was in effect giving his blessing to the violence about to be committed.[19]

As this mass of the Roman nobility bore down on the assembly, their high priest at their head, no man dared stand in their way. The Gracchan supporters yielded and ran. In vain Tiberius tried to rally the people with a speech. Behind the senators came their own adherents, with the clubs and staves they had brought from home. The senators themselves tore the weapons from the hands of the Gracchans.

Then suddenly, from where he had been hiding in the temple of Jupiter, sprang the tribune Satureius, 'dripping with sweat, his eyes blazing, his hair on end, and his toga awry', and ran forward towards Tiberius. Even while the herald was trying to call for order for Tiberius' speech, Satureius planted his foot on one of the benches that had been laid out for the assembly and tore a leg off it, calling on the others to do the same.

Tiberius began to pray to the gods, but the senators with their wooden weapons attacked his bodyguard. A man in the crowd shouted, 'Fly, Tiberius, fly. Can't you see? Look behind you.' The bodyguard was put to flight. Tiberius turned to run, and as somebody grabbed at his toga Tiberius let it go and took to his heels in his tunic. But as he tried to swerve round the back of the temple he tripped over the bodies of men who had already fallen.

It was as he was struggling to his feet that Satureius caught him and struck him on the head with his chair-leg. Tiberius fell, and tried to rise again. But this time a man called Rufus swung at him with a cudgel and broke his skull open. Without a cry the great tribune fell dead on the steps above the archway of Calpurnius, near the gates of the Capitoline area and close to the statues of the old kings of Rome.

Trapped on the isolated hilltop of the Capitol, some two to three hundred of the Gracchans were killed on the spot, either with sticks and chair-legs and stones or else hurled bodily over the Tarpeian rock, where criminals were usually executed. None of them was killed with an iron weapon, it is recorded. So powerful was the taboo—for iron was strictly excluded from all Roman sacrifices. Tiberius and his friends had been butchered like sacrificial pigs.[20]

Despite the request of young Gaius Gracchus that he be

allowed to bury his brother, the bodies of the dead were thrown into the Tiber.[21]

*

The sense of shock produced by this one day of riots and murder was never forgotten at Rome. Was this the end result of nearly four hundred years of peaceful evolution in domestic politics and unparalleled military successes abroad? Something unthinkable had happened.

When Appian wrote his history of the Civil Wars that had finally brought Augustus to the imperial throne, he began with the tribunate of Tiberius Gracchus, for 'until then no sword had ever been carried into the assembly nor had there ever been a political murder'. Plutarch recorded that 'since the kings were driven out this was the first civil unrest to be settled by the blood and murder of citizens'. 'Here was the beginning of civil bloodshed and the unpunished use of swords in the city of Rome,' wrote Velleius; 'from this moment on, the law was overborne by force, might was regarded as right, and disputes between citizens were settled with the sword.'[22]

In a dialogue set in the year 129 Cicero gave the clearest account of the watershed that had been crossed, by posing the question, 'Why in our one republic do we now have two senates and virtually two separate peoples? For you can see how the death of Tiberius Gracchus, not to mention the whole character of his tribunate, split a united people into two.' It left a double legacy of violence and division, as Appian showed. 'It was the first such evil crime in the assembly but not the last, for the precedent was then regularly followed. Yet the city was split between grief and joy over the death of Gracchus, with some people rejoicing that all their wishes had been fulfilled while others wept for themselves as well as for him, afraid that their constitution was now replaced by the rule of force.'[23]

At the moment when politics had only just begun to polarize into two broad groupings, the attitude of each side was immediately dominated by memories of violence, and dreams of vengeance. Plutarch felt that 'the rich' had been motivated by hatred and anger rather than the pretexts that they put forward, and in evidence points to their savage and lawless abuse of the dead tribune's body. Reflecting the opposite view, Cicero spoke of Nasica, 'who though a private citizen restored the state to freedom from the tyranny of Tiberius Gracchus', and of Tiberius' slayers, 'who filled the whole world with the glory of their names'. Valerius Maximus denounced Tiberius as a man 'who preferred his own aggrandisement to the safety of his fatherland'. Scipio Aemilianus, aloof and triumphant in far-away Spain, welcomed the news with a lordly quotation from Homer:

So perish anyone else who tries to do the same.[24]

But despite the bitterness (and this sneer came near to costing even Scipio his popularity) there was also a universal feeling that a remarkable man had died, a man for whom no praise seemed too great. He was 'easily the first in birth, in good looks, and in eloquence'. 'He far surpassed his contemporaries in wisdom and speaking ability, and indeed in every accomplishment.'

After comparing their achievements Plutarch concluded that Tiberius outshone his brother and the two Spartan kings in virtue. It is hardly surprising that a rather sentimental picture gradually emerged, of the good man who went tragically wrong, 'who died in the pursuit of a most excellent policy, just because he pressed it too hard'.[25]

Tiberius turned the state upside down, although his birth was high, his talents worthy of his grandfather Africanus, his education superb and his spirit noble.

He shattered the stability of the republic; but what a man he was! What a speaker! What a leader! In no way did he fall short of his father's and his grandfather's outstanding virtues, except that he broke with the senate.

A man totally free of any fault, brilliant in intellect, honourable in purpose, adorned with every noble quality that an ideal character and an ideal training can instil into the human frame, yet when he became tribune he broke away from the good men, passed his land laws, offered the citizenship to the whole of Italy, stirred up greed everywhere, confounded the highest and lowest elements in the state, and brought the whole country into extreme and terrifying danger.[26]

Yet these psychological studies tell only a small part of the story. Tiberius Gracchus fascinates most when seen clearly in his context. He found Rome facing a great complex of problems. Perhaps with Appian we should accept that the military and manpower crises were the most urgent, but these in turn rested on a tangle of social and economic difficulties.

To deal with these Tiberius' personal position was always anomalous. In a Rome seamed with divisions between families and social classes his background tore him both ways. He could have sided with Scipio as easily as with Appius Claudius, he could have stood in the ranks of the conservative senators as easily as among the reforming tribunes. He was sprung from the heart of the nobility, yet alienated from it by the Mancinus affair. Today's verdict must be that his intentions were honourable and his patriotism sincere, and yet he died an outcast.

Looking back it is easy to see that land reform alone was not enough to solve all the problems. Yet merely trying to follow up this initial move brought him immediately up against serious constitutional problems and formidable opposition. He did too little for his country's needs and yet too much for his countrymen to accept. But it is not surprising that he ran into these harsh realities, the limits of the tolerable, for his tribunate was unprecedented in a way that is not always recognized. It was, in fact, the very first time that anybody had tried to govern Rome in the modern sense, by considering the problems and searching for answers. It was nobody's job to do this under the existing constitution. Rome had no effective government. Power was in the hands of the nobles who accepted responsibility for nothing except success in war (and not always that). The total absence of any coherent alternative programme is one of the most remarkable features of the whole business.

In this as in so many ways, what a contrast there was between Romans and Greeks, who whether in republic or monarchy always produced such a rich and even embarrassing flow of plans and policies. The conservative Romans seem to have had no ideas for coping with their problems nor even to have seen the need for them. No doubt if more nobles had faced up to their responsibilities they could have worked out some programmes of modest change, with due regard to the over-riding national interest and the preservation of social harmony, as did their opposite numbers in nineteenth-century England. But the basis for doing this never existed in Rome. And so change brought bloody conflict.

In the original programme there was no ideological content. To redistribute the people's land, whether fair or not to the existing tenants, was not to launch class warfare. But to push such change through in the way Tiberius was forced to do was to tread a revolutionary path. This challenged the established way of doing things, it threatened the dominant role of the landed gentry, it posed for the first time the question of real and effective popular sovereignty.

Most significant of all, in Tiberius and his friends we see for the first time those different interests in the state coming together which were to crystallize as the popular movement. Nobles who wanted regular voting support, reformers who wanted to solve Rome's problems, poor men who wanted only land and jobs and corn, adventurers and desperadoes who wanted only self-advancement, in the popular cause they could all stand together.

Perhaps Tiberius did try too hard, and showed himself too ready to accept the possibility of violence. Perhaps, carried away by the magnitude of his task, he became too intolerant and maybe too ambitious. Yet he had laid the foundations and shown the way, apparently the only way, in which Rome could be made to change. His brother was to learn these lessons and make it change.

But what of the nobles who finally lost their patience on the Capitol hill? They saw the threat all too clearly. That they struck out so savagely is not surprising. Their world was in danger. But in acting as they did, instead of patiently struggling through the courts and the electoral assemblies to regain control, they made the fatal mistake which was to destroy their world without trace. They created a legend and a martyr. It was they who split the state in two. Reconciliations became impossible.

From that moment on every Roman had to be either for or against the memory of Tiberius Gracchus. Either you hated him, or you hated his murderers. In Roman politics nothing could ever be the same again.

8 A Showdown with Scipio

Tiberius Gracchus was dead, but his cause and his brother lived on. And although for the moment his far-sighted younger brother held cautiously back from the glare of public life, yet the cause flourished. The reign of Tiberius had provoked assassination, yet the hard core of his policies survived.

Those who had resisted the whole concept of reform from the outset were isolated and forced into a position of weakness. The land reform that Tiberius had dreamed of became a dynamic reality that profoundly changed the republic. And yet it created its own fresh opposition; it was forced to a dramatic showdown involving the lofty figure of Scipio Aemilianus; and it left an inheritance of even more complex problems to challenge the political genius of Gaius Gracchus.

*

Tiberius Gracchus was dead, along with two hundred or more of his followers, and their bodies were thrown into the Tiber.[1]

Such treatment was offensive but perhaps for the best. A Roman funeral could be an evocative affair, as Mark Antony was to show. But Rome was not yet the city of Julius Caesar. The machinery of government held firm, the instincts of the aristocracy took command, and worse trouble was averted.

For this the credit must go to the consul Scaevola. Although his support for the Gracchan movement and his sustained hostility to Scipio Aemilianus cannot be doubted (his contacts with Scipio's friends Laelius and Rutilius notwithstanding) Scaevola was above all a great and patriotic lawyer. He had ruled that Tiberius' old commander Mancinus had forfeited citizenship by his act of surrender.[2] He had been more moderate in his politics than his brother Crassus. On that fatal day of 133 he had tried to settle the dispute by process of law, refusing to take up arms for either side.

Now as consul he was in charge of the state. Blood had been shed. Cicero called it 'a terrible crisis, when the omens showed great dangers menacing the state'. The people raged furiously against those who had done the deed. Tribunes who remained loyal to Tiberius organized an immediate inquiry, summoning the senators and demanding to know the name of the actual murderer, and only Scipio Nasica was bold enough to admit responsibility and even claim credit for doing away with a tyrant.[3]

For a moment his candour quietened the mob. Then Scaevola himself came forward and gave his view that Nasica's use of violence had to some extent been justified. Whether he actually praised the murder might well be doubted (Cicero had his own reasons for suggesting that he had), but by his words he damped down thoughts of immediate vengeance. Perhaps it was by his suggestion that the mysterious Sibylline books were consulted, and on their advice priests were sent to the sanctuary of the goddess Ceres in Sicily to expiate the crime, while thrice nine maidens sang in a ritual to purify the city.[4]

In fact a deal had been done. Scaevola did not press for vengeance, and indeed perhaps he was one of those who had begun to feel Tiberius was going too far. What mattered to him was the original goal of land reform, and for this he secured his greatest success. For in return for the restoration of order the senate was persuaded to make its own concession and permit the distribution of public land to continue.

It might have been difficult actually to repeal or void the land law, but the implication seems to be that administrative barriers were withdrawn. The senate showed its wisdom, commented Valerius Maximus, alike by punishing the tribune and by preserving his law, for by doing so it destroyed both the author and the cause of the trouble. Another land commissioner was needed to replace the dead tribune and the people chose Scaevola's brother Crassus, father-in-law to Gaius Gracchus, so that the commission remained a family affair as it had begun.[5]

But if land reform were to go ahead then Nasica had to be sacrificed, since he had led the opposition on this very point, while most other senators had objected mainly to Tiberius' later and more extreme behaviour. The pressure on Nasica built up again, with threats of prosecution and violent abuse. Fulvius Flaccus, the one leading senator known to have been with Tiberius at the end, engineered a judicial challenge against Nasica and proposed Scaevola as arbiter. The tactless

Nasica rejected the great lawyer as prejudiced, which further annoyed the senate, and though he tried to turn the affair with a joke he was by now in evident danger. It would be better for everyone if he could be put out of the way.[6]

Fortunately an opportunity arose quickly, and again Scaevola's hand can be traced. To secure the work of land reform he needed Tiberius' settlement of the province and revenues of Asia confirmed. But there things were happening quickly. The pretender Aristonicus was already in open revolt against the transfer of his country to the Romans. Quickly he won over several cities and many poor people and slaves, offering them freedom and calling them 'Citizens of the Sun'.[7]

The senate had formally accepted the bequest of Attalus before 24 September 133 (the date of the Pergamene New Year), and a month later it acted to reassure its supporters there with a further decree ratifying all the official acts of the Pergamene kings. At the same time an embassy was sent out to try to quench the revolt with whatever loyal forces were available on the spot. Nasica was chosen to lead this inauspicious mission. Understandably it achieved very little, and after travelling up and down the country with nothing to his credit he died there a little later.[8]

Scaevola had done very well indeed, checking the violence, rescuing the land reform, and removing its main opponent. There was only one trick he failed to take. The consular elections must have come almost immediately after Tiberius' death, with no chance now of passing the law needed to permit the re-election of the main Gracchan candidate Appius Claudius. In the absence of any ready alternative the centuries voted for two hostile candidates, Popillius and Rupilius, the latter a particularly close protégé of Scipio Aemilianus.[9]

Once these two took office in 132 it became clear how valuable Scaevola's restraining hand had been. Now the senate passed a very different decree, that 'the consuls should punish, after the fashion of our ancestors, those who had supported Gracchus'. It is not to be supposed that the great noble leaders of the reform movement were the target of such an exercise, but their lower-born allies were brought before a formal inquiry on which Scipio's old friend Laelius sat as adviser to the consuls.[10]

Punishments of the utmost severity were handed out. Blossius of Cumae managed to get away and fled to join the revolt in Asia, but others were less lucky. Diophanes the teacher of rhetoric was executed and an unknown C. Villius was done to death by being locked in a cage with poisonous snakes.[11]

Yet not even these heavy-handed consuls had everything their own way. One intended victim, Vettius, called on the young Gaius Gracchus to defend him, which he did with such spirit as to stir up frantic enthusiasm among the people and some alarm among the conservative senators.[12] Perhaps the warning was taken and the inquisition allowed to lapse. Scaevola's policy had proved wiser, and the result of this savage consular outburst was only to swing the pendulum further in the Gracchan direction. And now it was becoming clear just what an immense political force Tiberius had unleashed.

*

Scipio returned from Numantia, but victory over the tough Spanish hillmen had brought him little in the way of prisoners, booty or glory. His triumph in 132 disappointed even his own soldiers, who received a bounty of only 7*d.* apiece from the proceeds of the campaign, whereas Scipio's father had handed out 100*d.* each after the battle of Pydna a generation before.[13] None of this helped Scipio's cause or his friends, and it seems that his ally Rupilius was actually refused a triumph despite settling the war in Sicily, with all that that meant for the security of Rome's grain supplies. After watching his brother's defeat at the next consular elections, despite Scipio's support, we are told that Rupilius finally took his own life in shame.[14]

Victory was passing into other hands. The brilliant Crassus Mucianus, brother to Scaevola, had already been elected land commissioner the previous year. Now he was chosen consul for 131. When news of Nasica's death came through he was also elected high priest to succeed him.

Then the senate decided that one of the new consuls should take active military command of the war in Asia. Although no high priest had held such a command before Crassus promptly threatened to fine his colleague, who happened to be a junior priest, if he left his religious duties in Rome. The popular assembly remitted the fine but told the other consul to obey Crassus. When somebody proposed instead that the job should go to Scipio the city's most experienced commander received only two tribal votes out of thirty-five, and Crassus went off to the East.[15]

This was a marvellous chance to win yet more fame and glory, with an important political goal too. For the treasure of Attalus, which held the key to land distribution, had still not reached Rome, and Crassus made this his main objective rather than the pursuit of the rebels.[16] So he took even further that eastern connection which runs so persistently through the Gracchan story. Victory and treasure from Asia, added to his strong political base at home, could have given Crassus a golden opportunity. If it had worked out that way . . . .

Work on the land programme was meanwhile gathering speed. Over the years the Romans had enough practice at surveying and allocating land to settlers to develop it into a highly systematic activity, and a whole literature has survived on the subject. Boundaries were marked with stones erected according to precise rules, and to our very good fortune several of the actual stones used for the Gracchan distribution have survived to this day.

Of at least eleven original Gracchan stones eight can confidently be ascribed to the years 132-131, because they bear the names of the land commissioners of that time. A typical stone takes the form of a pillar. On its shaft are inscribed the three names of C. Sempronius (Gracchus), Ap. Claudius, and P. Licinius (Crassus), always in that order, with their official title of 'three commissioners for assessing and allocating land'. On top of the stone lines are cut to indicate direction, and code letters to fix its position in the survey. All eight stones were found in south-west Italy, six in the fertile Vallo di Diano above Salerno and two more on the edge of the foothills behind Naples. Elsewhere, at Pesauro in the north-east, we have another stone erected half a century later which purports to restore the work of these same commissioners.[17]

No doubt surveying the land and checking the status of owners and applicants posed severe administrative problems. But it is clear that preliminary work was making good progress, even though the delays in obtaining the money from Pergamum meant that not enough of the new land was actually settled in time to affect the census figures of 131. Meanwhile two major wars were over and the grain supply from Sicily was secure again. Things were looking better for the Roman people.

It was of this period that Cicero wrote of Appius and Crassus leading the 'slanderers and enemies of Scipio', and it is perhaps significant that for the first time in history two plebeians were elected censors in 131. Both of them, Metellus and Pompeius, had shown personal hostility to Scipio, and both had joined in the attack on the later behaviour of Tiberius, not on land reform as such.

Pompeius had always been a popular figure, while Metellus revealed an almost Gracchan concern for social reform and the manpower problem. He adorned his term of office with a famous speech urging all good Romans to take themselves wives and produce children. He even suggested that marriage be compulsory, and handed down an often-imitated commonplace of public speaking: 'The trouble with women is that we cannot live with them pleasantly nor without them at all.'[18]

As the Gracchan revival flourished it became more respectable to support its wider aims even while refusing approval for Tiberius' later behaviour. For example Annius Rufus, praetor in 131 and probably son of the Annius who had attacked the tribune so effectively, even saw fit (whether during or after his term of office) to claim credit for his own efforts at land reform. He carved the deed on a milestone which he erected in the same Vallo di Diano, 'I was the first man to make the herdsmen on public land give way to the farmers.'[19]

*

By now, in fact, the revival was strong enough to make further headway against even the popular Scipio Aemilianus, a job which was tackled by the talented yet sinister figure of C. Papirius Carbo, one of the most forceful young men of the day.

The same age as Tiberius Gracchus, and of comparable talent in Cicero's view, Carbo had seized the opportunity offered by the growing number of semi-political trials and lawsuits (especially since the secret ballot now made it harder to bribe the jurors). Maybe his speeches were described as crude and short of legal expertise, but he had mastered all the advocate's tricks. He could be polite or sarcastic, fierce or melodious, as the need arose, and so earned the reputation of an advocate who won cases.[20]

For all that he was a man born out of his time, more akin to the unprincipled adventurers of the next century. Such at least was the stereotype image of him that grew after he had ignominiously changed sides, been accused of murder, and poisoned himself. The family was ill fated, for other members also met with evil reputations and violent deaths.[21]

Having backed Tiberius in 133, this remarkable man became tribune himself in 131 with what looks like a carefully drawn programme. First he pushed through the third of a series of laws to establish secret ballots, this time in legislative assemblies. This would reduce the influence that rich men (and Scipio more than any one else) could bring to bear by mobilizing their personal supporters and pressurizing their social inferiors and dependants.[22]

Remembering how uncertain Tiberius' voting support had become in the latter days of 133, Carbo was preparing the way for his next and more radical proposal, a bill to permit a man to be re-elected tribune as often as he wished. As the issue that had decided the fate of Tiberius, this provided an opportunity to debate the whole Gracchan programme.

The proposal came under vigorous attack and passions rose again. Carbo wept for the murdered tribune, and used all his flattery to win support. Gaius Gracchus spoke for the bill, while Scipio Aemilianus led for the opposition with all the weight of his personal authority and dignified style of speaking, backed in turn by his faithful shadow Laelius.[23]

In the event Scipio's following remained loyal despite the temptations of secret ballot, and the bill was rejected, leaving the legal position as unclear as it had been two years before. But Carbo's main purpose, to stir up political feelings again, was well achieved, and the debate was chiefly remembered for a famous argument into which Scipio rashly allowed himself to be dragged.

Carbo simply asked what Scipio thought about the death of his brother-in-law Tiberius Gracchus. Scipio had been scornful at the safe distance of Numantia, but it was a very different thing to speak his mind in open assembly at Rome. Yet he stood up and declared that Tiberius had been justly killed, adding only the saving clause (according to one account) 'if indeed he had been planning to take over the state'.

A tremendous uproar burst from the assembly, whereupon Scipio made matters worse with ill chosen sneers against the people as well as their champion.

'I never feared the shouts of whole armies,' he told the assembly, 'so don't expect me to be bothered by your noise, you who are only Italy's step-children.' For by now the Roman assembly included a fair number of people who had been foreign-born slaves and captives, or were descended from such.

'Should I care,' he asked, 'about men whom I myself led into captivity and sold off as slaves?'

When both Gaius Gracchus and Fulvius Flaccus pressed the same question he continued to give hostile replies. But from now on Scipio's public appearances became the object of frequent interruptions and hostile demonstrations such as he had never faced before. A great leader's popularity had crumbled, and this was Carbo's real achievement. With Nasica dead Scipio Aemilianus was the chief opponent to the Gracchans, especially to the process of land reform, and for the moment Carbo had neutralized him.[24]

*

The Gracchan movement should now be thought of as commanding broad acquiescence, if not open support, across a very broad span of Roman politics, including the chief dignitaries of state: censors, high priest and leader of the senate. All was set fair for Crassus to return in triumph from the east with the elusive treasures of Attalus. Until one day bad news arrived.

'More intent on the booty than the war', Crassus had left too much of the fighting to an impressive parade of Eastern monarchs. Nicomedes of Bithynia, Mithridates of Pontus and Armenia, Ariarathes of Cappadocia, and Pylaemenes of Paphlagonia, all had hastened to show their loyalty to Rome. But during the winter Crassus, apparently acting independently, had been badly beaten in an assault on Leucae. His army broke in flight and he was captured by the pretender's Thracian guards.

A consul in the hands of rebels jeopardized his own and Rome's dignity. The recent fate of Hostilius Mancinus did not encourage any compromise. So Crassus deliberately struck out at the Thracians with his riding cane, blinding one of them, and was butchered on the spot, 'so avoiding both disgrace and captivity', yet also 'paying with his own blood the price of his rash greed'.[25]

His death was a heavy blow to the Gracchans, especially when the leader of the senate Appius Claudius died during the same winter in Rome. But the ranks were reformed with remarkable speed.

Scaevola himself was chosen as high priest in his brother's place.

To lead the senate the censors chose the aged L. Lentulus, who had been consul a quarter of a century before. Lentulus was probably an enemy of Scipio since he became one of the main butts of Scipio's friend, the satirist Lucilius. Certainly by choosing him Metellus and Pompeius deliberately snubbed Scipio, the only other living patrician ex-censor, who must have regarded himself as the obvious candidate.

It was moves such as these that fully justified Cicero's sad lament that even with Crassus and Claudius dead the slanderers and enemies of Scipio still managed, under the leadership of Scaevola and Metellus, to keep half the senate opposed to him.[26]

Two new members of the land commission had also to be found to replace the dead, and the people chose Carbo and

Fulvius Flaccus as the most prominent of the out-and-out Gracchans. Carbo had just been in the public eye, but it was Fulvius who effectively replaced Appius as leader of the movement. Although noted by Cicero as more a student of literature than a strong speaker in his own right he was a competent soldier and a vigorous hot-tempered politician, thoroughly at home in the new and more turbulent Rome. He had been close to Tiberius Gracchus in those last moments on the Capitol and joined in the attacks on both Nasica and Scipio.

Like Carbo, Fulvius had perhaps inherited some streak of unruliness. His grandfather had shown lawless cruelty in the great war against Hannibal; in 174 his father or uncle had been expelled from the senate by a brother who had ended a distinguished career by hanging himself. The Fulvian family had given Rome almost a score of consuls, but the Gracchan leader was to be the last of the line.[27]

Fulvius and Carbo were men of lesser standing than Claudius and Crassus, but they could be expected to push even harder for reform. And now good news came from Asia at last. The new consul Perperna, possibly a supporter of the Claudian family, had raced out to the army of Crassus and swiftly pursued, trapped and captured the pretender Aristonicus. The rebel was strangled in Rome. The consul took ill and died in Pergamum, and another Appius Claudius was elected in his place. And the vital treasure was safely shipped to Rome and sold at auction.

Wealthy Romans shamelessly competed to buy from this breathtaking collection of precious objects and works of art. Amassed over a century and a half by prosperous and cultured tyrants and kings, the treasure of Pergamum must have outshone even the booty of Corinth or Macedon. Pliny moralized that it was from this auction that the Romans finally learned to lust after the show of wealth, not merely to admire it. What mattered politically was that the financial constraints on land distribution were at an end.[28]

Now the three commissioners could press ahead with their work on the land. Again we have surviving boundary stones, naming Fulvius, Gaius Gracchus and Carbo (in that order), found farther inland than the earlier ones, in the hill country near Benevento.[29]

The census figures give some idea of the pace of development. In 136 fewer than 318,000 adult male citizens had been counted, the lowest figure for thirty years, and in 131 still only 319,000.

But by 125 the number had leaped to 395,000. Despite doubts about what the figures exactly mean, the huge increase must represent the results of land reform and shows how much was at stake.

Whether more men became qualified for the census or whether there was more interest in counting them, the overall result was to raise Rome's effective manpower resources by a quarter. Even by 131 the reform had gathered enough pace to reverse the decline. But once the tedious preliminary work of surveying and adjudicating had been well advanced, then the younger and more aggressive commissioners of 130, with the proceeds of the Asian treasure in their pockets, were able to accelerate the distribution to bring about the dramatic results revealed in 125.

To create 80,000 jobs inside eight years would be an important achievement for any modern government. For Rome it was a colossal feat. This was the Gracchan triumph. Tiberius had not lived or died in vain. Yet it was no wonder that such work created difficulties and stirred up opposition which now brought the reformers to a showdown, and in doing so inextricably linked the dominant theme of Tiberius' tribunate, land reform, with that of his brother's, the people of Italy.

*

The sharp deterioration in the political atmosphere under the revised commission, in 130 and 129, is clearly recorded. Livy states that 'seditions' were stirred up by the new commissioners and Scipio set himself to oppose them. Appian adds a more detailed account.

Those who occupied public land had been slow to register their holdings, and so the new commissioners called for informers to come forward. Immediately many difficult judgements fell to be made. Whole districts had to be investigated because one estate had been sold or divided. Contracts and title-deeds were lost or ambiguous. Some owners were made to exchange orchards and buildings for empty ground, or cultivated fields for swamps. Farmers had been free to cultivate any public land adjoining their own, so that the boundaries had been quite obscured. Time had changed everything. The rich were being unfairly treated but by how much it was impossible to tell. With all the moving and resettling, everybody's affairs were in a muddle.

The muddle was universal but, Appian adds, it was 'the Italians' who could not tolerate the upheavals and the harassing adjudications. And so they turned to their old friend Scipio to champion their cause and prevent their wrongs.[30]

Again Appian has brought the Italians into the centre of the picture, and his evidence is well supported. A later Roman scholar left us this explanation. 'Scipio had taken up the cause of the Latins, according to their rights as allies, against Gaius Gracchus and his fellow commissioners, to prevent their land too from being divided.' And Cicero went even further into the subject, by trying to recapture the uneasy days of 129 in a fictional dialogue between Scipio and his friends. Some passages are full of foreboding.

The slanderers and enemies of Scipio [*now led by Scaevola and Metellus*] . . . will not permit him to help us in this emergency, although he is the only man who could do so, when the allies and Latins are storming with fury, their treaties have been broken, these subversive land commissioners plot some new trouble every single day, and all good men are in despair.

If we cannot reunite both senate and people again we shall be in the most serious trouble.

A little later a gap in the manuscript leaves us with this tantalizing fragment.

. . . Asia Tiberius Gracchus looked after the citizens but neglected the rights and treaties of the allies and Latins. If this lawless behaviour spreads and changes the basis of our empire from justice to force, so that those who willingly obeyed us can be controlled only by terror . . . then I fear for our descendants and for the immortality of our republic.

And the 'Dream of Scipio', the famous final scene of the book, contains this moving appeal to the great man.

The whole state will turn to you and you alone. The senate, the good men, the allies and the Latins will depend on you. The safety of the republic will rest on your shoulders. It will be your duty to become dictator and restore the state—if only you can escape the murdering hands of your relatives.[31]

But what on earth was going on, and why had the Italians come into the centre of the picture? How can we reconcile Appian's belief that the Italians were intended beneficiaries of the land law with this evidence that they were more upset by it than anyone else?

We can be sure that Cicero was following very closely, even if embroidering, the events of 129. He and Appian are clearly discussing the same people, so that 'the Italians' must include both the privileged 'Latins' and the more loosely bound allies in the rest of the peninsula. This alone rules out the tenacious theory that Appian was referring only to those Roman citizens living outside the capital. Roman citizenship was precisely what the Italians had not got and were eventually to fight for, as Appian well knew.

The only logical answer is that those Italians who stood to gain were not the ones who felt aggrieved, and this makes very good sense.

Who might gain? Poor landless Italians hoping to receive land not needed for Roman citizens. Whether or not the reform was originally meant to help them, later Gracchan propaganda was bound to claim so, once Gaius had made the Italian cause his own. And from the· military standpoint extra Italian manpower was almost as valuable as extra Roman.

But, no matter who benefited, who was bound to lose? Wealthy Italians who already occupied public land which was being taken away from them for distribution. In Scipio's eyes and Cicero's these were the leading citizens, the Italians who mattered, and they had a real and bitter grievance.[32]

So here is how the crisis must have developed. The first commission had set to work quickly, working mainly in the south and no doubt starting on the least controversial sites. But gradually arguments about what was and was not public land became more of a problem. The more aggressive second commission of 130 sought to overcome this obstacle by a more ruthless deployment of their judicial powers.

In so doing they stirred up bitter resentment among the Italians, and the reason is obvious: the commissioners found it a good deal easier to bully Italian occupiers of the public land than those who were full Roman citizens.

This had to be so, for Romans rich enough to hold surplus public land would be more likely to have powerful friends in the capital than the average Italian would. But we can speculate further.

The political tide had been running in the Gracchan favour, and it is not too much to suppose that the commissioners had encouraged this by relaxing their efforts against citizen occupiers and concentrating against those who had no votes (or only limited voting rights, as the Latins had). So allied landholders were being pushed off land which they had long farmed, as a result of legislation passed in Rome for the prime benefit of Romans. And it was in this sense that they could reasonably complain that their rights, status and treaties had been unilaterally violated by the Romans. Here was material that a generation later would set the peninsula ablaze with civil war.

But who would champion the Italians in their distress? Most rich and powerful Romans must have welcomed this diversion of the commission's interest. And so the allies turned to Scipio, the man who would put honour first.

Scipio's recent misfortunes seem to have taught him discretion, for when he spoke in the senate early in 129 he carefully avoided criticizing the principle of the Gracchan law, which would have enraged the people. Instead he merely emphasized the practical difficulties that had arisen, and proposed that the adjudications should be entrusted no longer to the land commissioners, who could hardly command the confidence of the landholders, but to somebody else.[33]

The argument seemed fair and the senate ruled that the disputes should be judged by the consul Tuditanus. He promptly saw what a difficult and unattractive job this would be and vanished north to fight a war in Illyria. And suddenly, with no way of resolving the disputes, the commissioners were unable to secure more land and their work ground to a halt.

Again the people vented their fury on Scipio. Once their darling, whom they had twice helped to an unlawful consulate, now he had turned against them to assist the Italians. Personal enemies alleged that he had decided to bring the land law itself to an end and would not stop short of bloodshed to do so. Was this the proposal to make Scipio dictator, that Cicero hints at? No wonder that friends of Gaius Gracchus called out to 'kill the tyrant', at which Scipio boasted that it was hardly surprising if men who tried to sabotage their own country should want to kill him. 'For Rome cannot fall while Scipio stands firm. Nor could he live on if the city succumbed.'[34]

While panic gripped the people, Scipio found himself again the centre of a crowd of admirers. Cicero paints a dazzling picture of 'the finest day of Scipio's life' when, one evening after the senate had risen, he returned home escorted by a great cavalcade of senators and commoners, Latins and allies.

But the same day had been tarnished by a particularly virulent attack from Fulvius Flaccus in the forum. On the morrow Scipio was expecting to be denounced at further public meetings, and perhaps to face serious legal proceedings. Yet before composing the speech with which he would defend himself before the people, he calmly lay down to sleep.[35]

In the morning the hero was found dead in bed.

Bloodshed and dictatorship had been averted.

The land reform was free to continue.

9 Gaius Takes up the Cause

While his brother's political heirs did battle against Nasica, the consuls of 132, and his own cousin Scipio, Gaius Gracchus kept himself quietly in the background. His reticence has puzzled many people, at the time and since.

About his vigour, energy and fire there could be no doubt. Plutarch's judgement, already quoted, is confirmed by the furious pace he set in office, and echoed in other, more hostile, appraisals.

> His brother had drifted from excellence to ambition, and only then to wickedness, but Gaius was naturally turbulent and a willing rogue.... So his schemes were even more pernicious and his behaviour always bolder and more outrageous.
>
> He was luckier in his style of speaking than in his theme, for he used his blazing genius to subvert the state, when he could have been its staunchest supporter.

Thus Dio and Valerius Maximus.[1]

Yet his energy was more under control than this would suggest, and there were other sides to his character. Plutarch flatly denies 'the widespread view that Gaius was a demagogue pure and simple, even keener than his brother for popular acclaim—the fact is that he seems to have been forced into politics rather than to have chosen it'.

To begin with he withdrew from the forum and lived quietly by himself, as though planning to continue a modest and inactive life, 'so that he even found himself criticized for despising and rejecting his brother's policies'. Appian notes that Gaius 'had for a long time kept quiet after what had happened to his brother', and Plutarch explains why. 'It was either because he feared his enemies or else as a way of forcing them into an invidious position.'[2]

To be sure, he had other things to do. He chose to serve

twelve years in the army rather than the statutory ten before seeking election. Born in 154 he must have joined up in 138, at the earliest possible age of sixteen. Apart from major foreign campaigns like Numantia (where he fought with Scipio), we are not to suppose that military service was a full-time occupation for a privileged member of the officer class, but he enjoyed it and was as well trained for war as for the law-courts (P).

Furthermore, whether or not he really meant to stand for tribune during 133 we know that he was elected land commissioner. In view of the heavy commitments of his colleagues it is likely that, as the youngest member, Gaius was charged with the main burden of administration and travelling. For it was during these years after 133 that he made it plain that his quietness was not to be an excuse for an idle and soft life, nor one wasted in drinking and financial speculation (P).

Some time after 131 Gaius linked himself more closely to his brother's friends by marrying Licinia, daughter of the late high priest, consul and land commissioner Crassus. Licinia's mother may have been a Clodia, and so perhaps related to the other Gracchan leader Appius Claudius, although after her first husband's death in the east she seems to have gone on to marry the redoubtable Brutus, whose political interests were very different.[3]

His marriage mattered to Gaius, for later he is found lamenting that out of the whole Scipio-cum-Gracchus family only he and his one son survived, and suggesting that perhaps even then he should withdraw from politics to ensure the survival of the breed. This anxiety for the family could have been encouraged by his mother Cornelia, who had now apparently retired to her country home at Misenum but kept up a steady correspondence to her son's house on the Palatine hill.[4]

Another passage of Plutarch also captures this rather wistful fancy for the quiet of family life, shared by many statesmen.

> After seeing the striking ill fate of his brother, Gaius withdrew as far from public life as he could. But eventually, infuriated by the contempt and abuse heaped on him, he had his own try. Quickly he became weary of the pressure of affairs and public opinion. But when he tried to give it up and yearned for peace again he found no way of laying down his power, for it had grown too great. Instead he perished first.[5]

Indeed a Gaius Gracchus could hardly expect to live in obscurity, and his rare political appearances were always exciting events. After carefully developing a speaking ability 'that could raise him to the heights' he began by defending Vettius, probably in 132. His talent, which 'made the other speakers appear no better than children', immediately alarmed the opposing leaders, who began to murmur that they would need to prevent this Gracchus from becoming tribune too (P).

His speech in support of Carbo's electoral bill in 131 carried an even clearer note of warning.

> You scoundrels who killed Tiberius, the best of all brothers: watch and see how I return like for like.

Then over the next couple of years we have seen him involved with the 'seditions' of the land commissioners, the pressure on the allies, and the attacks on Scipio.[6] When Scipio so suddenly and opportunely died it is not surprising that foul play was suspected and the name of Gaius attached to it. Yet he came out of it fairly clean. The main suspicion centred on the hot-tempered Fulvius Flaccus (P) or else on Cornelia, mother of the Gracchi, and their sister Sempronia, Scipio's loveless and unlovely wife (A). Later on Carbo became the prime suspect.[7]

Slaves were said to have testified under torture that murderers had been let in through the back door during the night to suffocate Scipio (A). The evidence is confused but it seems that the body was unmarked (except in Plutarch's account). Poison was the favourite theory. One view was that he killed himself in despair of attaining his ends (A). It could also well have been a natural death, perhaps a stroke brought on by the great excitement.

Politically what mattered was that the affair was hushed up. There was no judicial inquiry, for the people were relieved at Scipio's death (A) and had no wish to see Gaius implicated in the results of any investigation (P). For the man who had done so much for Rome there was not even a public funeral (A). But Scipio's family and friends seemed content to let it pass.

The faithful Laelius, in a splendid funeral speech composed for delivery by Scipio's nephew Fabius, simply commented that 'illness removed him at the very moment when his life could have been of the greatest service to you and to all who love our country'. Metellus also did his best to heal the wounds. Despite his own personal enmity he greeted the news of death with the sad epitaph, 'The walls of our city are overthrown,' and insisted that his own sons should carry the funeral bier.[8]

*

Scipio's death had an importance more symbolic than real. In a sense he was the last of the old leaders, the statesmen who tried to remain grandly outside the intensifying political struggle. Yet his own career had bristled with constitutional anomalies. His military reputation rested on patient siegecraft rather than any tactical brilliance, and his real contribution to the problems of a difficult period was no more than modest. That notorious arrogance with which, for example, he summed up the consuls of 144, 'The one has nothing, nothing can satisfy the other,' was hardly justified.[9] But for all that there was no man of such stature to take his place in the state, and Cicero imaginatively describes the alarm then felt by the conservative nobles.

> When Carbo and C. Cato were supporting Tiberius Gracchus, Gaius was not very conspicuous, but now he burns with enthusiasm [*Laelius is speaking a few days after Scipio's death*] . . . . And so we have reached such a situation that it must be our duty to watch out for the dangers facing the state. Our old political traditions have already swerved from their normal track. Tiberius Gracchus tried to seize regal power, or rather he really did reign for a few months—when had the Roman people heard or seen such a thing before?
>
> Even after the death of Tiberius his friends and relatives followed his cause, and what they did to Scipio I shudder to tell. We have put up with Carbo as best we could, in the little time that has passed since Tiberius paid his penalty.
>
> But what am I to expect when Gaius Gracchus becomes tribune? I do not like to forecast. Events are unrolling and once they gain momentum they will rush us headlong to disaster. Now I seem to see the whole people estranged from the senate, and the greatest affairs of state settled according to what the mob thinks.
>
> More people will learn how to start trouble than how to resist it.[10]

Yet Cicero overestimated his hero, and the immediate effects of Scipio's death were limited to the issue that had preoccupied his last years, that of Italian land. Appian claims that the occupiers still managed to postpone the division by spinning out their arguments and excuses. But Dio reports that with Scipio out of the way the power of the nobles was again diminished so that the commissioners could 'ravage' (a strong word to use) the whole of Italy. Livy says that the 'seditions' of the commissioners now flared out more fiercely than ever. It must be concluded that Scipio's attempt to reduce them to idleness failed with his death.[11]

The fact that Scipio's behaviour had brought him so much unpopularity must indicate that even in 129 there was still a great pent-up demand for land among the citizens. Friction with the Italian occupiers continued, and we must deduce that the work of distribution continued over the following years, up and down the length and breadth of Italy, to the great annoyance of the Italians.

Unfortunately no further Gracchan boundary stones have yet been found, but another source makes it possible to assess the overall scale that land distribution finally reached.

This is the curious 'Book of Colonies' compiled under the later Roman empire, a garbled list of Italian and other settlements. Most of these colonies were established by the emperors. But for more than thirty of them the list specifically refers to the land boundaries laid down by surveyors working under Gracchan legislation. Some land was assigned under these laws but later redistributed by an emperor; in other cases it seems that the Gracchans merely did the surveying work without any formal allotment. The fragmented document is of monumental obscurity, but the evidence of those names is vital. Many are obviously prime sites for settlement. Some are close to where Gracchan stones have been found, in south and central Italy. At some on the east coast the marks of rectangular land divisions can be seen today, with a criss-cross pattern easily traceable from the air. Gaius may have been responsible for some of these allotments, but Tiberius' original land law was the driving force behind them.

The form and state of the book suggests that the list is far from exhaustive, and it must powerfully reinforce the conclusion that the Gracchan surveyors made themselves felt throughout the country. They had a massive total impact on the pattern of land settlement, and therefore on the jobs and economic life of rural Italy. The original and prime aim of the Gracchan movement was accomplished. By the censorship of 125 perhaps all the available public land had in fact been distributed. The fact that land hunger did not end there, and poverty and unrest were not thereby eliminated from the Roman world, set a new challenge for the reform movement. Reform was more complicated than had been thought.[12]

Perhaps working on the land programme still kept Gaius busy; perhaps with Scipio out of the way there was less reason to rush into public life. Having completed his ten years of military service he could have stood for quaestor in 129 or 128 but did not do so. He still shrank from politics and public speaking, yet felt unable to resist the appeals of the people and his friends. When he finally stood and was elected quaestor for 126 he claimed he was glad of the chance to leave the city, for by chance he had drawn an assignment to accompany the new consul Orestes to Sardinia (P).

Yet this picture of self-denial is not wholly convincing. The rebellion in Sardinia was the year's major military commitment, and so the best chance for glory. In view of the island's history as almost a family fiefdom (his great-grandfather conquered it and his father fought there twice) it might be doubted whether the ballot was totally left to chance. Gaius was to do well there, which helped his career as much as Spain helped his brother's.

Similarly his delay in standing for office can be overstressed. He became quaestor at twenty-seven, two years older than his brother but not old by normal standards. This would not hinder his career. It is even possible that he simply waited for the prospect of an important foreign campaign, for the two previous years seem to have been as bereft of military glamour as any in Roman history.

In other words Gaius knew what he was doing, and once this is realized then the period of withdrawal loses its mystery. As a young man badly shocked by his brother's murder, what must his priorities have been?

First to keep his head down and avoid a similar fate. Second to see the land reform, for which he had a personal responsibility, successfully carried out. Third to develop his own skills at speaking and soldiering. Fourth to choose the moment to make a noteworthy entrance on to the public stage. All these things he did. We may guess that there were already signs of trouble in Sardinia before he stood for election, and perhaps a friendly candidate for consul. His apparent reluctance to step forward until overwhelmed by public demand looks only like shrewd public relations. For then he went further, and in an obvious throwback to the mystique of his grandfather Scipio Africanus brought supernatural influences into play as well.

'I have had a dream,' he told his friends, 'that my brother Tiberius came to ask me why I was delaying—for as champions of the people the same life and the same death awaited us both.'[13]

What matters is the truth behind the façade. 'He was seized with the same madness as his brother,' says Velleius, 'whether his purpose was to avenge his brother's death or to seize regal power for himself.' Florus says that, 'He burned with the same ferocity both to avenge his brother's death and to champion his laws.' Appian notes that many of the senators treated him contemptuously and it was this that led him to work against the senate. But the best witness is Gaius himself, when he told the Roman people in a later speech that, 'Nobody comes and speaks before you for nothing, but what I ask you for is not money but that you think well of me and hold me in honour.'[14]

The clear picture is of a proud and bitter noble determined to re-establish his position in the state, yet careful and far-sighted enough to plan a much stronger power base than that which had collapsed so unceremoniously under his brother. And so, while following wholeheartedly the direction set by his brother, he began to prepare for political action on a much wider scale. His brother's fate showed that his support had been too fragile to carry out worthwhile and lasting reform, while the course of the subsequent decade made it clear that a broader approach was needed. Turning over one stone had merely revealed how widespread was the rot in the Roman state. More needed to be done, and to do it much more support was needed.

So after 133, and much more after 129, Gaius Gracchus and his friends began to prepare such a movement and such a programme. Four great interests in the state were to dominate his political activity, and in different ways they all came into focus during these preparatory years. What were these four?

The knights, with their flourishing business interests.

The Italians, resentful about land and their inferior status.

The citizen poor, hungry for land and food, with a massive if unreliable voting strength.

The provinces of a neglected and under-exploited empire.

About all these Gaius thought more clearly than anyone had ever done before. By juggling these interests he brought about a realignment of Roman politics more profound than his brother had achieved. From now on politics developed as a kaleidoscope of shifting alliances as leaders tried to build power groups strong and stable enough to achieve change—or to resist it.

This development became clear only when Gaius came to power. Until then we have but scanty records, tantalizing snapshots of manoeuvres hard to interpret. So at this stage it is most convenient simply to record these successive stepping-stones which brought Gaius to power, and only then to consider how he tried to fit them together into a coherent political whole.

*

The first move towards mobilizing the latent political power of big business came in 129. Leading businessmen headed the companies of financiers, public contractors and tax farmers, whose importance had been vastly multiplied by the spread of empire and the inflow of wealth. Their organization and activities embraced the entire Mediterranean world. They also had social standing, which was never far removed from wealth in Rome. For, just like the senators and those many rich men who must have lived only the simple lives of non-political country gentlemen, these leading businessmen were members of the eighteen centuries of Roman knights, proud possessors of the traditional right and duty to fight for the state on a horse provided at public expense.

Such businessmen will have had much in common with the senators of all but the very grandest noble families, and indeed they stood together against Tiberius Gracchus. Yet their interests were not and could not be expected to be identical on all points. Could they not be prised apart?[15]

In 129 a proposal was put before the Roman people to enact that men who entered the senate should hand back their public horses and thus cease to be knights. Here was no obscure technicality, for Cicero, well aware of all that was to follow from it, put these words into the mouth of Scipio.

'How sensibly the social orders, age-groups and classes of voter are organized, as well as the centuries of knights in which the senators also vote. Too many people are now stupidly trying to wreck this useful system; they are searching for a new kind of bribery, proposing some kind of law for the return of horses.'[16]

Since such a rule was in force by the end of the republic it is likely that it became law in 129, after the death of Scipio, judging from Cicero's reference. A formal and permanent distinction had been established between the first two social orders, the senators and the knights. The dominant voice in the eighteen centuries had passed from the nobles of the senate to the most influential financiers and contractors. A new political-force was born.

In the charged atmosphere of 129 it was only reasonable to put into Scipio's mouth so strong a condemnation of what must be regarded as a Gracchan measure. But the reference to bribery may give a further clue. Perhaps this was also the occasion for passing another measure to give the knights (now excluding the senators) the much treasured privilege of fourteen reserved rows of seats at the public games.[17]

But the knights had an even more urgent reason to look round for political support. Two inscriptions found in Asia Minor have preserved for us a battered account of a dispute considered by the Roman senate, probably in this same year 129. It concerned businessmen who had apparently taken the contract to collect taxes in the new and just-pacified province of Asia, the former kingdom of Pergamum, a rich land dear to Gracchan hearts.

It was an important case, examined in detail by a committee which probably included Metellus and Laelius, and it turned on the precise boundaries separating the territory of the city of Pergamum from the rest of the province. The city was exempt from Roman taxes, and the trouble taken by the citizens to preserve this record argues that the decision went in their favour and against the business interests. No doubt the senate was anxious to show favour to the new province, which had already been milked to finance the Gracchan land programme. But the dispute must have made it easier to drive the wedge between business and senatorial interests. There is no direct evidence that Gaius Gracchus was involved in any of these events, but it can safely be inferred. His closest ally Fulvius Flaccus, probably praetor in 129 or 128, is known to have been active at this time in 'dissension over new legislation', a phrase which would fit this context perfectly.[18]

*

In the next episode, a bold attempt to win the support of the Italian allies, both of these popular leaders were openly involved. It may have begun as an attempt to soothe Italian resentment about land reform, or that resentment may have opened Gracchan eyes to the political possibilities. Land reform had exposed the vulnerability and inferior status of the Italians as never before.

So alarming was the prospect suddenly opened up that its opponents launched an equally bold pre-emptive strike to prevent Fulvius from being elected consul for 125. This is the most convincing explanation of the notorious proposal by Junius Pennus, tribune during 126, to expel all foreign-born residents from the city of Rome.

Even Cicero described it as an inhuman measure, while the

new quaestor Gaius Gracchus vigorously denounced it before sailing off to Sardinia, lamenting that the Italian peoples had now lost their own political rights on top of everything else, thanks to Roman greed and stupidity.[19]

The proposal can be best understood as an anti-Gracchan measure intended to keep the Italians away from the consular elections, for fear that they would demonstrate on behalf of Fulvius and that some of them, the Latins, might even exercise their right to vote for him. Pennus carried his law, for we know that even the father of the recent consul Perperna was forced to leave the city. But Fulvius still won his election, presumably with the all important voting help of those eighteen centuries of knights that he had helped in 129. No doubt business interests among the next rank of voters, the seventy centuries of the first class, supported him too.[20]

So as consul in 125, Fulvius Flaccus tabled his great and revolutionary plan, to extend full Roman citizenship to any of the Italians who wanted it, and to others the treasured right of appeal to the Roman people.

Appian explains this move in two rather different ways. The most common view was that it was a prop to land reform, so that in sheer gratitude the Italians would stop quibbling about their land. Indeed they greeted the proposal with delight, admitting that they preferred citizenship to hanging on to their disputed lands.

But there was much more at stake, and in a separate passage Appian comments that Fulvius was the first Roman openly and publicly to inflame the Italians with a desire for Roman citizenship, as a means to become partners in the empire rather than subjects. Here once again the dual personality and the dual aims of the Gracchan movement come clearly into sight. Concern with the immediate economic interests of the Roman poor marched hand in hand with this broad view of the strength and health of the entire state, composed of subjects and allies as well as Romans. This dichotomy provides their claim to greatness, and was to be their undoing.[21]

Fulvius kept up the strongest pressure for his proposal. But the senators were indignant at the idea of giving equal rights to subject people, says Appian, and their view prevailed. The Gracchans were outmanoeuvred, deprived of their best speaker because the senate decided to keep Orestes in Sardinia for another year and Gaius had perforce to stay with him. The other consul Plautius also seems to have opposed the scheme, for which Gaius later attacked him. So strong was this opposition that Fulvius was reluctant even to enter the senate house. When he did he was alternately urged and warned with such force to drop his proposal that he felt unable, or refused, to reply, which was thought to be a display of singularly bad manners.[22]

At last the senate found the ultimate answer, an excuse to send the consul off to fulfil his prime and overriding duty of waging war. The people of Marseilles sent an appeal for help and Fulvius had to go to fight the tribes of southern Gaul. He did very well, and won a victory important enough to earn him a triumph, but the war kept him away from Rome and so amid great popular disappointment the franchise bill lapsed.[23] But what is revealing is that if the senators felt they had to resort to such a manoeuvre to remove Fulvius, then they must have expected that otherwise those same centuries that had elected him consul would approve his law. Considering the extent to which the wealthier classes dominated the assembly of centuries, the inference must be that wooing business interests was already paying dividends for the Gracchans.

Meanwhile in Sardinia Gaius Gracchus was also having a good war. Plutarch enthusiastically records:

> He gave every proof of a fine character. Whether fighting the enemy, dealing justly with the subjects or showing respect and loyalty to his commander he far surpassed the other young men, while his moderate, frugal behaviour and readiness for hard work outshone even his elders.
>
> A harsh winter came and sapped the strength of the soldiers, so the general ordered the local communities to provide them with extra clothing. But they appealed to Rome, where the senate accepted their pleas and told the general to find some other way. He had no idea what else to do, and the soldiers were suffering terribly, whereupon Gaius went round the towns and persuaded them to send clothing of their own free will.
>
> When all this was reported to Rome the senate was even more alarmed, regarding the incident as a clear forerunner of new political disturbances.[24]

Gaius and his commander were kept on the island for another year while Fulvius tried for his franchise bill. His failure was followed by two further threats to the tranquility of the Roman world.

First came a disastrous blow to the grain supplies. A terrible plague of locusts destroyed the crops of North Africa, to be followed by a widespread pestilence that killed, we are told, hundreds of thousands of people. Supplies and prices were affected all over the Mediterranean for several years. Grain was to be a major political issue two years later, with emergency supplies being shipped to Rome from as far away as Spain. Yet right in the heart of the crisis an African king, Micipsa, sent some of his own precious grain stock to help out the troops in Sardinia, 'in honour of Gaius Gracchus'.

Now Micipsa was the son of Masinissa, who many years before had been a close friend to Gaius' grandfather, the elder Scipio. Again the family tree was bearing fruit, in a way that could hardly harm Gaius' electoral prospects but earned the royal ambassadors a chilly dismissal from the senate in Rome.[25]

The second blow was even sharper. Revolt flared up in Italy itself, not sixty miles from the capital in the historic Latin town of Fregellae. This old colony had been a bulwark of the alliance in the bitter war against Hannibal. A generation later it attracted thousands of settlers from the hill country. Only the greatest pressure could have brought so prosperous a town, 'whose splendour illuminated Italy', as Cicero described it, to the point of revolt.[26]

The stimulus for revolt must have come from the great passions aroused by the franchise bill of Fulvius Flaccus. Rome was terrified by the fear of insurrection flaring through the alliance, for the many accounts we have use sinister words to tell of treachery, conspiracy, dangers and civil war. One report has it that a second town, Asculum, joined the plot. Another testifies that other Latin dissidents were only held back by the speed of Rome's response. The praetor Opimius was sent out with an army, the town was betrayed to him and utterly destroyed, even though the inhabitants were spared.

Yet although revolt could always expect the harshest reaction from the Romans, Cicero's comment that Opimius had saved the state from the greatest dangers has to be viewed in the light of later events, that showed Opimius as the fiercest opponent the Gracchans ever met. The revolt was directly related to the internal political struggle within the capital, and an ominous portent of the violence to come. Though at least the senate had the tact to refuse Opimius the glory of a triumph.[27]

*

In the five years that had followed Scipio's mysterious death the Gracchan movement had found a keener cutting edge. Land reform had been pressed home, business and Italian interests mobilized. Fulvius Flaccus had shown powers of leadership, while young Gaius had at last emerged from private life, to demonstrate talents and popularity no whit inferior to those of his martyred brother.

Gaius now wanted to hold office as his brother had done, the voters seemed likely to give him it, and much of what he intended to do must have been clear. The conservative anti-Gracchan group, which now dominated the senate, had reason to feel anxious. Tiberius had shown how the senate could be by-passed. For one crucial year Gaius had been kept away from Rome, with Fulvius consul and Fregellae in revolt. But what would happen next? The elections of summer 124 would be the next testing time, and we can judge that everything pointed to a Gracchan victory.

So a last attempt was made to stave off the crisis. At the beginning of 124 Orestes was again told to remain in Sardinia, his command extended for a third year. Naturally Gaius was expected to remain there also.

Instead in a fury he broke precedent and sailed home on his own authority. The people clapped and cheered to greet his sudden arrival in the city, but such precipitate action brought him much criticism, not merely from his personal enemies. He was summoned before the censors, as guardians of public propriety, who at this time were the strict but popular leader L. Cassius and the conservative Cn. Caepio.

But Gaius easily fended off the charges. Did the censors realize, he asked, that he had served twelve years in the army when other men only had to do ten? He had remained with his commander into a third year although the law permitted him to return after only one. He was the only man in the army who had taken a full purse to Sardinia and brought an empty one back, while the others had even stuffed their wine-jars with gold and silver to bring home. So well did he speak that he left the hearing with a clear name and even some sympathy for having been unfairly criticized.[28]

In a speech to the people he then developed this theme further, contrasting his own honest behaviour in the province with the corrupt manners that had become so common.

On provincial duty I conducted myself in the way that I thought would best serve your interests rather than most further my ambition. I kept no drinking shop crowded with pretty young slave boys. Your sons had to behave as carefully at dinner as when on duty.

I made sure that nobody could truly claim that I had

accepted a penny in gifts, or that anyone else had been put to expense on my account. I spent two years there, but if in that time any harlot was brought into my home, or anybody's slave boy solicited on my account, then think of me as the lowest man on earth. So if I even kept my hands off their slaves you can judge for yourselves how I lived with your sons.[29]

Quite apart from the striking insight that these remarks give into the behaviour standards of the day, this theme of honest provincial government was a fruitful one. No doubt the two years Gaius spent in Sardinia did much to mature his ideas, but the subject was already very much in the public eye because of a notorious recent trial involving again the rich province of Asia.

After Perperna had died in Asia the consul for 129, Aquillius, took over the command there, imposed a final peace, and with the aid of ten commissioners settled the affairs of the province. In 126 he returned home, to triumph through the streets of Rome, and then face the indignity of prosecution before the standing law-court on provincial extortion. Prosecuting were aged P. Lentulus, the new leader of the senate, and Scipio's friend Rutilius Rufus, neither of them friends of the Gracchan cause. With or without their connivance, Aquillius secured acquittal by open bribery of the senators who composed the court, an event which Gaius scathingly criticized, and to which he was to find an answer.[30]

It may be a sign of Gracchan influence that the consuls of 124 founded a new colony, Fabrateria, to replace the flattened Fregellae.[31] Good news kept coming of Fulvius Flaccus, successfully campaigning in the valleys east of the Rhone, an area which until then had interested Rome only as a high road to Spain. Gaius cleared himself of new charges, that he had been party to the conspiracy at Fregellae and even encouraged the allies to revolt (although some communication between the Latin rebels and their Gracchan sympathizers can surely be taken for granted). And then at last he formally declared himself a candidate for the coming elections, to stand for the office of tribune in 123.[32]

The tide was unstoppable. A couple more fragments of his speeches at this time survive. 'How can the man who speaks favourably of villains help attacking honest men?' 'If I can secure what the people want I shall prove it is to the benefit of the whole state.'[33] Plutarch says that in the election campaign all the nobles opposed Gaius, presumably meaning that fewer supported him than had backed his brother. Which is likely enough, for already he was a more controversial and, with his wide spread of interests, a more dangerous man than Tiberius.

But huge crowds of voters came in from the countryside to give Gaius their support. Instead of the confines of the Capitol the election was this time held in the wide spaces of the Campus Martius, the field of Mars. Even this was not roomy enough for all the voters. Many, after failing to find lodging for the night, had to be content with shouting their support from the roof-tops, helped no doubt by allies who as yet had no vote and hoped to be given one. The nobles won this much of a victory, that of the ten tribunes elected in summer 124 Gaius was returned not first, as expected, but fourth. But his margin was clear enough.[34]

On 10 December 124 Gaius Gracchus, brother of the martyred Tiberius, younger son of the great censor, grandson of the great conqueror Scipio Africanus, took office as tribune of the people. And his cause? It was reform, revolution and revenge.

10 Revolutionary Power

What the evidence of the last two chapters has made clear beyond question is that the nine years following the murder of Tiberius Gracchus were utterly dominated by Gracchan politics. It is time to abandon the usual picture, of a near vacuum interrupted by sudden and inexplicable storms, and terminated out of the blue by the extraordinary eruptions of 123. Instead, carefully examined, even our scattered evidence reveals a pattern of steady development.

Sharp reaction followed the tribunate of Tiberius Gracchus. Both sides showed anger and intolerance. But slowly a broader-based Gracchan movement began to emerge. The live tribune had been a goad and an irritant; martyred he became a symbol and his work was carried on. Quickly self-confidence returned to the movement, bringing further confrontation and ending in the death of an over-strained Scipio. Land reform was achieved.

New leaders, Fulvius Flaccus and young Gaius Gracchus, began to look for new targets, new causes, and new allies. As with reform movements throughout history, the first step forward proved to be only a beginning, not an end.

Such a view is fully confirmed by the hectic pace that Gaius set when in office. Roman laws were complex documents, not to be drafted in a week. So much was done in that year, in a turmoil of legislative and administrative activity not to be repeated until the dictatorship of Sulla in 81, that it can only be understood as the end product of years of planning and intriguing. Bearing in mind the long absences of Gaius in Sardinia and Fulvius in Gaul, and their continued involvement with the land commission, the talk and preparation may well have begun as far back as the death of Scipio. It is easy to imagine that it was after the removal of that one towering figure that Gaius began seriously to plan his own career, and to give careful thought to the difficult task of completing the work that his brother had left only half-begun.

The sequence of events by which the new tribune went to work is the subject of controversy, for historians have been tempted to divide his work and career into 'moderate' and 'extreme' phases according to which of his policies they happen to approve of. That is hardly a satisfactory form of analysis. In fact dispassionate examination shows that the Gracchan policies were much more of a piece, evolving largely in response to identifiable pressures and quickly changing circumstances.

Because of the problems that crop up later on, the only way of making sense is to date all the legislation actually passed to 123, and the unsuccessful proposals to 122. As to the development of his ideas, what can be traced is that the great judiciary law did indeed emerge in two stages, before and after the mid-123 elections, while the most controversial proposal of all, the franchise bill, was deliberately left till last, perhaps along with other more radical schemes.

Although elected only fourth of the tribunes for 123, Gaius dominated the scene from the outset. It is an enviable characteristic of aristocratic government, from which Rome benefited again and again, that it can bring talented and self-confident young men to a level of deep political maturity while their energies are still fresh. Gaius Gracchus exemplifies this principle as much as any man in history. A great man had come to power, whose vigorous driving force and irresistible speaking ability brought him instant mastery over the Roman state.

It was for Gaius Gracchus that Cicero, although no political sympathizer, reserved his most glowing enthusiasm when reviewing the long line of Roman orators.

But now we come to a man of the greatest ability, of intense application and thorough education. Compared with Gaius Gracchus you cannot imagine anyone better or more richly equipped for public speaking. Of the earlier speakers he is the only one I think you should read.

His untimely death was as great a loss to Latin literature as to the Roman state. If only he had shown as much loyalty to his country as he did to his brother!

How easily a man of such talents would have matched the glorious achievements of his father or even his grandfather, if only he had lived longer! In sheer eloquence I think he would never have found an equal. His words were sublime, his arguments were shrewd, and his whole style was earnest.

Admittedly his works lack the finishing touch, and what was so well begun was not always brought to full perfection. But I am sure that the young men should read Gaius Gracchus in preference to any other statesman, for his words will strengthen as well as exercise their minds.[1]

Such praise is echoed on every side. Plutarch emphasizes that he immediately became foremost of all the tribunes, with his 'incomparable' power of speaking, as well as a loud and robust voice essential for anyone trying to dominate the open-air Roman assemblies. Livy, Velleius and Dio all stress that he was a far better speaker than his brother. The historian Tacitus and the philosophical emperor Marcus Aurelius both read his speeches with devotion.[2]

But how were such talents to be deployed? What motives drove him on? The passionate personal commitment, over and above the principles of reform that he was struggling for, come over equally clearly in the ancient writers. At one point even Cicero shows some sympathy with this personal motivation.

'Gaius Gracchus was roused by the death of his brother; and his own loyalty, grief and indomitable spirit drove him to avenge the shedding of his family's blood.'

Plutarch confirms that Gaius sought vengeance for a brother 'slain not by the law nor by senate's decree nor even at the hand of a magistrate'. As soon as Gaius became tribune he kept speaking with great emotion about the death of his brother, using every excuse to remind people what had happened.

'Your ancestors would go to any lengths to maintain respect for the tribunes. But these men, before your very eyes, clubbed Tiberius to death and dragged his corpse through the city to throw it into the Tiber. His friends were arrested and killed without trial, contrary to all our old-established practices.'[3]

The same bitterness showed through when some opponent was rash enough to speak slightingly of Cornelia, mother of the Gracchi. 'How dare you insult Cornelia, who bore Tiberius?' Gaius lashed back. 'How can you even compare yourself with her? Have you borne such children as she did? Why, you are a man but the Romans know that she has kept off men longer than you have.' The coarse style was apparently not untypical of Gaius' exchanges in the forum.[4]

This strong personal feeling gave his politics a more vigorous and partisan tone than those of his brother. Immediately on being elected he began to plot against the senate, says Appian. Diodorus comments on his tremendous popularity with the mob, and his speeches threatening to establish democracy in the place of aristocracy. But it was above all the energy with which he worked that impressed men most. 'Such was the man who pitted himself against the established constitution and accepted no limit to his words or deeds,' wrote Dio, and Velleius echoes the same view. 'He left nothing unchanged, nothing tranquil, nothing at peace: he left absolutely nothing in the same state that it had been in.'[5]

*

Many attempts have been made to classify the legislation of Gaius Gracchus into political and non-political measures, but without success. There is hardly a move that does not contain elements of tactical manoeuvre and of long-term reform. Above all the power base had to be maintained—and how can we guess what promises had been made to whom before Gaius came to power? And yet these successive moves are so closely linked with one another as to reflect a depth of analysis of Rome's problems never again matched under the republic.

Which is not to say that all details were worked out in advance, for politicians must react to events. But the theme and style are consistent. And it must be remembered that when Gaius came to power he could only expect one year of authority, one year in which there was so much to do . . . . His plans, as Velleius saw, were both greater and more controversial than his brother's. Unhappily they never commanded such broad support among the nobility as his brother's first measures had. His own revolutionary drive served to inflame and unite the opposition. It is noteworthy that with Tiberius we know the names of more supporters than opponents. With Gaius the opposite is true.[6]

After stirring up the sympathies of the people Gaius began with a measure directly related to the central crisis of his brother's career, the deposition of his fellow-tribune Octavius. He proposed a law that any magistrate deprived of office by the people should not be permitted to hold office a second time. The effect of this was to smear Octavius directly and, more important, to reinforce the principle that the people had the right to depose. He was warning off anybody who thought of following the example of Octavius, and the threat alone was enough. At his mother's request Gaius withdrew the law, to spare Octavius who may even have faced the threat of exile under it. This act of charity pleased the people and raised Cornelia's esteem even further. But to the best of our knowledge no tribune dared to veto Gaius for the rest of that year.[7]

No such second thoughts came to the rescue of the next victim, Popillius, the heavy-handed consul of 132. A law was passed to provide that no Roman citizen should be sentenced to death except by order of the Roman people. It probably also extended the protection against sentences of exile, regarded as virtually a 'living death' since it meant deprivation of civil rights, and against flogging.[8]

This new protection was badly needed. As military commanders, and heirs to the privileges of kings, the consuls exercised general powers over the Roman state except where restrained by the law. The right of appeal against harsh punishment had been established over the centuries, but did not seem to give clear protection to the victims of a formal inquiry conducted by the consuls at the instruction of the senate. It could be argued that enemies of the state were fair game, but the consuls of 132 had used their powers with sweeping abandon. The new measures accordingly gave a firm warning that violence must not be used by consuls or senate to override the will of the Roman people. They were intended to put the matter beyond doubt, with what success will emerge shortly.

To drive the point home, the law was given retroactive effect and Gaius proceeded to prosecute the surviving consul of 132, Popillius. In a series of passionate speeches he reminded the people of the tortures that had been inflicted, of the wholesale massacre of free men within the city, and warned his enemy that it was now too late to repudiate his crimes. And so Popillius himself was driven into exile, forbidden access to water or fire, as the legal phrase had it. His supporters escorted him out of the city with tears, for their cause had been badly hit. Cicero, who suffered a similar punishment himself for similar behaviour, repeatedly laments this use of tribunician violence against a man who had been consul.[9]

So, with great speed, Gaius had secured his rear against the misfortunes that befell his brother. His laws were safe against veto now that the principle of deposition had been reaffirmed, for it was not to be expected that the people would ever refuse to depose a man who pitted himself against Gaius Gracchus. Similarly his person was now safe against violence, even after he laid down the protection of office, for who would now dare use violence except at the people's bidding? It must have seemed inconceivable that the people would ever sanction a repeat of what Popillius had done.

*

How and why this elaborate insurance policy fell apart so dramatically will be seen later. The attempt to predetermine the future is the occupational failing of politicians. But now in a great surge of confidence Gaius was free to move on to the offensive. The common people of the city dominated Rome's voting assemblies. They had missed out on the benefits distributed by Tiberius, which by definition were confined to those people who actually returned to the land. In return they had withdrawn their support and let their champion go to his death. Gaius now tackled their basic economic problem, brought them a share in the benefits of empire, and bid for their undying loyalty with a law to establish permanent supplies of subsidized grain for the inhabitants of Rome.

Every month, it was enacted, grain would be sold to the citizens at the special price of six and one-third bronze asses per Roman peck, or quarter-bushel. This price was lower than the normal market price (P) and, what was quite unprecedented, it was subsidized out of public funds.[10]

Now the price and availability of grain had been a problem even before the time of Tiberius Gracchus. Since then Sicily had begun to recover from the slave revolt but the important supplies from North Africa had been badly hit by the terrible plagues. Gaius had found a special consignment of grain very welcome in Sardinia, while this very year Fabius sent a special gift of grain from Spain to Rome. Pirates based in Majorca had now become such a nuisance that the new consul Metellus had to be sent to put them down, and no doubt grain shipments from the western Mediterranean had been one of their targets.[11]

The problem was real enough, therefore, yet despite the comment of Velleius, that the corn was 'given' to the poor, the set price was not exceptionally low. At the turn of the century we know when special circumstances made it possible to sell Spanish or African grain in Rome at the 'cheap' price of four asses or the 'very cheap' price of two. In the fertile Po Valley Polybius had seen grain regularly sold at one and one-third asses, and a century before a Metellus had celebrated a triumph with a special sale at only one as.[12]

In the light of these figures the exact price selected by Gaius is revealing. The as had recently been devalued, and now counted sixteen to the silver denarius instead of ten. Six and one-third new asses was the nearest possible equivalent in new coinage to four old asses, which had been regarded as a low but not rock-bottom price in the past. In silver the new price was still almost exactly 0.4*d*. In other words the proposal was highly conservative, and yet there was a subsidy element which became controversial.

So the best way of making economic sense of the law is that it did not cut prices to some abnormally low level: it must have been an attempt to stabilize them at what was commonly regarded as a 'reasonable' level in the face of economic pressures that were forcing prices upwards. It was an exact parallel to the efforts of British governments in the 1970s to use subsidies to preserve 'the three-shilling loaf'. Gaius was reacting to the currency change as well as the supply problem, and struggling to get back to 'the old price', the price that people could pay. For the violence with which prices could fluctuate is shown by an exceptional level of 5*d*. a peck recorded in grain-rich Sicily.[13]

This analysis corrects any suggestion that Gaius was pauperizing a whole nation. However many people were resettled on the land could not alter the fact that Rome was becoming an 'exploding city' in the modern fashion, attracting a fast-growing population without any stable economic base of regular employment. In such circumstances it was hardly unreasonable to make it a state responsibility to make grain available at acceptable prices, so that it was no harder than it need be for the ordinary man to feed his family. What else was the empire for? Moreover Gaius did what he could to ease the burden on the exchequer by building huge granaries alongside the Aventine hill, for holding large buffer stocks would make it easier to avoid having to buy at the top of the market.

So Gaius had introduced the welfare state on a moderate scale which Rome could certainly afford. Juvenal's sneer about bread and circuses could not have been applied to the Gracchan age. Not until sixty years later was the subsidy turned into a free distribution, so institutionalizing rather than alleviating the problem of urban unemployment.[14]

But the law was evidently a vote-catcher too. He was aiming 'to gratify the people and overthrow the senate' (P). 'He plotted against the senate and by this one proposal quickly won the leadership of the people' (A). Orosius felt that Gaius 'stirred up the Roman people to fierce seditions with his lavish bribes and promises', and Diodorus denounces him for 'using up the public treasury for unsuitable and disgraceful expenditure so as to make the masses look to him as their leader'.[15]

It is left, curiously enough, to the obscure writer Florus to give the clearest justification for what Gaius was doing. 'What could be fairer than to let an impoverished people feed themselves from their own public purse? But the idea came to a bad end, for the cost of buying the corn exhausted the treasury, wherein lie the sinews of the state.'

There was the rub. Cicero admitted that a modest corn subsidy might be 'acceptable to the state and invaluable to the people; but the corn dole of Gaius Gracchus was a great bribe that exhausted the treasury'. Elsewhere he embroiders this criticism.

'Gaius Gracchus passed a corn law that was very agreeable to the common people because it allowed them to live without the trouble of working. But the good men tried to resist it, for they felt it would divert the people from toil to indolence, as well as emptying the treasury.' But this was hardly fair. Under Gaius the recipients had to pay and so to work. The switch to a free dole happened only two years before Cicero made that remark, and the man who brought it about was Cicero's bitter personal enemy.[16]

One distinguished Roman fought the bill there and then, and even managed to put Gaius at a momentary disadvantage. This was his 'mortal enemy', Piso Frugi. For when Gaius summoned him before the assembly, and the stewards asked which Piso he meant, he was forced to indicate 'the honest one', since that was the meaning of the surname Frugi given to Piso after his famous law on provincial extortion a quarter of a century before. Ignoring this reputation, Gaius savagely attacked his opponent's private life, from the follies of youth to the scandals of his old age, but Piso was unabashed. When the law had been passed despite his efforts, the old statesman was seen queuing up for cheap corn like everyone else.

How dared he draw benefit from a law that he had so bitterly opposed? Gaius demanded. But Piso replied coolly, 'I would object just the same, Gracchus, if·you were to divide all my personal belongings among the citizens, but I would still try to get a share back for myself'.[17]

An important reform had been introduced, and Gaius had paid the first important dividend to his supporters. No doubt he believed that the burden on the treasury would not be severe except in unusually bad years, although it is characteristic of such open-ended subsidies to turn out more expensive than their authors expect. Sudden upsurges in prices are rarely as temporary as politicians fancy, and if Gaius had misjudged the immediate market situation he could quite unintentionally have brought about the sudden drain on the exchequer that so upset Cicero. Certainly attention would now have to be paid to the public revenue, but Gaius had ideas for this as well. As an extra benefit, establishing this stable market with ample storage capacity must have helped and encouraged suppliers of grain. From this moment the commitment to safeguard the corn supply became one of the major pivots of Roman politics, and was to end up as a prime responsibility of the imperial civil service.

*

Gaius Gracchus had established himself already as a powerful and innovative force in Roman politics, but it is at this point that the sequence of events becomes obscure. Of the four authors who give us anything like a time sequence, Plutarch, Livy and Velleius describe a great deal of legislative activity as if it took place before the next tribunician elections, whereas apart from the corn law Appian concentrates it afterwards. Moreover none of the four distinguishes between when the new tribunes were elected, around July 123, and when they took office the following December.

Appian's silence before the election can largely be discounted, however, for in fact he ignores most of the legislation anyway to concentrate on a small number of major issues. If the Gracchan laws were indeed all passed before the new tribunes took office in December, then there is no reason to reject the majority of our sources and their clear implication that most of the laws had already been tabled and openly discussed before the elections, even if not yet passed into law. Our sources, it must be remembered, are only giving brief summaries of longer accounts that were available to them but not to us. That they abbreviate and collapse a chronological sequence is always to be expected, but that they arbitrarily reverse it is not.

The only direct contradiction posed by this solution concerns the judiciary law, the most important and complex of all. But though Appian puts it after the election the others place it firmly before, and there can be no doubt that this sensational proposal played a key part in the new election campaign, even if it only reached its final form afterwards.

Leaving aside the contents of the legislation to the next chapter, we are to imagine a feverish scene in which a greater variety of laws were being discussed, proposed, debated and voted on than the Romans had ever seen before. The corn and capital punishment laws are the only ones we can be sure were passed early in the year but several others may have been. And it is quite clear from the surviving accounts that all this activity, and the administrative work which flowed from it, had a quite mesmeric effect on political life. In particular it dominated the election campaign and determined its rather surprising result.

In one savage attack Diodorus describes the whole tribunate in terms of cynical election bribery. Gaius built up credit with every class in the state, making all men support and pursue his ideas in the hopes of their own private gain. 'He deliberately fomented unrest and divisions in the community as a way to win power for himself.'

In all this activity the judiciary proposals played the most striking part. With them Gaius destroyed all the harmony that previously existed between senators and knights, Diodorus felt, and made the best elements in the state subordinate to their inferiors. He had no sooner put the people in his debt than he sought to do the same with the knights (A). It was in forcing this law through that he displayed his greatest efforts (P). While speaking in its support he shifted the whole constitution from the appearance of aristocracy to that of democracy by the simple practice of turning to face the open spaces of the forum to speak instead of the cramped area in front of the senate house.[18]

The judiciary law fundamentally altered the balance of power between senators and knights, and as a result Gaius acquired something very like royal power during this pre-election period, with even the senate yielding to his advice (P). He proposed laws and supervised their administration, unwearied by his massive duties. With amazing speed and energy he tackled each job as though it was the only one before him, so that even those who hated and feared him were impressed by his powers of business.

The common people marvelled at the sight of their hero attended by crowds of contractors and engineers, ambassadors, magistrates, soldiers and scholars. He handled all of them easily and with a courteous dignity, so giving the lie to those who called him truculent, vulgar and violent. In negotiations and the management of affairs he turned out to be an even more powerful figure and a truer leader of the people than when haranguing them from the platform.[19]

To help cope with this press of business Gaius was the first Roman to organize an inner cabinet of confidential advisers, while admitting other followers only into more open gatherings.[20]

So by the middle of 123 Gaius Gracchus had attained something very like the reign—the almost royal or dictatorial power—that his brother had been accused of grasping. But now the elections were drawing near, and the Gracchans chose a very surprising name indeed for their principal candidate. None other than Tiberius' old friend M. Fulvius Flaccus, land-commissioner and already consul in 125, now offered himself for election as tribune of the people. His two years in Gaul had been crowned with victory over three separate tribes, and he had returned to Rome in triumph early enough to help Gaius with the corn law. It was unusual and perhaps unprecedented for so grand a figure to stoop to what was traditionally a young man's office, but Fulvius showed all his family's determination to finish the job he had not been allowed to complete in 125, to pass a law to enfranchise Rome's allies.[21]

Another distinguished man seemed to be on the same side. The historian C. Fannius, who had scaled the walls of Carthage alongside young Tiberius Gracchus, now stood for consul. Suddenly Gaius was seen walking Fannius down to the Campus Martius and canvasing in his support. Whether any deal was struck between them is uncertain. Fannius had been a friend of Scipio, son-in-law to Laelius and a student of Stoic philosophy, and so perhaps sympathetic to the allies. But what counted was that Gaius urgently needed to keep out the other leading candidate for consul. This was the sinister figure of Opimius who had so ruthlessly crushed the rebellion of Fregellae and even claimed a triumph for doing so. Nothing could be more vital than to prevent Opimius from being consul in a year when Italian franchise was again to be under discussion.[22]

But what of Gaius himself? The possibility of re-electing tribunes to office had been raised by Tiberius in 133 and again by Carbo in 131, but the legal position had not been clarified either way. And Gaius may not originally have contemplated re-election. He was having no difficulty with his legislative programme for 123 and was committing himself to a good deal of administrative work for 122, when Fulvius could be expected to take on the burden of law-making.

On the other hand Plutarch depicts him carried away on a tremendous wave of popularity during the run-up to the elections. When he told the people he would be asking a favour from them the city was full of rumours that he would seek to become tribune again and consul as well.

The latter bizarre idea he averted by giving his support to Fannius. As for a second tribunate, Gaius neither offered his candidature nor pressed for support, but the people were wildly enthusiastic for him and elected him all the same (P). 'For a law had by now been passed laying down that the people could choose from the whole body of citizens if there were not enough candidates for tribune' (A). In other words Gaius did not fall into his brother's mistake of pressing his own suit from the start, but a technical situation developed which allowed his election. The suggestion that there were not enough candidates seems unlikely; it would be more reasonable to suppose that not enough of them achieved the basic requirement, namely to be chosen by a majority of the thirty-five tribes.

Such an anomalous result would be difficult to organize in advance, which supports the idea that Gaius had not sought re-election. But this had happened before, and an ancient law laid down that if fewer than ten were elected the presiding officer must carry on to fill up all the vacancies. Presumably this old law had been reinstated or modified by the law that Appian mentions, maybe in 130 after Carbo's attempt to clarify the position. In any case, in 123 the support for Gaius was so overwhelming that whatever mysterious loophole existed in the law was exploited to the full.

Gaius Gracchus was re-elected tribune for 122, and the legality of his re-election was never, to our knowledge, put in question.

Fulvius Flaccus was also elected tribune; and with Gracchan support (P) Fannius was chosen consul.[23]

With a massive base of popular support, with a complex legislative programme well under way, and now with this brilliant success in the elections for 122, it seems that the Gracchan age had arrived at last. The revolution had come to power. Now it is time to examine more closely what it was that Gaius Gracchus was trying to achieve.

11 Vision of Empire

If ever a man in history tried to build an empire by passing laws, that man was Gaius Gracchus. With no armed forces at his back, nor any special constitutional position, his only powers were those of persuading the free Roman people to vote his proposals into law. Yet with a dozen or more laws the thirty-one-year-old tribune probed every corner of the Roman state. He sought to restore it to health, to establish a new balance of powers and rewards among its various elements, and to make it better fitted for its newly won task of ruling the world.

In the early chapters of this book great stress was laid on that astonishing process whereby Rome became, almost overnight, master of the Mediterranean world. The heroic age of conquest began with one Scipio and ended with another. Young Tiberius Gracchus, first blooded at Carthage, spanned both periods, but Gaius was wholly a child of the new age of empire. His genius lay in his grasp of the changes that were needed.

The centrepiece of his reform programme was the great judiciary law that transferred control of the law-courts from the senators to the knights. Here lay the key to domestic politics, the expansion of the revenue, and the government of the empire. To this all the other laws can be related. But first, who precisely were these knights, that remarkable group of businessmen and squires whom Gaius thrust into the centre of the political world?

On 15 July every fourth year it had long been established that the Roman knights should ride in ceremonial procession to parade before the temple of Castor, of which three columns of Athenian marble still remain standing in the forum, a tribute to the republic's favourite gods and a cherished site for ceremonies, speeches and riots.[1]

The origins of the parade were military, and the knights had acquired political and social status long before they came to the attention of Gaius Gracchus. To begin with they were simply the cavalrymen, the chevaliers of the state. From among the richest citizens the censors selected 1,800 knights to fight on horseback on horses provided at public expense.

To serve was a duty, to be chosen to serve was an honour as well as a mark of wealth. A man had first to possess the qualifying amount of property and then to be selected by the censors, who might also choose to take away his public horse as a mark of dishonour. Livy tells us of men who were rich enough but were not awarded the public horse. In the first century the minimum wealth required was 100,000*d*.[2]

From the qualifying citizens the censors would in general choose the richest and those of the best-known families, especially the sons of established knights. But there was nothing to prevent any man of ability from acquiring the wealth and winning his way to this great distinction, which entitled him to wear the cherished golden rings. Men who had the wealth but were not chosen could still be called upon to serve on horses provided at their own expense, but this brought no dignity. They were just horsemen.[3]

Their political status developed through the fact that in practice the knights were the officer class and only they could stand for senior elected office, and so enter the senate. Moreover they controlled eighteen centuries in the voting assembly, giving them a disproportionate influence on the election of praetors, consuls and censors. Within the eighteen centuries there was a select group of six, probably reserved for men of senatorial family, for until the law of 129 senators and even magistrates remained also knights in possession of the public horse.[4]

In the tight hierarchy of Roman high society, therefore, there were several thousand men rich enough to serve as cavalrymen. Of these 1,800 were awarded the public horse and they were the knights, strictly defined. Among them men of senatorial family occupied the six oldest centuries. The senators themselves numbered around 300 men, who after 129 were separated from the body of the knights. And finally, at the very apex of the pyramid, special status among the senators was reserved for the nobles who came from the old consular families.

Even after 129 it is clear that knights and senators cannot be regarded as rival corporations within the state. The senators were simply the upper fringe of the hierarchy. Knights would mix socially with them and many of them would be blood relatives, working together for their family interests at election time. The richer knights would be just as rich as the average senator, and many of them were simply well-off country gentlemen who deliberately chose not to seek the active political life of the senate. Some embarked on other careers of less than senatorial dignity, such as the career army officers. But others wanted to rise in politics, and while failure was common many managed to make the ascent, for it was from the ranks of such knights that the senate had to keep recruiting new members as the old families died out. Cicero has left a detailed account of how one man, Plancius, succeeded, although with difficulty, in breaking into the higher ranks of elected office after his family had been knights of distinction for generations. The greatest social distinction always remained that which separated knights and junior senators alike from the representatives of those great noble families who concentrated in their own hands the republic's past glories and most of its current political power.[5]

But there was also an economic distinction of profound importance. Since the Claudian law of 218, supported by the popular leader Flaminius, senators and their sons had been forbidden to own cargo ships 'because profit from trade was deemed beneath their dignity'. The law was in force, if increasingly ignored, right up to Cicero's time, and they were also banned, apparently, from bidding for public contracts.[6]

As the wealth of a new empire flooded into Rome, during that century which separated Flaminius from Gaius Gracchus, the principal forms of business activity other than investment in land were formally and effectively closed to the senators. And so the leadership of the developing business community fell naturally into the hands of the most important men outside the senate, in other words the knights.

The Mediterranean had long been a world of traders and small manufacturers, but the large-scale capitalism that characterized Roman business grew out of the republic's need for organizations that could handle large public contracts. 'Publicans' were the men who undertook them, both the supply contracts for erecting buildings or equipping armies and the tax-farming contracts under which they paid an advance sum to the state for the right to collect a defined tax.

The great war against Hannibal made the huge military supply contracts necessary, just like the American Civil War. In one case businessmen who had already profited from the war agreed to supply the Spanish army on credit, a remarkable proof of financial strength. As the empire spread the system grew in importance. Publicans handled the great public building contracts and ran the lucrative state mines in Spain, and no doubt they also carried out much of the private building work in the city, although tax contracts were apparently less important at this stage.[7]

Inevitably there were frauds and rows, and there is evidence of keen competition. In 184 the censors squeezed the publicans by letting the building contracts cheap and charging dear for the tax concessions. In 169 they refused to deal with those who had won the previous round of contracts. In 167 the senate closed down the mines in newly defeated Macedon, 'because there was no way of running them without the publicans, but if the publicans were allowed in there would be neither law nor freedom for the allies'.[8]

By the middle of the century the contractors were dealing in vast sums of money and highly organized into an elaborate system of joint stock companies. To operate they needed social contacts at the highest level, as well as an extensive capital base, because they had to be able to pledge landed property as security for the contracts as well as find their own working finance. For these reasons the chief publicans had to be knights. Indeed Cicero describes the publicans as 'the flower of the knights'.[9]

The extent to which the publicans and the knights overlapped, and were beginning to see their interests as one, was well shown in the dispute of 169.

'The censors took public horses away from many knights . . . so offending the whole class of knights . . . then added to the grievance by reassigning the contracts . . . so upsetting the previous group of publicans . . . who found a tribune to champion their interests and promote a law voiding the new contracts . . . and when the censor Claudius was brought to trial eight of the twelve centuries of knights voted to condemn him, as well as many centuries of the first class.'[10]

What the chief publicans, the knights who ran the big companies, provided above all was top management, high-level contacts, and risk capital. They were Rome's City of London. Mere trade was something else, less dignified, and largely left to Italians, just as new industrial developments seem to have been mainly in the hands of freedmen. But much of this activity, too, must have been ultimately financed by the publicans. What gave them their political potential was the simple fact that their companies were the only strong organizations to exist outside the senatorial class. Yet though individuals might quarrel over particular contracts the knights were not as a class opposed to the senate on any general matters of principle. Those knights who ran companies were interested in business, not politics, and of the senators the opposite was true. The interface between the two groups might function smoothly or not, but there is no evidence that it was called fundamentally into question until the appearance of Gaius Gracchus.

But if Gaius Gracchus seriously meant to reform the administration of the empire, and to make any inroads into the senate's absolute monopoly of political power, then the knights, with their high social and political standing and their almost global network of business interests, represented the only alternative base on which to build. Hence the judiciary legislation of 123.

*

From the earliest days the Romans were fascinated by law, both making and administering it. They liked constructing an elaborate legal system, many of whose principles remain active today, while in the practice of advocacy their public men could develop those debating skills needed for their political careers. Law and politics became irretrievably intertwined. But while it was the law that restrained the powers and actions of magistrates, it was the senate, itself composed of former magistrates, that controlled the law-courts, so that their status as an independent restraint was highly questionable. It depended on the very highest standards of honesty, and such standards were ceasing to hold good.

Inevitably the problem came most readily to the surface in the provinces, where senatorial governors wielded almost unlimited powers, open to temptations which they found irresistible. Piso Frugi had established a permanent court in 149 to deal with cases of extortion, the misuse of authority for purposes of illicit self-enrichment. Cicero regrets that before then no such law had been needed, but afterwards a whole succession of laws, each harsher than the last, did nothing to stop the allies from being everywhere pillaged and plundered whenever the courts could be set aside.[11]

In other words, commerce may have been beneath the dignity of a Roman senator, but bribery and loot were not. And the senators who manned the courts acquitted their own colleagues whenever they could. If they would not do it out of goodwill then they would do it for a share of the pickings. There is no reason to doubt the charge levelled by Gaius

Gracchus, that the courts were discredited because of bribery. The great Gracchan leader Scaevola had pursued the case of Tubulus, the corrupt praetor who had openly accepted bribes when presiding over the court dealing with murder in 142. Now Gaius denounced the recent acquittals of three 'notoriously corrupt' men, including Aquillius the governor of Asia, despite detailed and bitter accusations made against them by their victims.

The example of Aquillius was crucial, for just as the treasures of Asia had financed the reforms of Tiberius Gracchus, so Gaius was determined to exploit its revenues. But first he had to ensure that those revenues came into the treasury rather than the pockets of individuals. The law court on extortion was not merely a device for punishing wrong-doers and restoring their ill-gotten gains. It was also a prime arm of imperial administration, and Gaius Gracchus was determined to make it work.[12]

So it was with the triple purpose of curbing errant senators, improving the administration of justice, and securing the public revenues, that Gaius Gracchus passed his famous judiciary law, that transferred the law-courts from the senators to the knights.

In future knights rather than senators would man the juries and sit in judgement on the peculations of senatorial governors. It could reasonably be expected that this might improve the standards of provincial administration. What is certain is that it immediately and for ever destroyed one of the principal bulwarks of senatorial government, their un-questioned control of the administration of justice.

> Gaius already had the people in his pocket, and now he won over the knights as well . . . But once the law had been passed, with some support from senators ashamed of the corruption, then he was heard to remark that he had completely destroyed the senate's power. And so it turned out. For this new power of exercising judgement over all Romans and Italians and even the senators themselves, with authority to fine, dishonour or exile them, raised the knights into the more powerful position and reduced the senators to mere equality or even worse (A).
>
> The judiciary law was the one by which he most effectively cut away the power of the senators, who up to now, through their monopoly of the courts, had been able to intimidate people and knights alike . . . And when the people went on to insist that he should personally select those knights who

were to be jurymen then his power became truly that of a monarch (P).

What could seem fairer, Florus asks revealingly, than that the knights should be supreme in the courts to balance the rule of the senate in the provinces? Livy bluntly gives the law's purpose as 'to seduce the knights from their harmony with the senate'. Diodorus tells us that it was a hard won success. When the senate threatened open war against the tribune if he transferred the law-courts then he warned them in turn, 'I shall not hesitate to wrest this sword from the grasp of the senate even if I die in the attempt.' After winning the crucial vote by only one tribe out of the thirty-five he boasted that, 'Now the sword hangs over my enemies' heads—for the rest we shall be content whatever fortune decides.'[13]

All these references, and particularly Appian's strong words about 'all Romans and Italians', make it clear that this legislation was of wide scope, applying to all law-courts. It was not restricted to the extortion court, where naturally only senators could be charged. It put an end to what Polybius had so vividly described as 'the senate's most powerful weapon: the fact that judges are appointed from its ranks for most of the important public and private trials, so that ordinary citizens naturally feel wary of obstructing or resisting the senate's decisions'. We know from Cicero that several permanent courts had been established by now to deal with serious crimes such as murder, on the pattern of Piso's extortion court. The Gracchan law must have applied to them all, and perhaps to some of the civil courts as well.[14]

So wide ranging was the Gracchan interest that the judiciary law itself has to be fitted into a series of three or more laws, all sharing the common purpose: to prevent the senate from buttressing its own misgovernment by the manipulation of the legal system.

The law that has been discussed earlier, forbidding capital punishment except by order of the Roman people, effectively denied the senate's right to establish special tribunals with powers of summary execution, and so naturally takes first place in the sequence.[15]

Senators who instead tried to abuse the machinery of the regular courts to pursue their enemies, however, would fall foul of a second law. This sought to punish magistrates and senators who conspired to procure false convictions. The natural meaning is that it pursued the powerful men who gave the bribes, or exerted other forms of pressure, rather than the jurymen who succumbed to them. So it remained equally valid even when knights had replaced senators on the juries. We can be sure that it proved a powerful restraining influence, for Cicero was later to declaim with indignation against the terrible suggestion that the law should be extended to punish the acceptance of bribes by jurymen (in other words knights), arguing that in such an event they would never dare convict any rich defendant through fear of being themselves pursued under this law for conspiracy.[16]

But both these preliminary laws, as they are best regarded, were directed against senatorial attempts to oppress their opponents. Gaius' central purpose, however, was to bring the senators themselves under the control of the courts, which could never be done while it was they who manned the juries. So it was with this aim that, through the judiciary law proper, he changed the composition of the juries.

As a first step he seems to have considered the possibility of mixed juries. Three times Plutarch tells us that 300 knights were to be added to a list along with the 300 senators, and the juries chosen from all 600. Livy gives what must be a garbled version of the same idea, reporting that 600 knights were to be enrolled into the senate itself, an explosive and indeed fantastic suggestion for which no other evidence exists. Yet these reports do seem to indicate some half-way step towards the complete transfer featured in all other versions.[17]

There is, however, no evidence that mixed juries were ever established at this period (though they do turn up later), nor does any writer suggest that one law was passed and later changed. Bearing in mind that Plutarch gives his version before coming to the re-election of Gaius Gracchus, while Appian puts it afterwards, the best reconciliation is that Gaius proposed the mixed juries before the election. This compromise was supported even by many senators during that curious honeymoon period so vividly described by Plutarch. But then after his crushing election victory he felt able to strengthen the bill so that when it finally became law later in 123 the knights took over the juries completely.

Why did he modify it in this way? Perhaps he no longer felt any need to compromise. Perhaps his hot-headed friend Fulvius Flaccus urged him to do so. But above all the knights themselves pressed him to go the whole way. This is the clear implication of Appian's very next remark about the new-found strength of the knights. 'In return for supporting the tribunes at the elections they obtained in return whatever they wanted, and so more and more terrified the senators.' No wonder that the latter resisted this final version so bitterly.[18]

The question then arises of whether there was a further law dealing in particular detail with the special case of the extortion court, on which the greatest attention was so obviously focused. In his famous series of speeches denouncing Verres, the corrupt governor of Sicily, Cicero made elaborate reference to the law of Acilius Glabrio, 'which established the best law-courts and the strictest judges for dealing with cases of extortion'. He also comments that it had been passed against determined opposition. Now in that trial Cicero was going out of his way to praise juries composed of knights, and so it seems to follow that the Acilius in question was the man who first transferred the courts to the knights. He must have been one of the tribunes of 123 and have passed the law on behalf of Gaius Gracchus, who is bound to have used what help he could to see through a legislative programme of this scale.[19]

But while this further evidence, of how Gaius orchestrated his political machine by sharing tasks among his colleagues, is impressive enough, it remains an open question whether the Acilian law was the main Gracchan statute, covering all the law-courts, or whether yet another law was passed to cover the special case of extortion.

If it was the latter, then it is just possible that we have it still. In the museums of Naples and Vienna survive fragments of a bronze tablet, once in the possession of the Renaissance scholar Cardinal Bembo. On the smoothly prepared front of this tablet more than ninety lines of Latin had been engraved, and although three-quarters of the whole is missing enough survives or can be reconstructed to show that we have the actual text of a second-century law setting out the complete procedure for dealing with extortion suits.

> If any person of the allies or the Latin name or any foreign people, or anyone living under the guidance, authority, power or friendship of the Roman people, seeks from any former magistrate or son of a magistrate, or from any senator or son of a senator, the restoration of money in excess of the specified minimum for any particular year, which money has in the exercise of legal authority been carried off, seized, exacted, extorted or expropriated, from himself or his king, people, parents, slaves or dependants, then he has the right to sue and summon before a praetor . . . .

Majestically the long and complex clauses roll on, detailing every aspect of procedure right down to the size of the ballot boxes and voting tickets to be used by the jurymen, all ingeniously constructed to minimize the effect of outside pressure and secure the conviction of the guilty. And in particular this fascinating document lays down that the jurors for any particular suit shall be chosen from a standing panel of 450 persons none of whom may be a magistrate, senator or son of a senator.[20]

Several possibilities exist, despite the efforts of scholars to establish one or another as unquestioned truth. The simplest equation, and the favourite of many, is that the bronze law is the Acilian law is the main judiciary law of Gaius Gracchus. Unfortunately this just cannot be accepted. It has been clearly established that the main achievement of Gaius Gracchus was a comprehensive transfer of the law-courts to the knights. But the bronze law does not do that job at all; it is specifically concerned with the question of provincial extortion.

So what follows? Either the bronze law is a later codification of the extortion procedure, incorporating the general changes introduced in 123—which is possible but not very attractive, since it is not easy to fit such a law into a political context inside the crowded sequence of judiciary legislation that followed the Gracchan period.

Or, with greater probability, the bronze law forms a separate element in the Gracchan programme. As well as the general transfer of judicial power, Gaius also put through a comprehensive overhaul of extortion procedure. We may have no independent evidence that he did such a thing, but the bronze law is unmistakably Gracchan in its overall impact and in every line of its carefully constructed detail.

In any event, the Acilian law may have been the main Gracchan law about law-courts, or else the bronze law about extortion procedure. Neither is certain. All that we know is that it cannot possibly be identified with both.[21]

*

Whatever precisely constituted the judiciary legislation of Gaius Gracchus and his allies, we are in no doubt that what made it so overwhelmingly important was its profound effect on two aspects of Roman politics, the status of the knights and the administration of the provinces.

Gaius established the knights as a real political force in Rome. To be sure, we are again unfortunate that the surviving fragments of the bronze law fall short, by a tantalizing couple of words, of revealing the positive qualifications for being placed on the jury list. But for once the loss matters little. Once we know that past and present magistrates, senators, and their fathers, brothers and sons were all formally excluded, then we know that the jury lists were bound to be dominated by the leading knights, and the positive qualification makes little further difference.

Perhaps these were defined by strict reference to the 1,800 who held the public horse, but it would be more in character with Gaius' purpose if he used the wider definition, permitting jury-service to anybody possessing property worth 100,000*d*. Since the 1,800 were by definition the most distinguished of this wider class then they would still tend to be selected, as they would have been even without any minimum qualification: if the praetor were free to choose from the entire citizen body outside the senate he would still tend to select knights. That is how hierarchical societies function.

The wider definition is also more likely because those of the 1,800 who were willing and able to serve may not have been enough to fill the list. For the bronze law also lays down that only men who lived in or near the city of Rome could be chosen. Rome's equivalents to 'the knights of the shires' therefore could not be chosen. But as a result, those knights who wielded the new influence were inevitably those most involved in city life, the public contractors and the politically ambitious.[22]

In this way Gaius gave a new and dignified role, but also a new cohesion and common interest, to those Romans who stood immediately outside the ranks of the senate. The Gracchan jurors, however precisely defined, had become a power group to reckon with. At first they were known simply as jurors, but gradually the terminology became looser until all men financially qualified for the list were regarded as members of the order of knights, now a much wider concept than the 1,800 holders of the public horse.

At the same time, since the most active among them were the businessmen, they became identified with their interests too. By Cicero's time the jurors, the knights and the publicans could for many purposes be loosely regarded as the same group of men. As Pliny put it, a third body had been added to the state, in addition to the senate and the Roman people.[23]

It would still be wrong to suggest that the new knight-jurymen became a united pressure group fighting for common policies, despite the antiquarian Varro's judgement that by handing over the courts to them Gaius made the state 'two-headed' and so opened the way to civil war. General policy questions were not normally in issue between them: it was the courts themselves that become the bone of contention for senators and knights to squabble over for more than fifty years. The reason is that while the senate's power had been diminished, the freedom of the knights had been very much enhanced, above all their freedom to make money and exploit the potential of the empire.[24]

For Gaius Gracchus was also determined to mobilize the wealth of the Roman provinces. Concern for the nuts and bolts of finance was one of the striking characteristics of this rare man. He was ready to spend public money, with his corn law and other projects, but he also applied himself to finding the revenue to match, something that had never much bothered his conservative predecessors.

Since the abolition of direct taxes after the victory of Pydna, and apart from chance receipts of plunder from the wars, Roman revenues had mainly depended on a collection of indirect charges such as customs and harbour dues, income from public mines and land, and taxes on salt and the freeing of slaves. These were gradually developed and bolstered by an increasing flow of revenue from the provinces, notably Sicily.[25]

But it took Gaius to carry the whole system forward into a new order of magnitude, so that he could even style himself 'patron of the treasury'. By introducing new harbour dues and perhaps other minor tax changes he added to the revenue, but also provided more business for the publicans, who farmed such indirect taxes by paying an advance sum to the censors and then collecting them through their own organizations, pocketing any surplus left over.[26]

Then, on precisely the same principles, he reorganized the tax revenues of the immensely rich province of Asia.

It was Asia that transformed everything. Cicero spoke of it as Rome's greatest source of revenue even when a dozen provinces were yielding 50,000,000*d*. a year. Its impact sixty years before must have been overwhelming.[27]

But Asia was always a source of bitter controversy as well as of money. Its affairs had just been organized by its governor Aquillius and a special senatorial commission, but their settlement was violently attacked by Gaius, who argued that it did too little for the Roman revenues and too much for the open-handed rulers of neighbouring states. His speech on the subject to the Roman people is full of interest.

'I speak here to show you how to increase your revenues, so that you will be better able to manage the state's affairs and look after your own interests . . . But others who speak against this proposal are seeking money from King Nicomedes, not honour from you; those who support it want not your respect but the bribes of King Mithridates; while those who sit there saying nothing are the worst for they have taken bribes from everybody and are letting them all down.'[28]

What seems to have happened is that in return for bribes the corrupt Aquillius handed over the neighbouring region of Phrygia to the powerful King Mithridates of Pontus. But his misdeeds went further, for Mark Antony later claimed that the Romans had released the Asians from paying taxes until demagogues (meaning Gaius Gracchus) reimposed them, and the implication must be that it was Aquillius who provided this relief, in return for further bribes and at the expense of the Roman treasury.

For all this Aquillius came home to face prosecution for extortion, but now it was his turn to hand out the bribes and secure his own acquittal, probably in 125. However the following year Gaius Gracchus also came home, savagely denounced both aspects of the Aquillian settlement, and persuaded the senate to tear it up and declare Phrygia to be free.[29]

Then in 123 Gaius brought in his own law to secure the taxes of Asia, and he may well have had the senate's backing for this during the 'honeymoon' early part of the year, for his tax law only assumed its full political significance in the light of the judiciary law, passed later in 123.

So Gaius Gracchus passed a law, by which Asia was taxed at the rate of one-tenth of its annual produce. The tax was farmed out under contracts placed by the censors in Rome, and the law included provisions for remission of the contract fee in exceptional circumstances.[30]

There can be no doubt that the revenue was immensely strengthened. The treasury could now cope with the heavy commitments that Gaius had introduced, and it stood the pressure of heavy military expenditure later in the century far more easily than a generation before. The system of tax-farming adopted was one to which there was no practical alternative, for the Romans certainly had no direct civil service capable of all the complicated work of assessment and collection. Indeed, this sharp distinction now drawn between the job of governing and the job of tax-collecting could be expected to benefit the provincials too, by relieving them of all the arbitrary oppression inherent when revenues were left under the direct control of rapacious governors.

At the same time, however, the system was bound to prove a goldmine for the publicans. Money could make money as never before, for only the richest companies could possibly bid for contracts of this size. Whether their agents could then manage to recover more money from the provincials than their masters had paid for the contract in Rome would depend, more than anything else, on the degree of help or obstruction that they received from the governor on the spot. That much followed from the tax law. The difference that the judiciary law then made was to transform the relationship between the governors and the publicans by putting the former at the mercy of the latter. The result of gaining control over the law-courts, before which any provincial governor could be arraigned, at the same time as access to the huge tax contracts of Asia, was virtually a blank cheque for the publicans.

Cicero remarked that after this law had been passed then dishonest and greedy governors became the servants of the publicans and showered favours on any Roman knight who appeared in their province, for the knights were so united that an insult against any one of them earned the resentment of them all. But there is no reason to think that only bad governors felt vulnerable in this way. Diodorus felt that when there were knights in the provinces they could terrify the governors because of their powers as jurymen in any charges arising from provincial administration, and Appian makes the detail only too clear.

It quickly came about that political control was reversed, with the knights holding the power and the senators only the dignity. For now the knights had the upper hand over the senators, and they openly abused this far beyond what was proper. They went in for corruption on their own account, and having tasted the vast gains they pursued them with even less shame or restraint than the senators. They suborned false accusers against the rich, and managed to put a halt to prosecutions for receiving bribes. Corruption ceased to be investigated, and the judiciary law had generated new conflicts that lasted far into the future and proved much worse than what had gone before.[31]

Cicero boasted of the new importance of the publicans, 'those honourable and distinguished men whose activities and fortunes should be the concern of the whole state, for if taxes are the sinews of the republic then the men who bring them in are rightly regarded as the mainstay of the other classes'.[32] On the other hand critics could claim that the senators had been forced to become the slaves of the knights, that the transfer of the courts had wrecked the taxes, 'the patrimony of empire', and that by sacrificing the provinces to the arrogance and greed of the publicans Gaius had incited the subject peoples to a well merited hatred of Roman rule.[33]

Such charges cannot exactly be proven, and there must have been some basis for Cicero's claim that no knight-juryman was ever suspected of accepting a bribe to influence his verdict. But if the knights in the courts erred on the side of leniency, as seems likely from the small number of known convictions, the explanation is surely that most governors took very good care not to antagonize them. Those who did, like Rutilius who later helped reform the administration of Asia to relieve it of publican oppression, could be badly mauled in the courts. The knights had the whip-hand and were ready to use it.[34]

For all that, the system was a vast advance on what had gone before, and if the difficulties it later ran into were left too long uncorrected, then that was hardly the fault of Gaius Gracchus.

*

By a sequence of interlocking laws Gaius had stamped on bribery in the courts, transferred the juries to the knights, probably revised the legal procedure for dealing with charges of provincial extortion, and put the revenues of Asia into the hands of the publicans.

In doing so he had transformed the Roman world and laid the foundations of a great empire.

By these laws he tapped great revenues to use for the welfare of the Roman people and the maintenance of their armies. He began the development of a financial system, based on the organized accumulation and deployment of capital on a scale unmatched until modern times. He provided provincials for the first time with a means of redress that had some chance of being effective. He found a position in the state for all those prosperous and talented people who stood outside the charmed circle of the senate, and so immeasurably strengthened the administrative base of the Roman empire.

Above all, he decisively broke the monopoly of power that the senators had exercised collectively at home and individually in the provinces. There was a new order in the state, a new balance of power with new tensions and strains. The heroic old days of an empire ruled by a few men, unchallenged by right of birth, were gone.

This was the greatest single achievement of the Gracchan movement. But it·certainly opened up possibilities for the worse as well as for the better. The explosive possibilities of an empire whose administrative systems had at last begun to match its effective power could only too easily be misused, if it was exploited by men who lacked the insight and vision that Gaius Gracchus had brought to the task.

12 The Tide Turns

To illustrate the spirit in which Gaius Gracchus exercised that almost monarchcal power which he had gathered to himself in 123, Plutarch tells a simple story.

'Even the senate now listened to his counsel, but he was always advising them to do something honourable and to their credit. For example when Fabius, the governor of Spain, sent some corn to Rome; Gaius persuaded the senate to sell the corn, send the money back to the Spaniards, and reprimand Fabius for making Roman rule intolerable to its subjects. Such a noble decree, breathing the spirit of moderation, brought Gaius both fame and popularity in the provinces.'

A nephew of Scipio, Fabius was perhaps not so much lining his own pockets as trying to win a little popularity in Rome, at the expense of his unhappy subjects, with a view to the consular elections in 122. But quite apart from his own close personal and family ties with Spain, Gaius was further reinforcing the principle that Roman provinces were not private fiefs of the senators sent out to govern them.[1]

In such ways even his minor actions reveal the same purpose and breadth of vision, fortunately without raising such complicated issues of principle, as the great centre-pieces of his tribunate: the corn subsidy, the legal and tax reforms, and the political establishment of the knights. Wielding almost unfettered power Gaius continued with a series of reforms that penetrated every corner of the Roman state. In one way after another he made Rome better fitted to govern the world, while ensuring that its citizens were the beneficiaries rather than the victims of their own empire.

There is no clear guide to the chronology of the rest of 123, but it remains the year of high tide, when nothing is known to have gone wrong for Gaius Gracchus. So all his other successful legislation should be grouped into this same year.

For the tide was to turn sooner, and more decisively, than anyone could possibly have guessed at the time.

*

To raise the efficiency of provincial government and further limit the arbitrary nature of the senate's power, Gaius passed what seems to have been a comprehensive law to regularize the system whereby the two consuls for each year were assigned the two most important 'provinces', or spheres of duty. Cicero points out that 'Gaius Gracchus was the most popular leader of all, but so far from taking control of the consular provinces away from the senate, he even laid down that it should be the senate's task to assign them each year'. But from now on the senate had to take this key decision, which provinces merited the full authority of a consul with his army, before the consuls were elected rather than afterwards. Rules about when and how they should be replaced at the end of their tenure were also set out.[2]

The immediate provocation for the law was the stratagem by which the senate had suddenly assigned a Gallic war to Fulvius Flaccus in 125, to prevent him carrying his franchise bill. But it was more than a negative attempt to prevent such manoeuvres in future, for it also became the fundamental law governing, for example, the great debate about Julius Caesar's replacement in Gaul. What Gaius was trying to do was rather to prevent the senate from refusing the most important provinces to consuls of whom it disapproved. Now it had to define the tasks and leave it to the assembly to choose the men it wanted to fulfil them. Similarly the law seems also to have laid down that the allocation of consular provinces could not be vetoed by tribunes, so that nothing could stop the consuls taking the most important jobs. Quite how Gaius dealt with the obvious problem that an unforeseen emergency might suddenly need a consul's presence right away, we do not know. But it seems to have been covered because in the crisis of 113 the consul was able to bring German invaders to battle in the same year that their presence was reported.[3]

The Gallic war had meanwhile blown up into something more than a blind alley for Fulvius Flaccus. Fighting carried on for five more years, against tribes like the Allobroges and Arverni who were to figure so prominently in Caesar's campaigns. After Fulvius three other consuls won triumphs in a war whose permanent mementoes included colonies at Aix and Narbonne and a new high-road from Italy to Spain.[4] It was

Rome's most serious fighting since the great Spanish Wars, and it prompted Gaius to a series of military reforms.

First he enacted that conscripts be provided with a full kit of clothing at public expense without any deduction from their pay. This must have made a great difference to the poorer soldiers and paved the way for the regular recruitment of penniless citizens later in the century. No doubt the sufferings of the ill clad army with which he served in Sardinia had opened his eyes to the problem, which was but a continuation of those hardships associated with service life that had first interested his brother.

The recruitment of soldiers below the age of seventeen was stopped altogether, reinforcing an older rule even though the Gracchus brothers had both begun their own service at the age of fifteen (but as officers). Gaius also alleviated the harsh field discipline of the Roman army; we do not know how but Diodorus indignantly complains that he 'curried favour with the troops and so brought disobedience and anarchy into political life, for men who despise their commanders are hardly likely to respect the law, and so there followed the disastrous lawlessness and the overthrow of the state'.[5]

Soldiers not needed for the Gallic war were employed on another Gracchan project. In keeping with the established Roman principle that highways were the arteries of government. Gaius organized a large road-building programme throughout Italy. One milestone that has survived from 123 reveals that the consul Flamininus put his legions to work on the high road from Florence to Pisa and illustrates the scale of organization.

Construction work clearly caught Gaius' fancy, as it has done with many ambitious politicians, and he raised the standard of work towards that high level which became familiar during the empire. He took care to make the roads attractive as well as useful. They were built dead straight, of quarried stone on top of hard-pressed sand. Hollows and ravines were filled or bridged, while both sides of the roads were kept at the same height to give the work an even and handsome appearance. Along their course milestones and mounting stones for horsemen were set up (P).

Perhaps what interested him most, however, was the employment and prosperity created by so much building work, and the political advantage that followed in their train. 'For by bringing a vast array of contractors and workmen under obligation to himself, he made them ready to do whatever he should demand' (A). Once again the benefits of empire were being spread around, and Gaius was further cementing his own support.[6]

The combined effect of all this spending on public works, the army and the corn subsidy was to pump a great deal of extra money into the Roman economy, and some attempt has been made to gauge the scale of this from the evidence of coinage. Each year three officers issued coinage and usually marked it with their names. If we could accurately date each officer, then by counting the number of dies he used and estimating the number of coins struck from each die we could draw some conclusions about the quantity of new money issued in each year, which is probably to be equated with the level of public expenditure. The most detailed analysis suggests that the supply of new money in 123 did indeed soar to the unusually high figure of 15,500,000*d.*, three times the rate of the early 120s. Unfortunately the dating is tentative and the conclusions cannot be firm, even though the officers assigned to 123, C. Cato and M. Fannius, undoubtedly bear names closely associated with the Gracchan movement. That the overall level of financial activity, as evinced by the coinage, increased sharply from about the time of Gaius Gracchus cannot be doubted. The policy of economic recovery worked.[7]

In addition to whatever benefit the poor derived from his other measures, Gaius also sought to help by the direct device of settling them on the public land. To do this he passed a law on the same lines as his brother's, reiterating the ban on any citizen occupying more than 500 acres of public land, and continued to distribute land to the poor. Unfortunately the process was now less easy than it had been.

Despite the evidence of massive distribution after the death of Scipio Aemilianus, which may have accounted for all the then available supplies of public land, Appian makes it clear that even in 124 the land hunger was not abated. Indeed land seems to have been a problem which from now on was to require almost unceasing attention at Rome, just as employment does in a modern industrial state. Moreover two members of the land commission, Fulvius and Gaius himself, had been out of Rome for a couple of years and the third, Carbo, had receded from the limelight. So it was time to renew the pressure and no doubt Gaius made every effort. He drew up a new and precise definition of what land was liable to distribution and what was immune, which together with the fact that he now charged rent for the allotments suggests that he was laying hands on some new category of land that had remained inviolate until now. He also may have strengthened the land commission with the appointment of C. Crassus, the popular tribune of 145, to take the place of Carbo.[8]

Inevitably this activity aroused a good deal of the old resentment, perhaps made more bitter if he was in fact having to scrape the barrel to find enough land for his followers. Our sources speak of tumults, terror and sedition, and the anger of the senate against this further bid for popular favour. Cicero makes it clear that Gaius was associated with land reform just as closely as his brother had been, and insists that it was the struggle over land that caused both their deaths.[9]

Yet it is difficult to resist the impression that the actual acreage of land that Gaius could make available for classic piecemeal distribution was hardly enough to be worth stirring up so much hostility. After the great achievements of the commission his brother had established, the scope remaining for Gaius was so much less.

And so it came about that, with characteristic ingenuity, Gaius decided to give a new direction to his struggle to provide land, jobs and livelihoods for the Roman poor, a new direction that would also serve his empire-building ambitions. He would establish a whole series of new colonies, and these would not be confined to the mainland of Italy.

Most daring of all, he would colonize the site of Carthage, the home of Rome's greatest enemy, the very place where his brother, his cousin and his grandfather had all achieved imperishable military glory.

*

Founding colonies up and down Italy, numbering hundreds or thousands of settlers at a time, was an old Roman practice. Primarily intended to secure strategic positions, they also provided land for the landless and helped to spread Roman influence and culture, especially in the more recently conquered territory of northern Italy. For half a century the habit had died away, for reasons that presumably reflect the growing rift between the senate and the poor, as well as the economic pull towards the capital and away from the countryside. But undoubtedly the idea contained much that was bound to appeal to a man like Gaius Gracchus.

Our evidence for what he did reflects a perhaps inevitable confusion between proposals, laws and actual foundations. Livy and Appian flatly state that he founded 'many' colonies. One was certainly placed at Taranto, grandly named Neptunia after the god of the sea. Another was set up at Scolacium, also on the coast in the toe of Italy, and it could be guessed that both were sited with a view to sea-trading possibilities as well as agriculture. A third may have been placed at Capua, despite Cicero's claim that not even the Gracchi dared to lay hands on Campanian land.

Taranto and Capua seem to have played some special role, destined to receive a higher class of settlers than the usual destitutes, as befitted sites of such great commercial importance. Also Fulvius Flaccus, either now or during his Gallic campaign, may have founded Forum Fulvii in Piedmont and built a military road through it.[10]

In addition the thirty-odd Gracchan sites referred to in the obscure Book of Colonies may include some small settlements sent out by Gaius in the form of colonies rather than individual allotments. Further evidence is to be found in the bronze land law dating from 111 and referring to towns and colonies founded in Italy by commissioners under special legal authority. It seems to indicate that such foundations had recently been fairly common.[11]

In pressing for colonies in Italy Gaius was doing nothing unprecedented, nothing that other politicians had not done before him, most notably the powerful dynast Lepidus who had put 6,000 settlers into Parma, Modena and Luna earlier in the century. But Gaius was proposing to act on a much greater scale, and whatever the arguments in favour of colonies it was also true that their patron automatically acquired extra political influence by adding the support of his new colonists to his existing power base. Gaius gave extra offence by being careful to secure for himself the most important official posts connected with the major foundations, including the vital control of finance. No doubt he argued that personal supervision was the only way to ensure that the colonies were set up just as he wanted. The fact remained that he was cementing his own following at the public expense, and on two of the sites he was binding to himself a class of substantial citizens engaged in wide-ranging commercial activities.[12]

So the colonies gave his enemies further cause to fear and resent the spreading influence of the all-powerful tribune, who had conferred so many favours, remodelled so much of the Roman world, so irretrievably fractured the delicate machinery of senatorial government—and who now promised to wield even greater power in a second year of office. But the spark that ignited the smouldering suspicion was his precedent-breaking proposal to lead out the first colony ever to be established with full Roman citizen rights overseas, and of all places to lead it to Carthage.

Carthage! What a welter of emotional significance that name bore for Rome. The republic's deadliest enemy, defeated in three desperate wars that had spread over more than a century of time. Carthage, whose armies under Hannibal had marched to the very gates of Rome. Carthage, itself in origin a colony founded by the old Phoenicians, on a magnificent commercial site that had once made her the richest city in the western Mediterranean. Carthage, finally destroyed by Scipio less than a generation back. Carthage, whose site (did Gaius remember?) had been solemnly cursed, with bitter imprecations against anyone who should ever settle there again.

The law to send out a colony to Carthage was carried by a fellow-tribune, Rubrius, probably fairly late in 123. But because of the scale of the enterprise, and the many problems associated with it, Gaius reserved to himself the task of leading it out in the following year.[13]

Thus the great legislative programme of the year 123 was brought to its successful conclusion. To the best of our knowledge not a single project had failed, and there may well have been more of which we know nothing. After so many centuries we can still find ourselves lost in admiration for the colossal energy that Gaius Gracchus unleashed, the sheer drive and organizing ability needed to complete so much work. The complex phraseology of the bronze law is ample evidence of the detailed attention which was demanded. Still barely past his thirty-first birthday, Gaius had handled an army of advisers and specialists with great maturity, put his finger with uncanny precision on almost every one of those great problems which were to dominate the last century of the republic, and forced through reforms whose principles and effects endured far into the future.

*

On 10 December 123 Gaius entered his second year of office. This time his close ally Fulvius Flaccus was his colleague, and a friendly consul Fannius could be expected to give support after 1 January.

For the new year Gaius had reserved two major tasks.

One was to carry through the legacy of administrative work left behind by his laws: to see that the roads were built and the colonies established, and above all to organize the second foundation of Carthage as the crowning achievement of his tribunate.

The second was to pass the most ambitious law of all, to extend the Roman franchise to the Italian allies, the proposal that Fulvius had failed to push through in 125.

It was with every justification that Gaius postponed his great franchise bill to his second year of office, for it was indeed the most revolutionary of his proposals. This bill would finally reconcile those two contrasting Gracchan faces, that of the reforming imperial statesman and that of the ambitious popular leader.

On the one hand such an increase in the Roman citizen roll would massively strengthen the republic and give it the stronger base it now needed to rule its empire. Here was to be the first stage in the conversion of the Roman city-state into the Italian nation-state, to culminate as a world-state more than three centuries later when full citizenship was finally extended by Caracalla to every freeborn subject.

But on the other, its results must be to bring a huge new class of citizens into the voting assemblies as Gracchan beneficiaries, and so guarantee an almost unshakable Gracchan majority for the future. Here is the clearest indication we have of his long-term plans: to build a broad and diversified power-base with which he could wield enough authority, whether as a magistrate himself or working through friends, to guide and steer the Roman state exactly as Pericles had done in the golden age of Athens.

Perhaps Tiberius Gracchus had never aimed to establish a permanent 'reign', despite all the suspicions levelled against him. But this was certainly what Gaius had in mind. This is the only logical implication of a proposal for the culminating act of political patronage, the enfranchisement of an entire country.

But if this implication is obvious today, then so it was two thousand years ago.

Moreover, quite apart from the personal suspicion that such grand patronage was bound to stir up, the measure had one serious political weakness. It offered no direct benefits to any of the existing voters. So it had to be held back until Gaius had first won their favour by his other legislation, and achieved the strongest possible tactical position. In 122 it looked as though he would be even better placed than in 123. The Gracchan success at the elections of the previous year must have been taken as virtual endorsement of the idea, for the order of events given by Plutarch and Velleius make it clear that franchise had been an election issue, discussed from early in 123.

In any case, it was Fulvius' baby. He had brought it near to success in 125. His active support as tribune in 122 gave it the best chance of all. Or so it must have seemed at the time . . . .

The freeborn inhabitants of Italy fell into three main categories. Rather more than a third were full Roman citizens, including the people of the city itself, the citizen colonies, and most of old Latium which had been enfranchised in 338. Meanwhile a second concept, that of Latin citizenship, had been extended outside old Latium while many colonies had received Latin rather than Roman status. Latins had certain intermarriage and property rights, up to a point they could obtain Roman citizenship by migrating to Rome, and they had the right to vote at Rome but only within one of the thirty-five tribes.[14]

The rest, less than half of the total population, were merely 'Italians' or 'allies'. Racially and linguistically distinct from the Latin speakers, they were bound to Rome by treaties of several kinds but in no way participated in the Roman state itself. They fought for the empire but received none of its direct benefits. Some of them were quick to exploit the trading opportunities of the new world, but in Italy they were becoming an underprivileged class of social and political inferiors. When Fulvius offered them a choice between full citizenship and the right of appeal in 125, he showed that what mattered to them was not so much the vote as the privileges that went with it.

So in January 122 Gaius and Fulvius brought forward their franchise bill. To lessen the opposition they made it less radical than the 125 scheme, but its purport was still clear.

'Gaius proposed to give full Roman rights to the Latins, since the senate could not reasonably stand in the way of people of the same race, while to the other allies he offered the right to vote in the Roman assemblies which they did not have at present, hoping from then on to have their support in any future legislation' (A). In other words, as Cicero also makes clear, the bill concerned the allies and the Latins separately. The Latins were to receive full Roman citizenship and the Italians would move up one stage to receive Latin rights, including the vote in one tribe.[15]

Now the gradual extension of the franchise was one of those many customs which marked Rome's political genius and had done so much to build her strength. One striking example was the decision to grant Latin status to a curious community of half-breeds, the children of Roman soldiers serving in Spain.[16] The Gracchan extortion law had established that Roman citizenship could be given as a reward to a successful plaintiff. It may also imply that the elected magistrates of Latin communities were by now automatically receiving Roman citizenship, an enlightened principle that certainly existed a generation later and could tentatively be dated to 125 as a reaction to Fulvius' proposals. No doubt the senate felt that enfranchising such pillars of Latin society would help the spread of romanization, and encourage their loyalty, without much danger of filling the voting lists with dangerous radicals.[17]

So the slow spreading of the franchise was an established practice. What was radical about the Gracchan proposals was their scale. The Latins alone would be a substantial addition to the voting rolls, enough to hold the balance on most issues. But the two-stage approach carried the even greater implication, that Latin status was only a resting-place on the way to full franchise, that it would only be a matter of time before all the Italians moved on to attain that full citizenship which Fulvius had offered them in vain in 125. This is why the franchise bill would have been the culminating point of the Gracchan revolution.

That Fulvius Flaccus played an important role in the revised proposal there can be no doubt. A man of very distinguished family, a personal friend to both Gracchus brothers, a land commissioner, scholar, consul, and victorious commander, it might yet be questioned whether his vigorous and forthright manner was a help to the Gracchan cause. Plutarch refers to him as turbulent and hated by his fellow-senators, suspected of stirring up the allies even to the point of revolt, and tending to confirm these suspicions by his subversive and trouble-making policies.

'It was this more than anything that ruined Gaius, who had to accept a share of the hatred against his colleague,' although this and similar passages do read rather like special pleading by the followers of Gaius trying to find a scapegoat for his ultimate failure. The fact is that they worked closely together. Fulvius was 'an ally in the same madness'; his 'ambitions were as villainous'; and Gaius chose him 'as a partner to share in his own royal power'.[18]

And yet, formidable as this team looked, in 122 the conservative majority of the senate found the answer that had eluded them against Gaius the year before.

Early in the new year the Gracchan bill to enfranchise the allies was brought before the assembly of tribes, and the tribune M. Livius Drusus vetoed it.

The Gracchan tide had turned.

13 End of an Era

From the start of his second year in office, Gaius noticed with some concern the strength of the senate's hostility, while the supposedly friendly consul Fannius was proving somewhat cooler than expected (P). So perhaps it was at this point that he enlarged his colonial programme as a way of encouraging support for the franchise bill.

But the senate, afraid that he might become quite invincible, now tried a quite novel scheme to win the popular support away from Gaius, namely to overbid him for the people's favour. They would court the voters even if it meant acting against the public interest.

Now one of his fellow tribunes was Livius Drusus, a man inferior to no Roman in birth or upbringing, a man whose character, eloquence and wealth put him on a level with the leaders of the state. And it was to this man that the nobles turned, urging him to take their side and join battle with Gaius.[1]

But who was this Drusus, who was prepared to pit himself in a face-to-face duel with the most spectacularly successful politician ever to have trod the forum's paving stones? It comes as no surprise, in this in-bred world, that he came from the innermost ranks of the nobility. His father not only had been fellow consul with Scipio in 147 but was very probably his cousin too, for both appear to have been grandsons of the redoubtable Aemilius Paullus who fell at Cannae.

Cicero thought his speech impressive and his manner full of authority. Diodorus calls him a man of the greatest distinction, 'amazingly well-loved by the people for his birth and his virtue', while adding the revealing fact that his son became the wealthiest man in Rome. A marriage connection with a leading family of Capua may have helped the family fortunes. Perhaps he retained some personal sympathy for the allies, since they were given a concession on land tenure when he later became consul, after which he fought successfully in Thrace, was honoured with a triumph and elected censor. The enemies of Gaius Gracchus had evidently chosen a very talented young man to take up the challenge. Drusus was the truest political heir of Scipio Aemilianus, and he set about his delicate task with a shrewd application that amply merited his later acclaim as 'Protector of the Senate'.[2]

When Drusus vetoed the franchise bill in January 122 he took his enemies completely aback. He was careful to give no explanation for his veto (A), so it can be taken that he gave no warning of it either. Yet this was the turning-point for Gaius Gracchus. Before this veto nothing had gone wrong. From this moment on, nothing was to go right.[3]

Now what were the Gracchans to do? Drusus was a far more formidable opponent than Octavius had been eleven years earlier, so that the idea of trying to depose this tribune like his predecessor can hardly have seemed attractive. And there was no time available. Gaius was due to go off to establish his great new colony in Carthage, and arrangements for this must already have been made, which could hardly permit of delay. Indeed a special law may have had to be passed to give him, as tribune, permission to leave Rome for this task.

No doubt Gaius had counted on passing the franchise bill quickly, and himself being free to go overseas while Fulvius saw to the administrative consequences in Rome. Both would hope to be free in time to carry more legislation and rally their supporters before the next elections. But now that plan was wrecked.

On the other hand there was political capital to be won at Carthage, and no reason to suppose that Gaius could not handle Drusus and see the franchise bill through on his return. And so it was decided. Gaius went abroad, it can hardly have been any later than the beginning of February to allow time for what was to follow. Fulvius, who perhaps had already been on a preliminary visit to Carthage the previous year, was now left to hold the position in Rome.[4]

Such a task proved way beyond his abilities, however. For no sooner had Gaius crossed the horizon for remote Africa, than Drusus unveiled his plans in all their ruthless simplicity.

The nobles urged him not to use violence, nor come into headlong conflict with the mass of the people, but to exercise his office in the way that would please them most, giving in to them even when it would be more honourable to incur their displeasure.

And so, accepting this charge from the senate, Drusus began to draft laws which had no claim to be either honourable or useful. But he devoted every effort to one goal alone, that of outdoing Gaius in pleasing and gratifying the mob, just as in a play.

Plutarch was remembering the parallel scene depicted in the famous *Knights* of Aristophanes, where the crafty Sausage-Seller similarly outbid the great Athenian demagogue Cleon. But this was no comedy, 'for by adopting such a policy the senate made it absolutely plain that it was not so much bothered by the public policies of Gaius Gracchus as determined to humble and break the man himself' (P).

Drusus began the mock auction with a series of bills. To match the two important colonies that Gaius had in hand Drusus proposed, with the senate's full support, to send out no fewer than twelve colonies with 3000 settlers in each, chosen from the most destitute citizens rather than the better class envisaged by Gaius.

Then, bitterly though the senate had opposed the distribution of public land to the poor by Gaius, it was delighted when Drusus went even further and relieved it of the small rent that Gaius had charged. And now the people were so pleased with all this that they began to think rather less of the Gracchan laws.[5]

While speaking in support of his bills Drusus emphasized that the proposals came from the senate and showed its care for the people's welfare. This brought about the only useful practical result of his dealings, that the people became more friendly towards the senate. Drusus relieved the nobles of that burden of popular hatred and suspicion, and softened the bitter memories of past grievances. At the same time he took care to avoid even the appearance of self-interest in his own proposals, and named other men to manage the colonies and control the finances, in noticeable contrast to the normal Gracchan practice.

This extraordinary mixture of open bribery and pious rhetoric had an astonishingly rapid effect on the loyalty of the Roman voters. The absence of Gaius proved a fatal error, for it allowed Drusus to concentrate on the easier target of Fulvius and to probe away at the Gracchans' most vulnerable spot, the franchise bill itself, with which Fulvius was most closely associated and from which the Roman people had so little direct benefit to expect. Quickly the pressure began to tell on Fulvius. By abusing him and raking up all the old scandals that linked his name with Scipio's mysterious death, Drusus gradually won over his following among the people (P).

*

Meanwhile not everything was going well in Carthage, either.

Carthage was a very ambitious project. It was no after-thought that Gaius named his new colony Junonia, after the queen of the gods herself. Perhaps he had other overseas colonies in mind, one of which could have been at the equally attractive site of Corinth, destroyed in the same year as Carthage, where we know that the question of selling off confiscated land cropped up a few years later. But this whole concept of overseas settlement was controversial in the extreme, and Velleius tells of the fears that it aroused: 'Our ancestors stringently avoided such projects for they knew that all over the world the pattern was for colonies, like Syracuse, Marseilles, and Carthage herself, to become more powerful than their founder cities.'[6]

Rather oddly Plutarch suggests that Gaius was chosen only by lot to go overseas at this particularly inconvenient moment, and Appian says the senate contrived to secure his absence from Rome. Gaius had certainly secured his own nomination as one of the three founders, but perhaps we should conclude that he actually tried to duck his responsibilities at the last moment, seeing the strength of the Drusus counter-attack and the danger to his own popularity, and was somehow prevented from doing so.[7]

But in reality Gaius needed to go because there was so much to do there. On top of the destruction of the city in 146 the whole area had recently been ravaged by the plague of locusts. Yet the land here was so fertile, as Appian emphasizes, that it could not be left uncultivated. So determined was Gaius for success that unusually favourable terms were arranged for the settlers.

From the bronze land law we discover that some of the allotments in Carthage were as big as 200 Roman acres, which is confirmed by the evidence of modern aerial photography. This was more than one family could possibly handle without extra labour.[8] The allotments may also have been given freehold to the settlers rather than on the usual leasehold basis. Large freeholds could imply allotment to wealthy settlers, who were able to bring their own capital into the colony and could in turn give financial assistance to poorer settlers who perhaps operated as their tenants. We know that many of the settlers were poor and that the law allowed for an unusually large number of them, finally reaching 6,000, which with families added indicates that a large community was being established at a stroke.[9]

But there was still one problem of which Gaius had not taken sufficient account. After Carthage had been destroyed the weightiest curses had been pronounced on anyone who should ever settle there again, and the site itself had been abandoned for sheep to pasture on.[10]

As a result strange things happened when Gracchus and his men began their work. The very first landmark was snatched from its bearer's hand by a violent gust of wind and smashed to pieces. A whirlwind caught up the sacrificial victims lying on the altar and scattered them far outside the boundaries that had been established for the new city. Most sinister of all, once the boundary posts had at last been put in place, wolves came down in the night, tore them down, and either chewed them up or carried them off far into the open country.[11]

It would be foolish to ignore the possibility, or rather the near-certainty, that the hands of men hostile to the Gracchan cause were at work in some of these supernatural visitations. But the Romans were a superstitious people, and such bad news at the very inception of a new city was bound to be taken seriously, for this was a moment when it was vital that all religious matters be in order. Who could forget the traditional story of the ill omen that had menaced the foundation of Rome itself, when Romulus saw his brother jump over the half-built city walls—and killed him on the spot as a warning to future transgressors?[12] The strong conservative influence in the priestly colleges were available to reinforce the superstition. When letters arrived at Rome telling of the incidents, and revealing the deep anxiety of the soothsayers at the colony, the question was inevitably raised as to whether the whole idea should be abandoned for fear that it might threaten the peace of the Roman world.

Despite these distractions, Gaius raced through his work of establishing the new colony. In seventy days he had completed it all, urged on by the reports from Rome which told of the pressure on Fulvius and his own waning popularity. The people had had enough of his brand of politics, he was told, because many leaders were courting their favour and even the senate was gladly yielding to their wishes (P).

So at some time in April, as near as we can judge, Gaius found himself back in the capital, and with a great deal on his mind. Not only had Carthage to be kept going, and the franchise bill to be resurrected, but also there would soon be elections to fight, and the chances of further re-election to a third year of office were already receding.

The prospects for the consular elections were even worse. Of the two strongest candidates for consul, one was the Fabius whom Gaius had snubbed the year before over the matter of Spanish grain. The other was an even more hostile figure, the grim Opimius who had grown in popularity since Gaius had secured his defeat the previous year. The man who had crushed the Fregellae revolt, and had further cause for resentment against the Gracchan pressure that had denied him the honour of a triumph, now had an army of supporters. Should he become consul, as seemed likely, he was widely expected to be the undoing of Gaius Gracchus (P).

*

Again the political tension at Rome was rising fast. Both sides were playing for the highest stakes of all, and in an atmosphere of the greatest excitement Gaius Gracchus and Fulvius Flaccus once more brought forward their controversial franchise bill.

If only they could secure overwhelming popular support for the bill, then it should not be beyond their powers to win the elections and if necessary to force Drusus out of office. Not even now did they realize the strength and cunning of the campaign being mounted against them, for if they had done then perhaps they would have fought for the bill less doggedly. By abandoning or at least postponing it, maybe they could still have recovered their position. But instead they decided to play to win or lose everything.

So alarming was the situation that as soon as Gaius returned to Rome he moved house, from the spacious heights of the Palatine hill, where emperors would one day build their palaces, down to the slum streets near the forum. There he would be close to his poorer supporters (P).

Then he and Fulvius tried to rescue their beloved Carthage by flatly denying the whole story of the wolves, and furiously accused the senators of lying (A). They also tried to link the two burning issues of the day by opening the settlement lists for Carthage to colonists from all over Italy, whether enfranchised or not, and well in excess of the numbers authorized in the original law. That had been strictly confined to Roman citizens, and the change looked like an attempt at surreptitious enfranchisement. Or perhaps Gaius still believed his bill could not fail to go through.[13]

Then he formally tabled a whole series of bills, including the franchise proposal, and backed them with a famous speech of which several fragments have survived. In it he bitterly attacked the arrogance of Roman magistrates and their maltreatment of free allies.

A Roman consul and his wife recently visited the Italian town of Teanum. His wife wanted to wash in the public baths, so the local quaestor Marius was told to clear everybody out of them. But she complained to her husband that it had taken too long and the baths were not clean enough for her, and so this reputable man was brought to a stake erected in the forum, stripped and beaten with rods.

When the people of Cales heard this they laid down a rule against anyone using the baths if a Roman magistrate was there. The same thing happened at Ferentinum, whereupon a Roman praetor ordered the local quaestors to be seized. One of them was caught and beaten and the other flung himself from the town walls.

And let me give just one example of the intolerable behaviour of our younger men. This one was returning from Asia, where he had served as a junior officer, not even a magistrate, and was being carried in a litter through the territory of Venusia when an ignorant ploughman met the party, and jokingly asked if it was a corpse they were carrying. Our young man promptly stopped and had the rustic beaten with the binding straps until he died.

Now if behaviour of this kind was becoming at all common then the resentment of the allies is fully explained. Here was more than a grievance about land or plunder. And these were not obscure locations for crime, for the first three towns lay within a hundred miles of Rome itself. In these almost eye-witness stories we catch a rare glimpse of that arrogance which had so terribly corrupted the proud nobles of Rome.

But this was not all, for Gaius went on to attack the luxurious life-style of these same nobles, and denounced the money they spent importing fine wines to flaunt before their poor and frugal countrymen. Then the finest and most passionate orator of his time spoke to arouse sympathy for his own predicament.

You all know that my family is as noble as any. But now that I have lost my brother, who died for your sakes, then my young son and I remain as the only living descendants of Scipio Africanus and Gracchus the great censor. Yet supposing I were to ask and implore you to let me now retire from public life in the hope of preventing our line from utterly perishing, in an attempt to preserve some tiny branch of this great family—then how could I persuade you willingly to grant me even that wish?[14]

But would the Roman people continue to identify their own interests so closely with the Gracchan cause? Certainly that cause was becoming more and more radical. One of the laws introduced by that great speech was meant to reduce the strong class bias built in to the assembly of centuries. Since the centuries elected the senior magistrates, who in turn dominated the senate, it could have had the most far-reaching political effects over time, even though its immediate purpose was obviously to prevent the election of Opimius and Fabius as consuls that summer. Yet the only change involved would have been to call the centuries forward by lot to vote, instead of taking the wealthiest first and the poorest last. So little was needed to break the iron grip of privilege. And he may also have proposed a law for the reduction of debts or the postponement of repayments.[15]

Neither these proposals nor any others now introduced attained the force of law, but it could be argued that they indicate some shift in the Gracchan position. In his first year Gaius had passed a series of severely practical measures, designed to achieve specific reforms and rally defined groups of supporters. But the latest plans, and even the franchise bill itself, seem to reflect a more theoretical concept of equality more characteristic of Greek politics. Maybe he was being drawn, like his brother, from the particular to the general issue. Maybe the intransigence of the opposition had led him into the familiar predicament of the man who feels he cannot reform anything unless he reforms everything.

We do not know enough to be sure. But it is noteworthy that at this juncture Fannius saw fit to attack Gaius for the use he made of Greek advisers such as Menelaus. He also denounced his one-time friend for bribery, pointing out to the voters that corruption (by which we are to understand laws beneficial to the masses) had helped Greek tyrants like Phalaris and Pisistratus on the road to power. Was Gaius trying to emulate them?[16]

Moreover if Gaius was trying at last to grapple with the fundamental principles of a society in which power and privilege depended on noble birth and wealth, then this made it an opportune moment for Drusus to denounce his exquisitely born opponent for the extravagant purchase of silver dolphins costing 125*d.* per pound.[17]

Gaius and Drusus were desperately counter-bidding for the people's favours, and while coarse personal insults were nothing new in Roman politics, this open auctioneering was. But worse was to follow. The consul Fannius, whom Gaius had helped into office, the friend of Scipio and student of Stoic philosophy, was to betray his own ideals and introduce the most selfish note of all into the great debate. For the task he set himself was nothing less than to turn the Roman people against their own allies by convincing them that the spread of the franchise would erode their own living standards.

'If you once grant citizenship to the Latins,' he asked the assembly, 'do you imagine that you will ever be able to find room to stand at your own public meetings as you are standing now? Will you ever be able to find a place at your own public games and festivals? Can't you see that they will take possession of everything?'

No doubt he gave further illustrations, arguing that the allies would want a share in the colonies, the land distribution, or the corn subsidy, and that it could only mean less of a share for the citizens. The argument was effective just because it contained a grain of truth, and the speech in which Fannius rammed it home was praised by Cicero as fine and famous, 'the best of all those delivered at that period'. To be sure, it was widely suspected that many nobles had contributed to it, and that the whole speech had been fitted together and polished by the learned scholar Persius. But Fannius was playing with fire, for the wedge he drove on that day between the Romans and Italians was the first stage of the process that was to goad those allies into setting the whole peninsula ablaze with civil war a generation later.[18]

Yet this was not all, for Drusus had his own wedge to drive, this time within the ranks of the allies. His aim was to separate the Latins from the Italians. For now that the nobles had recovered their self-confidence and found leaders of ability, we can see them using in home affairs precisely those same ruthless tactics of 'divide and rule' which had so long guided their foreign policy. Drusus offered the Latins what fell short of the full citizenship proposed by Gaius but might be regarded as almost as valuable, namely a bill to prevent any

Latin from being beaten even when on military service.

This was a valuable privilege, for even Roman citizen soldiers had received such protection only within the past generation, and at least in theory it would fully protect Latin citizens from that arbitrary mishandling which Gaius had complained about. Technically it may not have been quite the same as the formal right of appeal offered by Fulvius in 125, but in any case it was offered to the Latins only. For the others there would be nothing. It was worth wooing the Latins, who had a limited voting right, but the Italians, it was made clear, now counted for nothing in Roman politics at all.[19]

Against these powerful hammer-blows from Fannius and Drusus we must imagine Gaius working flat out to muster all the support he could find. We can realize that however broad the power base he had built it must have been sadly lacking in depth and solidity for him to be thrown so quickly off balance. Yet his eloquence was greater than theirs, and he had his new legislative programme, which may have had more to offer than we know of. Even now he hoped to save his bills and win the day.

As the vote came near a great crowd of Gracchan supporters poured into the city from every direction. As well as Roman countrymen who would back Gaius with their votes, there came Latins and allies who would use either their limited rights or simply the moral support of their voices and, if need be, their fists, to see that their champion won them the prizes they still coveted (P).

Yet all was in vain. Now the senatorial leaders delivered their third and decisive blow. On their advice the consul Fannius issued a proclamation ordering that, 'Nobody who does not possess the right to vote shall either stay in the city or approach it nearer than five miles while these bills are being voted on.' It was a strange and almost unprecedented act, for he had repeated the idea used in 126 but this time relying on his own executive authority, rather than seeking legal sanction as had been done then. Now allies and friends of the Romans were simply expelled from the city, although Latins, whom Drusus had been wooing with such care, were presumably allowed to stay.[20]

Gaius was quick enough with his riposte. He issued his own counter-edict, denouncing the consul and promising to protect his supporters if they remained. But he was no longer in a position to do this. For when he saw one of his own personal friends being dragged away by the consul's attendants he passed by and did nothing. Either he feared to give proof that his own powers were declining, or else, as he himself claimed, he was anxious to avoid giving his enemies the opportunity they sought to come to blows with him (P).

Of course neither the voting rights of his supporters nor his own privileges as tribune were in any way formally suspended by the decree of Fannius. But its moral effect was devastating. While searching for broad principles, or calculating the narrow balance of interests, it is easy to overlook the extent to which an open assembly in a crowded Mediterranean town would be influenced by the crudest emotions and the most irrational shifts of sentiment. Gaius had built success on success; he had aroused a frenzy of enthusiastic support from every class of society and won the respect even of many senators for his energy and judgement.

But no sooner did he begin to look like a loser than all this support melted away like the summer snow. Evil omens had clouded the Carthage venture. Fulvius had cut a hopeless figure against the eloquence of Drusus. Now Gaius could not even protect his own supporters. He did not dare to veto the decree of Fannius. His glamour had faded. He had little left to offer.

The allies who had pinned their hopes on the franchise bill were kept out of Rome. In their absence, those voters who remained were no doubt intimidated by the triumphant consul and his attendants whom Gaius had not dared to defy. No doubt they were impressed by all those great men of the state who flocked around Drusus, accompanied by their own bands of clients and dependants and now openly denouncing the Gracchan programme.

Open public debate and demonstration must certainly have been stifled. The bills of Gaius Gracchus were rejected by the assembly. An era was over.[21]

14 Daggers in the Forum

It was Drusus who healed the wounds in the state that Gaius Gracchus had inflicted, Cicero felt. It was Drusus who shattered the great tribune's powers.[1]

With one young but determined leader, ready to tackle the Gracchans head on and capable of winning the enthusiasm of the voters, and with the firm support of the consul present in Rome, the massed ranks of the conservative nobility had thrown off the challenge of revolutionary politics at last.

Revenge was yet to come.

The elections were approaching fast, and in a desperate attempt to recover support Gaius made another mistake. A gladiatorial fight was to be staged in the forum, and several magistrates took the opportunity to construct seats all round and sell them to the public. In his role as tribune Gaius ordered them torn down, so that the poor would be able to stand and watch free of charge. But nobody took any notice of him.

So, waiting till the night before the show, he collected a force of workmen engaged on the public contracts under his control, and with their help pulled down all the seats so that at daybreak the space was clear. The poor praised him for a brave man, but his colleagues took umbrage. Just as over Carthage, when Gaius had ignored both the letter of the law and the warnings of religion, his behaviour again typified what any aristocracy must fear above all, that one of its members should try to exalt himself above his fellows. He was, after all, only one of ten tribunes, and to behave like this on his own was a piece of effrontery the others could not tolerate.

It was the last straw, and it cost him the elections. The story was that he still managed to win a majority of the votes, but that his indignant fellow-tribunes officiating at the election contrived to bring about his defeat. But this puts it the wrong way round. The previous year's events show us that re-election was possible only under special circumstances. To fix those circumstances must have needed the tacit if not the active support of his colleagues, and the real difference between the elections of 123 and those of 122 is that this time he had forfeited that support. The complex procedure governing the announcement of votes by order of lot gave ample scope for chicanery at the expense of a candidate whose influence was so evidently on the wane.[2]

Yet the incident is odd. One would have expected to find more Gracchan sympathizers besides Fulvius among the tribunes elected in 123. Perhaps like Fannius, some were never more than lukewarm in the cause, and some may have felt that Gaius like his brother was going too far. The more radical proposals tabled this year, not to mention the full implication of the franchise bill, may have turned away many a patriotic Roman who had accepted the reforms of 123. And so Gaius lost the election of summer 122. The following 10 December his legal authority and his personal inviolability as tribune would both come to an end.

In the consular elections immediately following, as expected, both Fabius and Opimius were chosen.

Gaius was bitterly disappointed, and not without cause. But when his enemies exulted over his defeat he turned on them with all his old fire, and warned that they were laughing bitter laughter, for they had no idea of the great darkness that would engulf them as a result of his political measures (P).

As a long-term forecast of the fate that was bound to overtake an aristocracy that governed as they did, it was accurate enough. But now it was Gaius who was more at risk than they were.

For the rest of his year in office Gaius seems to have busied himself with administrative work, on road building, land settlement and Italian colonies. No further attempts at legislation are known. His teeth had been drawn.

The counter-proposals of Livius Drusus are assumed to have been passed, but there is no evidence that his famous twelve colonies were ever sent out. The only hint of their fate comes when Appian remarks that thirty years later there were still several colonies in Italy and Sicily 'which had been voted long before but never established'. Meanwhile despite much controversy the work of establishing Carthage seems to have carried on to the end of the year.[3]

*

Came the new year, and the pressure began to build up. But

in view of the horrors to come, it is of some importance to consider the strength and nature of this pressure. Was a peaceful withdrawal from public life, such as Gaius had rather wistfully dismissed as impractical a year before, still in any way possible? On the contrary, the evidence suggests that the group of nobles who opposed him had now become completely dominant in the senate and were determined to force him into an impossible situation.

Early in 121 Fabius was sent off to continue the Gallic War, while the other consul Opimius and a tribune Minucius Rufus set to work whittling away the Gracchan legislative achievements. We are repeatedly told that Minucius actually repealed several laws, although we cannot be sure just what was scrapped.[4]

Certainly the great tax and judiciary reforms stayed, for there were too many vested interests in their retention. The land laws were not dismantled until afterwards. On the other hand, since most of our knowledge of Gracchan legislation depends on fragmentary evidence which by its nature applies only to those laws which had lasting effects, there must have been other laws which Minucius did repeal, and this may help to explain the extraordinary violence about to be let loose.

But the law that we know came under heaviest attack was that establishing the colony at Carthage. When the senate proposed that an assembly should be summoned to repeal the Carthage law, Gaius and Fulvius were enraged and bitterly complained that the whole story of the wolves and the boundary posts was a lie inspired by the senate (A). In other words they were the victims of a plot. Already the senate was disturbing the arrangements for the colony, and doing so deliberately to goad Gaius into some kind of action that would give it an excuse to get rid of him (P).[5]

Now the ultimate intention, which was achieved surely in this very year, was to cancel the colony altogether. But even before that the senate had taken the administration of Carthage out of the hands of Gaius, against whom even the gods had declared war. And curiously enough we know who was given temporary charge of it, for a fragment of a white marble boundary stone has been found there and can still be seen in the museum at Carthage. It is a later copy, but the original must be dated to 121 and the names of the post-Gracchan commissioners on it are fraught with interest.[6]

One was Calpurnius Bestia, consul in 111, a thorough anti-Gracchan, for it was he who carried the law to recall Popillius from the exile to which Gaius had consigned him.[7]

The second was the renegade Papirius Carbo. He had served on the Gracchan land commission and worked closely with Gaius in the attack on Scipio Aemilianus, but had since decided to change sides. This we know because at the height of the reaction, in summer 121, of all people Carbo was elected consul, and when he took office in 120 his main claim to fame was that he stood up in public to defend Opimius against charges arising out of the death of Gaius Gracchus. Carbo, of all people, was to claim that the death of Gaius was justified, Carbo who had so viciously abused Scipio for saying the same thing about Tiberius. Carbo betrayed the cause, and it would fit all we know of this unsavoury character if we guessed that the betrayal took place in Carthage, where his could have been the hand that secretly produced those special effects to indicate the gods' displeasure.[8]

But if one Gracchan could turn sides so could another. The third commissioner at Carthage was Galba, most probably the C. Galba who was Gaius' own brother-in-law, having married P. Crassus' other daughter. His future career confirms the suspicion. When the popular indignation finally caught up with the most hated nobles in 109, five men were convicted and exiled by 'Gracchan judges' specially appointed by the Mamilian law. The victims included Opimius, Bestia—and C. Galba. Galba was the first priest ever to be condemned by a public court at Rome, so we could very well explain his unpopularity by guessing that he had used his religious authority to give credence to the evil omens engineered by Carbo.[9]

So two Gracchan renegades, one a kinsman by marriage, not merely helped administer the rundown of the Carthaginian colony but may well have been personally involved in the plot to use religion to discredit it. Such was the emotional blizzard unleashed when Gaius decided to settle that accursed site, but these details also indicate how decisively the nobility had swung against him. And despite the fragmentary evidence it is possible to make some assessment of the strength of the anti-Gracchan forces now.

At least eight men who had already held the office of consul are known to have fallen out with Gaius or to have had reason for doing so. Of these, Piso Frugi and Fannius had actively opposed him in the two previous years. P. Lentulus, the leader of the senate, Q. Metellus, the conqueror of Macedon, and D. Brutus, who had married Gaius' own wife's mother, were all to do so during 121. Aquillius and, if he was still alive, L. Cotta had been attacked by Gaius over the small matter of corrupting the extortion courts. Plautius had been the butt of a speech in which Gaius had mocked the insolent manners of the senators who had once governed Carthage and Capua, with an implied warning to the Roman senate not to follow their example.[10]

In addition there were the many relatives of the above, as well as the survivors of the groups that had supported Scipio and opposed Tiberius Gracchus. These included the ex-consul Popillius, still languishing in exile, and Scipio's nephew Q. Aelius Tubero, who had broken off a friendship with Tiberius, never reached high office, but was still one of Gaius' most persistent opponents.[11]

Among younger politicians of note another dozen future consuls can be placed in the anti-Gracchan camp. These include the valiant tribunes Drusus and Minucius, and the commissioners Bestia and Carbo. The two other victims of the Mamilian tribunal were to be Sp. Postumius, a contemporary and old rival of Tiberius Gracchus, and C. Cato, who had once supported Tiberius and perhaps should be added to the list of turncoats. Gaius told L. Metellus, 'I know that you [*plural*] are thoroughly tired of me,' which confirms the hostility of not merely this Metellus but also his five consular brothers and cousins. And to this formidable list could be added other rising names, such as the future leader of the senate, Aemilius Scaurus, who later went out of his way to humiliate the man who dared to prosecute Opimius.[12]

To sum up, this weight of evidence makes it clear that whenever Gaius Gracchus set foot in that senate house from which the world was still governed, he must have met a reception of unwavering hostility. Old and young alike, the representatives of the great noble families detested him and everything he had done. And if the record of the Roman nobility shows anything, it is that the trait with which it won the empire was an unflinching resistance to any threat however formidable, which in turn meant that its resentment, once aroused, was implacable.

Greeks, Spaniards and Carthaginians had suffered agonies because the Roman senate, always slow to react, then never let go. And its ranks now stood virtually united in a determination not to let go of Gaius Gracchus. All means would be used to accomplish his destruction.

To combat this array, Gaius retained the loyalty of no men of distinction apart from Fulvius Flaccus, who was in any case perhaps more of a liability. The grouping of nobles that his brother had welded together had vanished without trace. Even the high priest Scaevola, whose support for land reform had helped set the whole movement going more than a decade before, had now withdrawn his favour. His religious, legal and historical preoccupations had turned him away from active politics, and he is not known to have intervened in the crisis. But afterwards he was prepared to blame Gaius for the violence.[13]

Nor was there anything left of the network of alliances that Gaius had forged outside the senate. We hear nothing of the knights, who must have been bought off by a senate promise not to repeal the legislation that concerned them most. Admittedly, it was not yet obvious how deep was the breach that Gaius had established between senators and knights. Sallust gives an account of how the counter-revolution was organized.

> The Gracchus brothers, whose ancestors had added so much to the power of the state in the Punic and other wars, began to assert the freedom of the people and to expose the misdeeds of the few. At this the nobility was as alarmed as it was guilty. Yet it managed to obstruct the Gracchan plans by working first with the allies and the Latins, and then with the Roman knights, whom it had separated from the common people with promises of friendship.[14]

And now that overwhelming power had been marshalled against Gaius Gracchus, it was time to strike.

*

At first Gaius put up with the provocation, and tried to oppose the countermeasures in a peaceful way. To his surprise he had no success at all, and to his disappointment he found the humiliation intolerable. Eventually Fulvius and his friends persuaded him it was time to take a stronger line, and gather a group of supporters prepared to resist the consul with arms if necessary—which may only mean that they would be prepared to defend themselves if the consul attacked them as Nasica had attacked Tiberius.

One story, not universally believed, was that Gaius was encouraged and helped by his mother Cornelia, from her retreat at Misenum. She was supposed to have secretly hired a bodyguard of Italians for him and sent them into the city disguised as reapers. At least this tells us that harvest time was coming round again, when such men could easily pretend they were looking for work. And so, in the warmth of early summer, tempers frayed, crowds filled the streets, and both sides steeled themselves with grim determination for the final confrontation.[15]

The day arrived for the crucial assembly, when the vote would be taken whether or not to revoke the colonization of Carthage. On the Capitol hill, on the very spot where Tiberius had met his fate, the Roman people would vote in their assembly of tribes. The consul Opimius was to preside, since we know that he conducted the preliminary sacrifice, although the tribune Minucius was also in evidence. As usual the official voting assembly was preceded by an informal gathering where speeches could be made, and to give support to their champions crowds of supporters from both sides began to take up strategic positions even before daybreak.[16]

With thunder in the air, the atmosphere must have been oppressive and the dawn gloomy and menacing. Fulvius was on the spot early, and even managed to make a speech, but by the time Gaius arrived with a much larger band of followers the main area in front of the great temple of Jupiter was already occupied, chiefly with his opponents. So he took up position in a portico which lay behind the temple and walked to and fro among his supporters, many of whom had weapons concealed beneath their clothing, while he watched to see what would develop.

Gaius, we are told, was in a nervous and agitated state, and reasonably so. There was every reason to expect that the other side would precipitate some act of violence, especially if Gaius genuinely hoped he could win the vote and defeat the proposed repeal. And yet to his consternation precisely the opposite happened.

An attendant passed by, carrying the entrails of the victim that Opimius had sacrificed. Antyllius, as he was called, found himself close to Gaius and spoke to him. What he said became the subject of natural disagreement later on. One version was that he provoked the Gracchans with an insulting gesture, brandishing his arm and crying out, 'Now you scoundrels, make way for honest men.' The alternative tale, which somehow rings less true, is that he came right up to Gaius, grasped him or even fell on his knees, and begged him not to use irreparable violence against his own fatherland.

Either way Gaius was taken aback and glared at the intruder, perhaps pushing him away. In so tense a situation the inevitable happened. Somebody thought the time for action had arrived, or that Gaius had been insulted, menaced, and wanted ridding of the man. Antyllius was seized and stabbed to death with voting pens that the Gracchans were said to have specially sharpened for the occasion. As so often happens, men who had armed to defend themselves had precipitated the very trouble they wanted to avoid.[17]

In vain Gaius berated his followers for so stupid a deed, that had at last given their enemies the opening they had been looking for (P). In vain he ran into the crowd to make his excuses. It was too late. Nobody would listen to him (A). The murder was the signal for battle, and Opimius acted on it. Panic spread across the assembly. At first people shied away from the Gracchans, the brawling became general, and the consul urged on the citizens to take vengeance.

At this moment, suddenly and providentially, the threatened rainstorm broke with such violence that the assembly had to be dismissed and the crowd broke up (P). But now there were other things to do.[18]

Quickly Opimius summoned the senate, and with a great show of indignation reported the murder and warned that they themselves would be attacked next. Gaius, it was now said, had deliberately ordered his men to kill Antyllius and make this the start of their own revenge.

Meanwhile the wretched victim's body had been taken up by his friends who organized an impromptu funeral procession. They carried it uncovered down through the forum and past the senate house, with many tears and lamentation. Out came Opimius and the senators, to add their complaints at this intolerable crime, although there were many in the crowd who bitterly contrasted this extraordinary demonstration by the whole Roman senate over one dead servant, who was at least partly to blame for his fate, with the callous way that the same men had tossed the corpse of Tiberius Gracchus into the river (P).

Having made the most of this oportunity, and whipped themselves up into a fine mixture of real and feigned terror, the senators reassembled and for the first time in Roman history passed the famous 'Ultimate Decree'. This formally instructed the consul to defend the state from harm, and perhaps added that he should put down the tyrant.[19]

*

More than a dozen times in the course of the republic's last hundred years, the Ultimate Decree was passed by a senate which feared violence, and yet its constitutional force remained uncertain to the end. Defence of the state was the consul's prime duty at any time, and yet in 121 there was no hostile army battering at the gates, only a sudden outbreak of violence which had already died down. There was nothing to suggest that established legal and constitutional machinery had been overthrown.

Perhaps it was under threat. The possible need for exceptional measures was certainly in the air, and, if the need arose, under what legal form could they be taken? Force had been used spontaneously against Tiberius Gracchus in 133. Yet as a result Nasica had been threatened with prosecution and forced out of public life. Gaius Gracchus had strengthened the law against arbitrary violence and driven Popillius into exile. Everyone could remember the rumours that Scipio would attempt a coup during the troubles of 129.

In the light of these precedents, the senate was anxious to ensure that this time any emergency action was taken within a clear constitutional framework, and so the Ultimate Decree was devised. It had no force of law behind it; it added not an iota to the consul's normal powers; but it urged him to remember his prime duty and use those powers to the full. In effect it promised the moral backing of the senate and its full support for whatever action he chose to take.

There is no government which cannot be provoked to use whatever force it can muster, regardless of the niceties of the law, against a threat to the fundamental interests of the state. Cicero embroidered the theme in a series of lapidary comments.

Let the safety of the state be the highest law.

Amid armed strife the laws are silent, and do not demand that we wait upon them.

The consuls are adequately armed by that tiny phrase [*of the Ultimate Decree*] even if it puts no weapons into their hands.

The law of Gaius Gracchus was passed to protect Roman citizens: but the enemy of the state cannot be a citizen, which is why the very man who passed that law had to pay the ultimate penalty to the state even without the people ordering it.[20]

Cicero, however, is hardly a neutral witness, for as consul in 63 he himself executed rebellious citizens under the authority of the Ultimate Decree, and a few years later found himself exiled for his pains. Hence he writes with a strong fellow-feeling for Opimius, and more than once describes the great trial of 120 when Opimius was himself prosecuted by Decius Subulo before the Roman people—and acquitted. In a clear legal analysis Cicero sets the position out.

> Opimius killed Gracchus. What does his case depend on? That he did so to defend the state, after calling the people to arms in obedience to the senate's decree. Remove this plea and he has no case. But Decius in turn denies its legality, so the issue must be whether the public interest and the senate's decree justified the act . . . . The question is one of general principle: should a man be punished for executing a citizen under a senatorial decree, and with the object of preserving the state, even granted that the deed itself were illegal?

But elsewhere he summarizes Decius' case against Opimius in these words: 'You had no right to put to death even the most criminal citizen without trial.' However often it was ignored, such in fact seems to have been the letter of the law. Consuls who ignored it always did so at their own peril.[21]

But passions were running high, and Opimius regarded the decree as authority enough and issued a call to arms for the following day. Senators were summoned with their retainers, and the knights were particularly asked each to bring two servants fully armed. The consul also made ready a band of foreign mercenaries, mainly Cretan archers. The fact that he had them ready at hand is ample proof that he had planned the affair well in advance, and suggests that he doubted the loyalty of any citizen troops that he might raise against the Gracchans.

Meanwhile the Gracchan leaders gathered in the forum, where Fulvius set about rallying a band of supporters. Gaius was in a more withdrawn mood, and walked across to stand quietly looking at the Sempronian Hall and the statue of his great father who had built it. As censor, consul twice and twice awarded a triumph, his father had been one of the most honoured leaders of the state. And now was this what his family had come to? Was this what his two sons had lived and worked for? One had been murdered, and now what fate awaited the survivor?

Gaius Gracchus burst into tears and with a despairing groan made his way home (P).

*

On the last evening of his life Gaius did not walk alone, however. Many of those who saw him weeping in the forum

were moved by the sight and blamed themselves for letting
him down. They followed him home and spent all night
guarding his doors. And at this point Plutarch draws an even
sharper contrast between the two popular leaders.

For those who guarded Fulvius spent all night shouting,
drinking, and boasting of what they would do. Fulvius was
the first to get drunk, and he spoke and behaved with a
coarseness that hardly became a man of such years.
But those at Gaius' house were more conscious of facing
some terrible public calamity. So in concern for what was
about to happen they kept themselves quiet, and passed the
night watching and sleeping by turns.[22]

From the middle of the night large crowds of people began to
gather in the forum. But Opimius made his preparations with
care. At dawn he put a strong armed force on top of the Capitol
hill, which overlooked one end of the forum, and then took up
his own station at the other end in the temple of Castor. Then
he sent heralds to summon the senate again, and waited and
watched (A).

In the morning the senate met and summoned Gaius and
Fulvius to come to the senate house and give an account of
their behaviour.

Perhaps even now there remained a chance of a peaceful way
out. Even if their power was gone, Gaius and Fulvius had no
reason to fear being put on trial before the Roman people—if
that was the intention. But the Ultimate Decree put that
intention in doubt. And to be made to appeal for their lives, not
before the people but before the senate, or even the consul
himself, was a very different proposition. And yet the leaders
were still in two minds.

Fulvius, we are told in Plutarch's contemptuous account,
was with difficulty awakened from his drunken sleep. But he
had already determined what to do, and immediately armed
his followers with weapons which he had once brought home in
triumph, the booty of his consular victories in Gaul. Then he
led them off to the Aventine hill, which had the merit of being
a strong position in its own right and the best part of a mile
away from the forum and the troops of Opimius.

Gaius, on the other hand, was unwilling to arm himself
properly, and set off just as if to the forum, wearing a formal
toga and just a small dagger. With their young son beside her,
his wife Licinia gave him her last farewell, which Plutarch has
worked up into a sad little speech.

'It is not to the political platform that I am now seeing you go, as tribune and lawgiver as I used to; nor to some glorious war where you might at least meet an honourable end. But this time you are going to meet the men who murdered Tiberius.

'You do well to go unarmed, for you may suffer a crime but you will not commit one. Yet your death will be no benefit to the state. Already evil has prevailed, and right is determined by violence and the sword.

'If your brother had fallen at Numantia, then at least his body could have been returned to us under truce. But now it is from the rivers and the seas that I shall have to beg the return of your body, like his. For what trust can men put in the laws or in the gods since the murder of Tiberius?'

But Gaius gently pushed his weeping wife to one side and walked away in silence with his friends. She swooned to the ground, and her servants carried her unconscious to the house of her brother Crassus.[23]

On the Aventine hill Gaius joined Fulvius, and they occupied and fortified the temple of Diana. With them they had some of their domestic slaves already armed. In addition they are said to have sent a herald round the city offering freedom to any other slaves who would come and join them, but in vain. It sounds like an invented story, although Opimius was in fact arming slaves and mercenaries against them.[24]

In further discussions Gaius urged a conciliatory approach, and finally Fulvius agreed to send Quintus, the younger of his two sons, down to the forum to try and negotiate a peaceful agreement. The handsome young man, only seventeen years old, spoke modestly and with tears in his eyes to consul and senators, many of whom were half persuaded to accept terms. But Opimius persuaded them to reply that they would not discuss the matter at second hand. If Gaius and Fulvius wanted peace, then they should lay down their arms and present themselves in person like responsible citizens, to submit to judgement and beg for mercy. The young messenger was warned to come back on these terms or not at all.

The prospect of begging for mercy before a senate already convinced of their guilt was hardly enticing, yet Plutarch says Gaius was still ready to give it a try but could not persuade the others. Quintus was sent down again to attempt a compromise, whereupon Opimius arrested him and gave the signal for a general attack.

At the consul's side marched P. Lentulus, who had been consul forty years before and was now the honoured leader of the senate. Metellus who had conquered Macedon and begun the resistance to Tiberius Gracchus was there. So was Brutus, who finished off the war in southern Spain and had more recently married Licinia's mother. Many other distinguished men joined the force.[25]

As might have been expected, from his truculent nature and his fine military record, Fulvius seems to have led the resistance. Brutus headed the initial assault, advancing up the Publician slope which led from the cattle market to the top of the Aventine. For a long time the battle was fierce and its outcome uncertain, and in the thick of the combat the frail and aged Lentulus was badly wounded. But eventually the Cretan archers mobilized by Opimius began to prevail.[26]

Their arrows rained down on the close-packed Gracchan forces, which finally broke. Fulvius and his remaining son ran for cover. Whether they hid in a derelict bath-house and were accidently discovered, or in a friend's workshop and betrayed, or barricaded themselves in a private house only to have the walls pulled down about them, they were caught and stabbed to death. Somewhere among the buildings that crowded round the lower slopes of the Aventine hill, a Roman consul had met his end.[27]

All this time Gaius was showing little enthusiasm for the fight. Indeed Plutarch insists that he refused to join in or even to defend himself, still more reluctant to do wrong than to suffer it. But as Opimius and Brutus pressed up the slope Gaius fell back again to the temple of Diana. Here he made up his mind to meet death at his own hand, by falling on his sword. Here too, perhaps, the great orator uttered his last recorded words. Their highly emotional style was typical of so many of his speeches, yet other speakers, even Cicero, were not ashamed to copy them for their own use.

'Unhappy me! Where now can I fly? Where shall I turn? To the Capitol? But it is soaked with my brother's blood. Or to my home? To see my wretched mother weeping in despair?' And Cicero says with admiration, that so passionate and vivid were his words and gestures that even his enemies wept, or would have wept, to hear him.[28]

At this point, however, two friends tore away his sword and persuaded him still to try and save himself. But first he fell on his knees to pray to the goddess that the Roman people should never be freed from servitude, in return for their ungrateful betrayal of him. For having at last broken down the stubborn resistance put up by Fulvius, Opimius had now offered to spare anyone who changed sides and many were doing so. The fight was almost over. Gaius and his two friends, Pomponius and Laetorius, ran for their lives.

Unhappily, as he leaped down the hillside from the temple of the Moon, Gaius sprained his ankle. Past the Triple Gate he hobbled, where the city walls came down to the river just north of the Aventine, and with difficulty managed to reach the bridge.

This was the oldest and most famous bridge in Rome, the wooden Sublician Bridge that a king had built 500 years before, lying just behind the Triple Gate. This was the bridge that the deathless hero Horatius had held long ago, to keep a hostile army at bay. When Gaius at last reached it, with his enemies close on his heels, as good Romans his two friends remembered:

> How well Horatius kept the bridge
> In the brave days of old.

So there, on the narrow bridge, they stopped, turned, and fought their pursuers to give their half-crippled leader what chance they could.[29]

While his friends fought and died for him, Gaius pressed on, accompanied by only one remaining servant, Philocrates. Across the Tiber he met people who encouraged him, just as if he were running a race, but nobody dared to help him, still less to offer him the horse he badly needed. With his bad ankle he had neither the strength nor, perhaps, the will-power to go very far. After a while he turned off the road into a grove that was sacred to the goddess Furina, sometimes equated with those avenging spirits the Furies. As his enemies burst into this last refuge, Gaius Gracchus, determined not to be taken alive, bared his throat to his loyal servant, who killed him and then himself.[30]

Now followed the most macabre scene of the whole story. In an evil moment Opimius had promised that he would give its weight in gold to whoever brought him the head of Gaius Gracchus. So now it was cut from his shoulders, but the man who bore it off was robbed by one Septimuleius, a personal friend of Opimius. But when he brought it in, stuck on the end of a spear, the head weighed in at the extraordinary figure of nearly eighteen pounds, in gold worth 18,000*d.* For the cold-blooded Septimuleius had taken out the brain and filled the cavity with lead. Or so the story went. But the men who brought in the head of Fulvius went empty away.[31]

In the heat of the fighting on the Aventine some 250 Gracchan supporters had been killed, and their bodies were flung into the Tiber, with those of Gaius and Fulvius, just as had happened twelve years before. But Opimius was 'as cruel in inquisition as he had been brave in battle', and on his authority no fewer than 3000 friends, clients and supporters of the Gracchan movement were put to death. His relentless pursuit seemed to be inspired by private hatred as much as any concern for the public welfare, comments Velleius. The houses of Gaius and Fulvius were looted and their property confiscated and sold. Their wives were forbidden to wear mourning, and Licinia the wife of Gaius could not even recover her marriage portion until her uncle, the high priest Scaevola, had publicly admitted that Gaius was to blame for the riot.[32]

Yet amid this horror one deed stood out for its wanton cruelty. Quintus, the younger son of Fulvius Flaccus, the herald who had played no part in the fighting and was innocent of any crime, was taken down to the dreaded Tullianum, the grim death cell in the prison which still stands at the foot of the Capitol. There Opimius offered him simply the choice of how to die. One story is that he killed himself by smashing his own head against the prison wall.[33]

The Gracchus brothers were dead, but the Roman people remembered them, and later set up statues to them and consecrated the places where they were killed. There they brought the first fruits of the harvest, and some even sacrificed and fell on their knees as if at the shrines of the gods.

The brothers were dead, but their mother the wise Cornelia lived on, and she bore all her sorrows with a noble and brave heart. The sacred places where her sons had died were, she said, tombs worthy of them. In her retreat at Misenum she kept up a busy social life, and talked pleasantly to visitors about the life and manners of her father the great Scipio.

But everyone marvelled at the way she spoke of her sons, without tears and without grief. To anyone who asked, she would tell of their achievements and of their fate, just as though she were telling the stories of some heroes of olden days.[34]

15 The Fatal Legacy

The Gracchus brothers were dead. It remained to add insult to injury. After the city had been solemnly purified of the bloodshed, the senate ordered the consul Opimius to restore the great temple of Concord which stood at the head of the forum, built to celebrate the reconciliation of plebeians and patricians in 367.

Opimius was a man of grand ideas. In restoring the temple he made the first large-scale use of concrete in architectural history—its massive foundations are visible today—and next to it he built a public hall to celebrate his own name.

But there were many Romans who thought Opimius was the very last man to be making so much of the spirit of Concord. Refused his triumph over rebellious allies a few years before, he was now celebrating the death of Roman citizens. During one night somebody crept up to the temple and scrawled this slogan on its walls:

A deed of mad Discord produces this temple of Concord.

Saint Augustine, who was so impressed by the Gracchan revolution and its impact on the fortunes of the republic, hazarded the guess that the spirit of Concord deserved to be shut up in the temple as if in a prison, for the crime of deserting the hearts of the people.

For unremitting discord in the state was the fatal legacy that the Gracchus brothers left behind them, and it finally brought the free republic down.[1]

*

Over and above the immediate human drama, the deeper fascination of the Gracchan story is that it poses with rare clarity the central paradox of political experience, the ease with which able men, applying themselves to fine ideals and careful policies, can yet end up achieving results nothing less than tragic. The ultimate consequences of the Gracchan adventure were riots, murder, revolution, counter-revolution, civil war and military dictatorship, a devastating toll of human misery to follow from such admirable ambitions.

On the one hand there was so much that was positive and good in what the brothers were trying to do. Their claim to greatness cannot be denied: they saw the need for change in the Roman world and they successfully identified those areas where change was most needed. Almost everything they touched became a central issue of political debate.

The provision of land, which meant food and employment, for the citizen poor, is a constant theme, particularly after Marius took the manpower policy to its logical endpoint by enlisting the poorest men into semi-professional armies, and so raised the question of how to provide for the discharged veterans.

Colonies became the classic means of romanizing the world, from the Clyde to the Euphrates. Franchise reform was blocked until the allies fought for it, but then the spread of citizenship became another great unifying force. It grew into the imperial concept that all men were equal citizens under one ruler, an idea that made Rome's influence so much more enduring than if it had merely stood for the subjection of other peoples to the will of the master-race. For all this the Gracchus brothers can claim some of the credit.

Their reforms of finance, the law-courts and provincial administration were perceptive moves. Above all their attempt to extend a share in real power to people outside the charmed circle of the senate and the noble families pointed the only way for Rome to develop. Emperors used the knights to counterbalance the senate just as Gaius Gracchus had done.

The Gracchus brothers, in short, inherited a political system which could not cope with the pressures of a rapidly changing world, and they sought to forge a system that could. No praise can be too high for the penetration of their analysis and the vision of their policies.

But, on the other hand, they failed.

Discord was the legacy they left behind them. The unity of the state had been under strain before, but it was the Gracchus brothers who shattered it. It was they who precipitated the crisis that set blood flowing in the city's gutters and inaugurated a hundred years of strife.

Opimius indulged in his cruel investigations. A year later he was prosecuted and acquitted, while Popillius was brought back from exile. Yet in 119 the pendulum began to swing again. The tribune Marius passed a law that brought greater freedom to the voting assembly. Young L. Crassus prosecuted the turncoat Carbo, driving him to suicide, and then encouraged the popular cause by founding another citizen colony in the provinces, at Narbonne.

Land reform was halted and for a time reversed, and control of the lawcourts changed hands more than once. But again outside events took charge. The senate's leaders found difficulty in winning a war against the North African prince Jugurtha, and failed miserably against German invaders from the north. To popular acclaim Marius was elected consul five times in a row until he had saved the state from its greatest danger since Hannibal. Politicians in the Gracchan tradition sided with Marius; new laws dealt with land, corn, colonies and the courts; rioting became general, until the senate again passed its ultimate decree and the consul Marius crushed his one-time allies in the year 100.

After further uneasy years and vicious political trials another Drusus came on the scene, the son of Gaius Gracchus' old enemy. After a familiar mix of land, colonial and judiciary laws he tried to extend the franchise to the Italian allies and was himself murdered in the streets. The allies broke out in open revolt, warfare ravaged central Italy, but in 90 the franchise was extended at last.

But the level of violence had risen out of control. The command against a foreign invader, who had overrun prosperous Asia, was offered to the consul Sulla, flushed with victories over Italians. When the people transferred the command to their old champion Marius, Sulla used the ultimate weapon, and marched his victorious army against Rome itself. Force finally prevailed over law. Three reigns of terror decimated the nobility before the dictator Sulla imposed a pre-Gracchan constitution that gave all power to the senate.

This settlement could not last. The consul Lepidus, the general Sertorius, the slave Spartacus, rebelled in turn. Again the senate's leaders could not cope, and the initiative passed to another Pompeius and another Crassus. Tribunes' rights were restored, then Pompey went east to fight the most dazzling war of all, triumphing over sixteen enemies and penetrating the holy temple of Jerusalem. Yet despite the eloquence and ideals of Cicero, politics in the city drifted further out of control, until one man emerged who combined the military talents of Pompey and the single-mindedness of Sulla with the political vision and the inspiring personality of Gaius Gracchus.

That man was Julius Ceasar. When the stubborn senatorial majority blocked his path he answered with force, and after titanic civil wars established his own dictatorship. When Caesar fell murdered in 44, his eighteen-year-old great-nephew and heir Octavian took over the cause, fought his own bloody wars and at last established peace. But also, under the new name Augustus, he founded a monarchy that was to govern Europe for more than four centuries. The agonies of the free republic were over at last, ninety years after Gaius Gracchus had met his end.[2]

*

The two brothers who had initiated such an awesome dance of death and destruction could hardly escape their share of the blame, and few ancient commentators found it possible to forgive them. Certainly not Cicero, who spent his life trying to cope with the terrible consequences of their revolution. Again and again he pays the highest tribute to their oratory and their fine personal qualities. But he loathed them for their destructive effect on the world he lived in. They had used their eloquence to overthrow the Rome their ancestors had built. That was the ultimate crime.[3]

But, as he recognized the greater ability of Gaius Gracchus, 'the most talented and eloquent of our countrymen by far', so it was for him that he reserved his greatest condemnation.

'After his brother came Gaius Gracchus. What genius! What eloquence! What vigour! What an impressive speaker! Good men could only weep that those wonderful gifts were not applied to a better policy and a finer purpose.

'Was it not through the catastrophe of Gaius Gracchus, and by means of those daggers which he boasted he had flung into the forum for the citizens to fight it out, that the power of the tribunes resulted in a complete revolution in the state?'[4]

Similar judgements abound in other writers. Livy condemns the madness of Tiberius Gracchus, and the pernicious laws and seditious tribunate of Gaius. Orosius denounced the whole family as one 'born for the ruin of its own country'. Power made Gaius intolerable even to his own supporters, and he was overthrown by his own methods. He had fomented riots in his own city, near his own home—the brothers were grandsons of the great Scipio and yet by their own blood they finally fed the cruelty of their enemies.[5]

It seemed to follow that the brothers deserved to die. Cicero numbered them among the ranks of 'those who have been justly killed', while Opimius was ranked as one of those great men 'under whose armed leadership the state has crushed traitors.' Repeatedly Cicero praised the men who had used force, and with approval quoted Carbo's question. 'What else had Opimius done except fulfil a consul's duty, consult the interests of his country?' Valerius Maximus neatly summed up this conventional view.

'The noble Gracchus brothers brought their energies and the highest hopes to our city. But because they tried to overthrow the state, their corpses lay unburied, and they were refused the final token of human respect.'[6]

To such critics the means whereby the Gracchus brothers brought about the destruction of the republic were evident. Their crime was that they had shattered its unity.

'They divided the Roman people, giving the state two heads instead of one.'

'The death of Tiberius, not to mention the whole character of his tribunate, split a united people into two.'

'Gaius made the republic two-headed, and so opened the way to civil war.'[7]

Such remarks formed, indeed, a commonplace of Roman political discussion. Livy used similar words to sum up troubles in the fourth century, when 'the citizens broke up into two factions, the sound element who supported the good men, and the mob of the forum'. The reason is that the terrors they lived through made both Cicero and Livy come to feel that the greatest of all political goods was civic unity and harmony. They believed it had existed before the Gracchan age: Cicero fought in vain to recreate it and Livy saw Augustus do so. To such men, and to all the other writers who echo their views, the greatest crime was divisiveness and for that they blamed the Gracchus brothers.[8]

Yet, if their analysis is understandable, it fails to give a full explanation.

The fact is that there were problems that needed solving in second-century Rome, and the blame for the violence cannot simply be laid on the Gracchan proposals for dealing with those problems. Their policies kept returning to the centre of the stage precisely because the pressures of the day put them there.

Florus acknowledges the appearance of justice in the Gracchan measures, and their genuine pity for the poor. Cicero can find occasion to admit that their crimes were less outrageous than what followed, that Tiberius was only slightly undermining the state, and Gaius only vaguely suspected of fomenting revolution. Sallust also lived through the troubles, and saw clearly that there was another side to the question.

'Opimius became powerful in the senate because, after the slaughter of Gaius and Fulvius, he made the cruellest use of the nobles' victory over the people.' It was when the Gracchi began to assert the freedom of the people and expose the misdeeds of the few that the guilty nobles took alarm, and slew first one and then the other. After the death of Tiberius the people were prosecuted, and after Gaius fell many of them were executed in the prison—on each occasion bloodshed was ended not by the law but by the caprice of the victors. But a few years later the war against Jugurtha provided the first opportunity for curbing the insolence of the nobles.[9]

The circumstances of the time dictated the Gracchan policies, but their real legacy was something more fundamental. Their period marked the division of the state into two warring groups. The supporters and opponents of Tiberius' original land-reform proposals swiftly evolved into the factions of the late republic, the populars and their self-styled betters, at odds with each other over every issue. And worse, from now on both sides were readier to use violence. Nasica attacked Tiberius; Gaius and Fulvius armed in self-defence; Opimius mobilized professional troops against them; Gaius threw the daggers into the forum and civil war followed. *But whose fault was it?*

It is clear that the Gracchus brothers set their feet on a difficult path. They cared for the poor and for their country. Nothing irresponsible can be found in their basic demands. If a charge can be fairly levelled against them, it is simply, as Machiavelli felt, that they pressed their demands too hard. Appian refers to a fine policy too violently pursued. Velleius laments that they misused their wonderful gifts and with greater moderation could have attained everything they sought. Sallust, who speaks so highly of them, accepts that in their enthusiasm they lost their self-control.[10]

But here we come to the nub of the argument. When the events are examined in careful detail they show conclusively that the Gracchans pressed their cause because they had to. There was no other way to make change happen. Appian speaks of the land law as 'fair and useful, if only it could have been fully implemented', and on this point Plutarch shows unusual perception.

'The brothers were caught up as if by a storm, because of the need to struggle against their opponents, and a passion that carried them beyond their natural inclinations, until they let the state drift into extreme danger.

'For what could have been more fair and honourable than their original aim, if the party of the rich had not determined to use violence and their inherited position to put down the Gracchan laws and involve both brothers in a struggle to the death?'[11]

Of all the lessons to be learned from the story, this is the greatest. Change was needed, but it was the resistance to change that made violence inevitable and precipitated the crisis. The Roman nobility would not let the Gracchans move more slowly. It refused to learn or adapt; it virtually refused to govern. It is not easy to judge the repeated charges that from now on personal greed and ambition became the notivating passions of the ruling classes, but certainly they were no longer facing up to their responsibilities.

Just as their grandfathers refused to compromise with Hannibal, so they now refused to compromise with the Gracchus brothers. But they had no alternative answers to the problems the brothers sought to tackle. They preferred to ignore them altogether.

For the moment the nobles won the victory. But they and the republic paid a dreadful price for it. From now on the only basis for reform lay with the popular movement, because the 'better men' had rejected it. Reform could only be sought in the teeth of the senatorial majority, and this meant that reform could only be attained if it was backed by force.

That was the fatal legacy left by the men who killed the Gracchus brothers.

*

The Roman people never forgot their heroes. They honoured the places where they died, and revered their mother Cornelia. Twenty years later a nobody could rouse the Roman people by claiming to be the son of Tiberius Gracchus, but the solemn word of Sempronia, who had so long survived her husband and brothers, was enough to secure his rejection.[12]

The popular politician Saturninus was once warned not to trust the Roman people overmuch, 'for the Gracchi lie unavenged'. Yet the people caught up with many of their enemies, not least Opimius, whose cruelty had always seemed to show more personal vindictiveness than honest public spirit. He died in lonely exile on the far coast of the Adriatic, leaving his name to a memorable vintage of wine.[13]

One branch of the Sempronius Gracchus family survived to hold obscure office under the empire. The great family of Fulvius Flaccus almost disappeared from history, although it is not fanciful to trace some shred of influence in the fact that it was the Gracchan leader's son-in-law, the little-known L. Julius Caesar, who in 90 passed the law enfranchising the allies.[14]

The Romans lost their freedom because of those same traits of pride and stubborn inflexibility that had won them the mastery of the world. The Gracchan revolution was the turning-point, when the chance of peaceful change was rejected. From then on it is hard to see what could possibly have saved the republic.

Today nobody can study this lamentable story without noticing the close parallels it presents to troubled modern times. Like the Gracchus brothers, we too have grown up in a world which finds it increasingly difficult to cope with change, which has so perversely missed the opportunities that seemed within reach.

Particularly in Britain can be seen those same Roman characteristics, the same pride in the past and the same neglect of current problems. Here is the same unwillingness to modify attitudes and institutions that once worked well, whatever their irrelevance to the new realities. Proposals for overcoming difficulties are put forward, but the arguments for rejecting them always prevail. Strong measures are needed, it is universally agreed, and strong measures are impossible, because society will not accept them. The case for doing nothing carries the day, and the problems grow worse.

If any society rejects peaceful change and accepts only superficial remedies for its ills, if nobody can be peacefully denied what he has come to regard as his rights and broad interests always have to give way to sectional demands, then the problems and the divisions can only grow worse until something breaks.

The lesson of the Gracchan revolution is that when governments abandon common sense and tolerance and honesty, then sooner or later the daggers will find their way into public life. The unthinkable happened, and it can happen again.

SOURCES

ROMAN MONEY
 1. Polybius, 6. 39.

INTRODUCTION
 1. Caesar, *Civil Wars*, 1,22: *populum Romanum factione paucorum oppressum in libertatem vindicaret*; Augustus, *Res Gestae*, 1: *rem publicam a dominatione factionis oppressam in libertatem vindicavi*. Compare Sallust, *Jugurtha*, 42: *Ti. et C. Gracchus vindicare plebem in libertatem coepere*.

CHAPTER ONE — BORN INTO A LEGEND
 1. Plutarch, *Gaius Gracchus*, 1. Early 162 is just possible, but 163 allows more easily for his military service from 147 to 138.
 2. Cicero, *De Inventione*, 1. 91.
 3. Plutarch, *Tiberius Gracchus*, 1; Cicero, *De Divinatione*, 1. 36; 2. 62; Valerius, 4. 6. 1; Victor, 57: *amore Corneliae coniugis*.
 4. Plutarch, T.G., 1; C.G., 19; Cicero, *Brutus*, 211: *filios non tam in gremio educatos quam in sermone matris*.
 5. Plutarch, T.G., 8, 20; Cicero, *Brutus*, 104; *De Amicitia*, 37; Valerius, 4. 7. 1.
 6. Plutarch, T.G., 8, C.G., 4; Pliny, *Natural History*, 34. 31. The portico of Metellus was later rebuilt as that of Octavia, and its gateway still stands. The statue was also given a new base, which was found in the portico in 1878 and can be seen in the Capitoline Museum. It bears a less partisan inscription, naming her father as well as her sons, and reading: *Cornelia, Africani f., Gracchorum* (Degrassi, 336). For the Flaminian Circus, a favoured rallying-point, see Taylor, *Voting Assemblies*.
 7. Plutarch, *T.G.*, 2-3; see also Pliny, *N.H.*, 33.147; Cicero, *De Oratore*, 3.225; Dio, 25 frag. 85; Valerius, 8.10,1.
 8. Cicero, *Philippic*, 8.23; Polybius, 29.27; Livy, 45.12.
 9. Ennius, Fragments 271, 209, 467: *moribus antiquis res stat Romana virisque*, 470.
10. Livy, preface.
11. Livy, 28.28.
12. Polybius, 1.1: τὸ παράδοξον.
13. Polybius, 1.37.
14. Polybius, 6.11.
15. Polybius, 6.3. Plato, *Republic*, 8.

16. Polybius, 6.11; 6.18: ἀνυπόστατον γίνεσθαι καὶ παντὸς ἐφικνεῖσθαι τοῦ κριθέντος.
17. Sallust, *Jugurtha*, 41: *ex nobilitate reperti sunt qui veram gloriam iniustae potentiae anteponerent.*
18. Plato, *Laws*, 942a; *Republic*, 4.431d.
19. Cicero, *pro Sestio*, 96.
20. Polybius, 6.56.
21. Consuls, praetors and curule aediles. Entry became automatic for plebeian aediles by 122, tribunes by 103, and quaestors after 81 (Gelzer, *Nobility*, 26).
22. Cicero, *Republic*, 2.39: *curavit ne plurimum valeant plurimi.*
23. The 89 centuries comprised 70 of first-class citizens, 18 of the even richer knights, and one of smiths and carpenters (Cicero, *Republic*, 2.39; Livy, 1.43; Polybius, 6.23; Dionysius, 4.21). For 400*d*. as the qualification for the lowest class see Polybius, 6.19; it was later reduced perhaps to 150*d*. (Cicero, *Republic*, 2.40).
24. Cicero, *pro Sestio*, 137, 97.
25. Polybius, 6.19.
26. Q. Cicero, *Commentariolum Petitionis*, gives a vivid analysis.
27. Sallust, *Jugurtha*, 85.23; Polybius, 6.54.
28. In the second century only seven 'new men' became consuls, including Cato (195), Octavius (165), Mummius (146) and Pompeius (141).
29. Sallust, *Jugurtha*, 63: *consulatum nobilitas inter se per manus tradebat.*
30. So said Demetrius of Syria (Polybius, 31.2).

CHAPTER TWO — A PROUD HERITAGE
1. Degrassi, 309, 310. Originals are in the Vatican Museum.
2. Vergil, *Aeneid*, 6.843: *fulmina belli.*
3. Livy, 21.46; Polybius, 10.3.
4. Livy, 22.53
5. Livy, 25.2
6. Livy, 26.18.
7. Livy, 26.19. But Polybius, 10.2 suggests that this was just showmanship and that Scipio's successes were simply due to care and forethought. Perhaps Polybius over-rationalizes his hero.
8. Livy, 27.19; Polybius, 10.40.
9. Polybius, 11.25-30; Livy, 28.24-9; 28.21.
10. Livy, 27.7.
11. Livy, 28.32.
12. Livy, 28.35, 38.
13. Livy, 28.40-5.
14. Livy, 30.27, 36-44.
15. Livy, 30.45.
16. Livy, 34.44, 54.
17. Livy, 35.14; Appian, *Syrian Wars*, 10.
18. Livy, 37.1-45; Polybius, 21.4-17.

19. Scipio's letter to Prusias, King of Bithynia, in Polybius, 21.11; letters to Greek cities of Heraclea and Colophon in Sherk, 35, 36; Delos inscription honouring the Scipios in Dittenberger, 617; Polybius, 10.40; Livy, 37.36.
20. Peace of Apamea, full terms in Livy, 38.38-9 and Polybius 21.42-5.
21. Livy, 38.54-60; Gellius, 6.19; Valerius, 4.1.8; Cicero, *De Provinciis Consularibus*, 18.
22. Livy, 38.50-3; Polybius, 23.14; Gellius, 4.18; Victor, 49. Details of these fascinating trials are irretrievably confused. Scullard, *Roman Politics*, gives the most detailed analysis, but he relies too much on the few facts in Polybius and too little on the many facts in Livy. Gracchus' tribunate and L. Scipio's trial must be dated to 187. So probably should P. Scipio's trial, usually assigned to 184.
23. Livy, 38.53: *bellicis tamen quam pacis artibus memorabilior*; Ennius, *Epigrams*, 4.23 (Vahlen); Polybius, 10.2; Cicero, *In Verrem*, 2.4.81.
24. Cicero, *Republic*, 6.9-26.
25. Livy, *Per.* 19; Livy, 24.16; Suetonius, *Tiberius*, 2; Gellius, 10.6; Valerius, 8.1.damn.4.
26. Livy, 24. 14-16; Valerius, 7.6.1; 5.6.8.
27. Livy, 25.16-17, 20; Valerius, 1.6.8; 5.1.ext.6.
28. The lists of magistrates and the family trees on pp. 229-34 to show how this handful of families attained great political importance in three successive generations. Many known examples of co-operation, friendship and marriage links between these families will be recounted; others can be deduced when they so often held office together or in succession. Such family groupings were neither rigid nor exclusive, but were none the less real and important.
29. Livy, 29.38: *admodum adulescens*.
30. Livy, 37.7: *longe tum acerrimus iuvenum*.
31. Livy, 38.57; Valerius, 4.2.3; Gellius, 12.8; Plutarch, *T.G.*, 4; Polybius, 31.27. Half of the dowry was paid immediately, the balance in 162.
32. Pliny, *N.H.*, 7.122; Cicero, *De Divinatione*, 1.36.
33. Livy, 39.5. Fulvius and Manlius were allies (Livy, 37.47).
34. Livy, 39.24, 33; although Polybius, 22.6 names Ti. Claudius rather than Gracchus.
35. Livy, 40.44.
36. Livy, 40.40: *cum summa concordia*. The friendly settlement is noteworthy since Fulvius had at first proposed to bring his entire army home, which would have left Gracchus dependent on raw recruits.
37. Livy, 40.47-50; Livy, *Per.*, 41; Polybius, 35.2; Appian, *Spanish Wars*, 43, 48.
38. Victor, 57: *Sardi venales*; Cicero, *Ad fam.*, 7.24; Livy, 41.12, 17, 28. The very old temple of the mother goddess, Mater Matuta, may be one of those whose traces have been found in the precinct

of Sant' Omobono just south of the Capitol.
39. Livy, 43.11-15.
40. Livy, 43.16: *tristis admodum atque aspera censura*; 44.16; 45.15;
    Plutarch, *T.G.*, 14.
41. Livy, 43.16; Valerius, 6.5.3; Cicero, *Republic*, 6.2.
42. Cicero, *De Oratore*, 1.38: *rem publicam iamdiu nullam
    haberemus*; Livy, 45.15; Victor, 57. Official disputes and
    misbehaviour are a recurrent theme of the decade (Livy, 40-4).
    For voting changes of 179 see Livy, 40.51.
43. Livy, 44.16; Livy, *Per.*, 45.
44. Livy, 45.40; Polybius, 18.35; Plutarch, *Paullus*, 30-4; Pliny, N.H.,
    33.56.
45. Polybius, 30.27-31; 31.1-3.
46. Cicero, *De Natura Deorum*, 2.11; *De Divinatione*, 1.33; Valerius,
    1.1.3.
47. Polybius, 31.15, 33.
48. Twelve children in Plutarch, *T.G.*, 1; Pliny, *N.H.*, 7.57; Seneca,
    Ad Marciam, 16.3; *Ad Helviam*, 16.6. Despite Plutarch most of
    them presumably died in infancy.
49. Cicero, Brutus, 79: *cum gravem tum eloquentem*; *De Oratore*,
    1.211: *reipublicae rectorem*; *De Divinatione*, 1.36: *summus augur
    et vir sapiens civisque praestans*; *De Natura Deorum*, 2.11: *vir
    sapientissimus atque haud sciam an omnium praestantissimus*;
    Republic, 6.2: *Claudii invidiam Gracchi caritas deprecebatur*.
50. Cicero, *De Provinciis Consularibus*, 18: *cuius utinam filii ne
    degenerassent a gravitate patria*; *De Officiis*, 2.43: *at eius filii
    nec vivi probabantur bonis et mortui numerum optinent iure
    caesorum*; *De Oratore*, 1.38: *pater, homo prudens et gravis,
    haudquaquam eloquens, et saepe alias, et maxime censor, saluti
    reipublicae fuit . . . at vero eius filii diserti . . . cum civitatem vel
    paterno consilio vel avitis armis florentissimam accepissent, ista
    eloquentia rempublicam dissipaverunt*; *De Finibus*, 4.65: *Ti.
    Gracchum patrem beatiorem fuisse quam filium, cum alter
    stabilire rem publicam studuerit, alter evertere*.

Earl, *Tiberius Gracchus*, assesses the elder Gracchus as 'above
all a political opportunist' and 'politically unreliable'. But this
seems too derogatory. Gracchus was tough, ambitious, and
nobody's creature, but there is no real evidence of any fickle
switching of sides. It was a brilliant career.

CHAPTER THREE — TIBERIUS GOES TO WAR
1. Plutarch, *T.G.*, 4.
2. Plutarch, *T.G.*, 4.
3. Appian, *Civil Wars*, 1.20: διὰ δυσμορφίαν καὶ ἀπαιδίαν οὔτ'
   ἐστέργετο οὔτ' ἔστεργεν. From now on the name 'Scipio' alone
   indicates Aemilianus, while Tiberius and Gaius Gracchus are
   normally referred to by their first names.
4. Appian, *Spanish Wars*, 49-54; Polybius, 35.4-5; Livy, *Per.*, 48.
5. Appian, *Libyan Wars*, 74-112; Livy, *Per.*, 50.

6. Appian, *Libyan Wars*, 127-135; Polybius, 38.19-22; Zonaras, 9.29-30.

7. Appian, *Libyan Wars*, 132; Polybius, 38.22; 2.21.

8. Polybius, 31.25; Diodorus, 37.3; Polybius, 36.9.

9. Polybius, 3.4-5.

10. Polybius, 32.13.

11. Plutarch, *Cato maior*, 27; Diodorus, 34.33; St Augustine, *City of God*, 1.30.

12. Livy, 39.7; Pliny, *N.H.*, 33.56: *populus Romanus tributum pendere desiit*; Cicero, *De Officiis*, 2.76: *finem tributorum*; Pliny, *N.H.*, 33.55.

13. Sallust, *Catiline*, 10; Velleius, 2.1; Pliny, *N.H.*, 33.150; Orosius, 5.8: *infamis de ambitione contentio*; note the bribery law of 159 which perhaps made it a capital offence (Livy, *Per.*, 47; Polybius, 6.56).

14. Velleius, 1.11, 2.1; Pliny, *N.H.*, 34.36, 33.57; Frontinus, *De Aquis*, 1.7.

15. Polybius, 6.17; Livy, 42.32; Cato, *Agriculture*, 135, lists manufacturing towns specializing in wagons, baskets or bronze utensils.

16. Livy, 41.28; *Per.*, 51.

17. Fates inflicted on Greeks before 169; on Ligurians in 173 and Illyrians in 171; and on the Epirots by Aemilius Paullus in 167.

18. Polybius, 31.10.

19. Polybius, 34.9.

20. Livy, 43.2; Pliny, *N.H.*, 17.245: *a quo tempore pudicitiam subversam*.

21. Appian, *Spanish Wars*, 44-66.

22. Appian, *Spanish Wars*, 67-75; Livy, *Per.*, 54; *Oxy.*, 54: *pacem deformem*.

23. Appian, *Spanish Wars*, 76-9: συνθήκας αἰσχράς; Livy, *Per.*, 54.

24. Livy, *Per.*, 55; Obsequens, 24: *mane, Mancine*; Valerius 1.6, 7.

25. Appian, *Spanish Wars*, 80; Plutarch, *T.G.*, 5; Livy, *Per.*, 55; Florus, 1.34.

26. Plutarch, *T.G.*, 6.

27. Livy, *Per.*, 55: *pacem ignominiosam*; Appian, *Spanish Wars*, 80: αἰσχίσταις πάνυ σπονδαῖς; Plutarch, *T.G.*, 7: δεινὴ καὶ καταισχύνουσα τὴν Ῥώμην.

28. Appian, *Spanish Wars*, 83; Plutarch, *T.G.*, 7; Dio, 23. frag. 79; Livy, *Per.*, 56; Cicero, *De Officiis*, 3.109; *De Oratore*, 1.181; *Pro Caecina*, 98; *Republic*, 3.28; *Ad Atticum*, 12.5.3; Victor, 64.

29. Scipio had supported the war from the start (Polybius, 35.4): σύμβουλος τοῦ πολέμου. His own name ran high in Spain, and perhaps he resented his younger cousin's celebrity.

30. Cicero, *Brutus*, 103: *turbulentissimum tribunatum, ad quem ex invidia foederis Numantini bonis iratus accesserat*; *De Haruspicum Responsis*, 43: *Ti. Graccho invidia Numantini foederis et in eo foedere improbando senatus severitas dolori et timori fuit, eaque res illum fortem et clarum virum a gravitate*

patrum desciscere coegit; Dio, 23 frag. 83: ἄκων ἐς τὸ κάκιστον ἐξώκειλε; Plutarch, *T.G.*, 7; Orosius, 5.8: *iratus nobilitate*; Velleius, 2.2: *graviter ferens aliquid a se factum infirmari*. Tiberius was also stimulated by personal rivalry with the young Sp. Postumius (Plutarch, *T.G.*, 8).

CHAPTER FOUR — THE STORM BREAKS

1. See above, page 114.
2. Cicero, *Brutus*, 82-108; 103 on Gracchus and Carbo: *utinam talis mens ad rem publicam bene gerendam fuisset quale ingenium ad bene dicendum fuit.*
3. Livy, *Per.*, 47; Cassiodorus.
4. Polybius, 35.4: ἐνέπεσέ τις πτοία παράλογος; Livy, *Per.*, 48: *consules cum dilectum severe agerent*; but more sympathetically Appian, *Spanish Wars*, 49: πολλῶν αἰτιωμένων ἀδίκους τὰς καταγραφάς. Taylor, *Forerunners*, discusses precedents, including levying disputes in 193, 191, 184, and 171.
5. Appian, *Spanish Wars*, 78; Roman soldiers now beaten with vines, not rods (Livy, *Per.*, 57); The minimum qualification had been 1100*d*. — see Livy, 1.43, and above, page 10.
6. Astin and Brunt argue that *civium capita* meant all adult males, Earl and Nicolet that it included only qualified men. But since the number of citizen troops sometimes exceeded 20% of the census figures, the latter can hardly have included many unqualified men.
7. Appian, *Spanish Wars*, 65.
8. Cicero, *Post Reditum*, 11: *certissima subsidia rei publicae contra tribunicios furores*; Asconius, 8C; *Scholia Bobiensia*, 148; Cicero, *In Vatinium*, 18; *In Pisonem*, 9; *De Haruspicum Responsis*, 58. The laws were passed 'nearly 100 years' before repeal in 58, but certainly predate the Gracchan troubles in 133. Cicero's glowing praise of the laws refutes the theory that they were designed to prevent a repeat of his hero Scipio's illegal consulate.
9. Cicero, *De Amicitia*, 96; Varro, *De Re Rustica*, 1.2.9: *primus populum ad leges accipiendas in septem iugera forensia e comitio eduxit*. The change was to the central part of the forum, in front of the rostra or speaker's platform, instead of the small area of the *comitium* behind the rostra and in front of the senate house. See Taylor, *Voting Assemblies*, and above, page 137.
10. Cicero, *Brutus*, 89-90, qualifying Galba's guilt with *ut existimabatur*; *De Oratore*, 1.227; Livy, *Per.*, 49; *Oxy.*, 49. On Galba and Crassus, Cicero, *De Oratore*, 1.239; Galba and Paullus, Livy, 45.35. On Piso, Cicero, *In Verrem*, 2.3.195: *ille Frugi qui legem de pecuniis repetundis primus tulit*; 2.4.56; *Brutus*, 106; *Pro Fonteio*, 39: *tanta virtute atque integritate fuit ut solus Frugi nominaretur*; Tusculans, 3.48; *Scholia Bobiensia*, 96: *fuit C. Graccho capitalis inimicus.*
11. Mancinus commissioned a picture of the siege to convince voters of what really happened (Pliny, *N.H.*, 35.23; Livy, *Per.*, 51;

Appian, *Libyan Wars*, 113-14; Zonaras, 9.29.

12. Valerius 6.4.2; Scipio unsuccessfully prosecuted Cotta in 138 (Livy, *Oxy.*, 55; Appian, *Civil Wars*, 1.22).

13. Suetonius, *Tiberius*, 1-2; Tacitus, *Annals*, 1.4: *vetus atque insita Claudiae familiae superbia.*

14. Livy, *Per.*, 53; *Obsequens*, 21; Dio, 22, frag. 74. The last unauthorized triumph had been in 294. Claudius' father in 177 and his uncles in 185 had similarly flouted custom and practice.

15. Plutarch, *Aemilius Paullus*, 38; *Sayings of Scipio*, 9.

16. Livy, 40.51; Dio, 22, frag. 76.

17. Cicero, *Brutus*, 96; *De Amicitia*, 77; Rutilius, frag. 7; Plutarch, *Sayings of Scipio*, 8.

18. Plutarch, *T.G.*, 8. The contents of his proposal are unknown, its date is a probable conjecture.

19. Tiberius and Claudia had three sons, the last born in 133 (Valerius, 9.7.2), as well as perhaps one daughter (Gellius, 2.13.1). All sons were dead before 122 (above, p. 173), the eldest on military service. This must mean that Tiberius married before rather than after his absence in Spain during 137, say in 140. Its political significance would then reflect the general drift away from Scipio after 142 rather than the specific row about Mancinus' surrender in Spain. On Metellus, see Cicero, *De Amicitia*, 77.

20. Appian, *Spanish Wars*, 70; Diodorus, 33.1; Cicero, *Pro Fonteio*, 23, 27.

21. Livy, *Oxy.*, 54; Dio, 22, frag. 78.

22. Gellius, 2.20; 3.4; 4.17; 6.11; Cicero, *De Oratore*, 2.258, 2.268.

23. Livy, *Per.*, 55; *Oxy.*, 55; Frontinus, 4.1.20; Cicero, *De Legibus*, 3.20.

24. Livy, *Oxy.*, 54; Cicero, *De Amicitia*, 41; *De Legibus*, 3.34-5; *Pro Sestio*, 103.

25. Cicero, *De Legibus*, 3.37; *Brutus*, 97; *Academica*, 2.13. Briso's resistance may not have involved a formal veto.

26. Plutarch, *Sayings of Scipio*, 15; Appian, *Spanish Wars*, 84.

27. Cicero, *Republic*, 1.31: *obtrectatores et invidi Scipionis*; Appius was *inimicus* to Scipio (Cicero, *Pro Scauro*, 32).

28. Heichelheim, *Ancient Economic History*, 3.38, argues this point, based partly on detailed study of price movements known from Egypt and Delos.

29. Cicero, *Brutus*, 85-6.

30. Obsequens, 27.

31. Diodorus, 34.2; Florus, 2.7; Livy, *Per.*, 56, 58, 59; Orosius, 5.9: *belli servilis contagio multas late infecit provincias.* For the Italian revolt of 133 see Orosius, 5.9 and Obsequens, 27b. For a coin of the slave king see Greenidge and Clay, 284.

32. Wars in Thrace and Illyria during 135, Livy, *Per.*, 56; Appian, *Illyrian Wars*, 10.

33. Plutarch, *Sayings of Scipio*, 15.

34. Cicero, *In Verrem*, 2.2.5.

35. Crawford, *Roman Republican Coinage*, at last establishes a probable date, around 141, for the crucial re-tariffing of the denarius. Undoubtedly the unofficial exchange rate between silver and bronze shifted first, and the official rate was at last altered to bring it into line. Crawford estimates that coinage was issued on a much larger scale in the early 130s, reaching over 10,000,000*d.* a year, and suggests that this destroys the theory of an urban recession. But his data are not really firm enough: the dates and sizes of issues are not precisely known and can have been affected by factors other than the level of economic activity, such as the re-tariffing itself.

36. Valerius, 3.7.3: *annonae caritate increscente*, followed by Nasica's arrogant reply: *tacete, quaeso, Quirites, plus ego enim quam vos quid rei publicae expediat intellego.* See Boren, *Urban Side of the Crisis.*

37. Dio, 23, frag. 81; Cicero, *Brutus*, 79; Livy, *Per.*, 56.

CHAPTER FIVE — LAND FOR THE PEOPLE

1. Lucilius, 200M: *deficit alma Ceres nec plebes pane potitur.* The context is unknown but must be around 133. Cicero, *Academica*, 2.15: *exortus est in optima re publica Ti. Gracchus qui otium perturbaret.*

2. Plutarch, *T.G.*, 8; Appian, *Civil Wars*, 1.7-8. (Future Appian references are all to *Civil Wars*, 1, unless specified.) 'Acre' in this book always means the Roman acre or *iugerum*, equal to 3,200 square yards, $\frac{2}{3}$ of an English acre, $\frac{1}{4}$ of a hectare.

3. The damage done by Hannibal should not be overemphasized. Pyrrhus had commented on its poor state in 280 as compared to the richer land near Rome (Dio, 9, frag. 27).

4. More profitable (Cato, *Agriculture*, 1.7; Cicero, *De Officiis*, 2.89).

5. Transhumance methods discussed in Varro, 2.2.9; 2.5.11: *hieme hibernant secundum mare, aestu abiguntur in montes frondosos*; Cato, 149.

6. Livy, 28.11.

7. Livy, 31.13.

8. Estimate from Brunt, *Manpower*, 121.

9. Cato, 1.7; 10.1; 11.1; 144.4; 2.7.

10. *Proceedings of the British School at Rome*, 1968, 145-8.

11. Apulia exported grain (Strabo, 6.3.9). Pliny, *N.H.*, 18.6.35: *latifundia perdidere Italiam*; but contrast Vergil, *Georgics*, 2.468 on the peaceful life of the farmer: *latis otia fundis.*

12. Estimate from Brunt, *Manpower*, 69-70.

13. In 189 and 177 immigrants into Rome had to be sent back home (Livy, 39.3; 41.8).

14. Sallust, *Jugurtha*, 41; Florus, 2.2: *depulsum agris suis plebem*; Seneca, *Moral Letters*, 14.2.39; Frontinus, in Thulin, *Corpus Agrimensorum*, 41; Livy, 42.1, 8, 19: *in vacuo vagaretur cupiditas privatorum.*

15. Cato, *O.R.F.*, 66; Cicero, *Pro Sestio*, 103: *locupletes possessionibus diuturnis moverentur.*

16. Plutarch, *T.G.*, 8: ἀναλαβεῖν τοῖς πένησι τὴν δημοσίαν χώραν.
17. Plutarch, *T.G.*, 9; Cicero, *Academica*, 2.13.
18. Cicero, *Laws*, 2.52: *Scaevolae pontifices maximi et homines acutissimi*. Q. Scaevola, consul 117, was augur and his namesake, consul 95, was high priest. For the annals, see Cicero, *De Oratore*, 2.52. For Scaevola and Blossius, Cicero, *De Amicitia*, 37. Scaevola was skilled at ball games and backgammon (Cicero, *De Oratore*, 1.217; Quintilian, 11.2.38).
19. Gellius, 1.13.10: Crassus was *ditissimus, nobilissimus, eloquentissimus, iurisconsultissimus, pontifex maximus*; Cicero, *Brutus*, 98, 127; *De Oratore*, 1.170, 216, 239, 240.
20. Valerius, 8.7.6; Quintilian, 11.2.50; Cicero, *Republic*, 3.17: a hundred million asses, presumably, rather than sesterces.
21. The first plebeians to act as consular military tribunes and masters of cavalry, in 400 and 368, were also Licinii. See above, pp. 44 and 47.
22. Livy, 6.35: [*lex*] *de modo agrorum, ne quis plus quingenta iugera agri possideret*. Livy, 34.4, but Cato's speech of 195 is not verbatim and contains anachronisms which make it an unreliable guide. Cato's speech of 167, *O.R.F.*, 66, Varro, 1.2.9, Valerius, 8.6.3 and Victor, 20, support Livy; Velleius, 2.6, gives no date: *plus quingentis iugeribus habere, quod aliquando lege Licinia cautum erat*; Diodorus and Cicero are silent.
23. Livy, 10.13, 33.42, 35.10, for transgressions of 298 and 196-3; see above, p. 56.
24. Cicero, *Pro Sestio*, 103.
25. Appian, 9: another 250 acres were allowed for each child. But perhaps for not more than two, since Livy, *Per.*, 58, and Victor, 64, set the limit at 1,000 acres.
26. Inalienability, sometimes criticized as an economic absurdity, is perfectly sound economics when new jobs and permanent settlements are the prime objectives. The Bronze Land Law (*C.I.L.*, 1.585) line 14. Other allotments in Livy, 39.55. Military service was an obvious aim of the measure, but since we are not certain that paying rent would disqualify a man from service we cannot infer that the land must have been rent-free.
27. Degrassi, 454, discussed later.
28. Appian, 9, 7, 8.
29. Appian, 10: ἐξ εὐπορίας ἐς πενίαν ἐσχάτην.
30. Appian, 11: οὐκ ἐς εὐπορίαν ἀλλ' ἐς εὐανδρίαν.
31. Plutarch, *T.G.*, 9-10; closely echoed in Florus, 2.1-2: *ne populus gentium victor orbisque possessor laribus ac focis suis exularet*.
32. Cicero, *De Lege Agraria*, 2.10: *amantissimos plebei Romanae*; 2.31: *Ti. Gracchi aequitate ac pudore*; 2.81: *Gracchorum benignitas*.
33. Appian, 10; Plutarch, *T.G.*, 9.
34. Appian, 10; Diodorus, 34.6.
35. Appian, 11-12; Plutarch, *T.G.*, 10. See also, Livy, *Per.*, 58; Orosius, 5.8; Florus, 2.2; Victor, 64; Velleius, 2.2.

CHAPTER SIX — THE REIGN OF TIBERIUS GRACCHUS

1. Cicero, *Laws*, 3.19; Livy, 2.33: *ut plebi sui magistratus essent sacrosancti quibus auxilii latio adversus consules esset.*
2. Livy, 38.52; 41.6; 45.21.
3. Livy, 10.37: *adversus intercessionem septem tribunorum triumphavit*; 38.36; see above, p. 48.
4. Cicero, *De Officiis*, 1.138; *Philippic*, 9.4; see above, p. 26.
5. Appian, 12; Plutarch, *T.G.*, 10; Dio, 24, frag. 83: διὰ φιλονεικίαν συγγενικὴν ἑκὼν ἀντηγωνίζετο; Cicero, *Brutus*, 95: *civis in rebus optimis constantissimus M. Octavius.* Perhaps Plutarch sentimentally exaggerates the reluctance of Octavius, and his mildness of manner during the quarrel, while Dio emphasizes his hostility.
6. Plutarch, *T.G.*, 10; Dio, 24, frag. 83. The legal machinery for stopping public business with a formal *iustitium* was probably a consular prerogative, but a repeated veto could have the same effect.
7. Appian, 12; Plutarch, *T.G.*, 11; Diodorus, 34.6. Appian places this second assembly on the day after the first, but with greater probability Plutarch allows an interval for the events of the previous paragraph. The chronology is confused but with care the accounts can be largely reconciled.
8. Plutarch, *T.G.*, 11; the ex-consul Μάλλιος is more likely to have been a Manlius than Scipio's friend Manilius.
9. Appian, 12; Plutarch, *T.G.*, 11-12. The accounts vary in emphasis but again the same sequence of events can be extracted: reference to the Senate, speech about Octavius, assembly on next day, seventeen tribes vote, final appeal to Octavius, bill carried. Again Appian stresses the value to Italy, but Plutarch the personal tragedy. Diodorus, 34.7, suggests a less likely version of the compromise offer, for a vote either to expel or to retain both tribunes. The final vote was taken on the Capitol hill (Cicero, *De Natura Deorum*, 1.106).
10. Plutarch, *T.G.*, 15.
11. Polybius, 6.16: ἀεὶ ποιεῖν τὸ δοκοῦν τῷ δήμῳ.
12. Cicero, *Brutus*, 95: *iniuria accepta fregit Ti. Gracchum patientia Octavius*; *Laws*, 3.24: *Gracchum non solum neglectus sed etiam sublatus intercessor evertit.*
13. Cicero, *Laws*, 3.20: *quid iuris bonis viris Gracchi tribunatus reliquit? Pro Milone*, 72: *per seditionem*; Livy, *Per.*, 58: *in eum furorem exarsit*; Velleius, 2.2; Orosius, 5.8: *his causis senatum ira, populum superbia invasit.*
14. Plutarch, *T.G.*, 12; Appian, 12; Diodorus, 34.7; Florus, 2.2: *praesenti metu mortis exterruit.*
15. Plutarch, *T.G.*, 13; Mucius rather than Mummius (Appian, 12) or Minucius (Orosius, 5.8).
16. Appian, 13; Plutarch, *T.G.*, 13; Livy, *Per.*, 58; Velleius, 2.2. Such family appointments were made illegal, presumably after the Gracchan era (Cicero, *De Lege Agraria*, 2.21; *De Domo Sua*, 51).
17. Plutarch, *T.G.*, 13: ὡς αὐτὸς ἀπεγνωκὼς ἑαυτόν.

18. Livy, *Per.*, 58. Scipio Aemilianus later attacked this law (O.R.F., 133).

19. Livy, *Per.*, 58: *heredem populum Romanum*; Plutarch, *T.G.*, 14; Florus, 1.35; Orosius, 5.8; Victor, 64; Justin, 36.4; Valerius, 5.2. ext 3; Strabo, 13.4.2; but strangely ignored by Appian.

20. Cicero, *Pro Lege Manilia*, 14. The proverbial wealth and corrosive luxury of Asia are a frequent topic, e.g. Livy, 39.6. Pliny, *N.H.*, 33.148, felt that the wealth flowing from this bequest brought more harm and less true benefit than earlier victories: *Asia donata multo etiam gravius adflixit mores, inutiliorque victoria illa hereditas fuit*. On Attalus, see Justin, 36.4.

21. Livy, *Per.*, 59: *[Asia] legata populo Romano libera esse deberet*. Decree of the city of Pergamum recognizing the will (O.G.I.S., 338): βασιλεὺς ἀπολέλοιπεν τὴ(μ πατρί)δα ἡμῶν ἐλευθέραν.

22. Orosius, 5.8: *Gracchus gratiam populi pretio adpetens, legem tulit ut pecunia populo distribueretur*; Valerius, 3.2.17: *profusissimis largitionibus favore populi occupato*.

23. The revolt was in progress before Tiberius died (Appian, 18, and Velleius, 2.4). See also Justin, 36.4; Florus, 1.35; Strabo, 14.1.38.

24. Polybius, 30.30; 31.1; see above page 26.

25. Plutarch, *T.G.*, 14; Orosius, 5.8.

26. Plutarch, *T.G.*, 14; Cicero, *Brutus*, 81.

27. Plutarch, *T.G.*, 14; Livy, *Per.*, 58; Annius, *O.R.F.*, 104–6.

28. Orosius, 5.8; Cicero, *De Amicitiá*, 37.

29. On Metellus, Victor, 61: *invisus plebi*; Cicero, *Republic*, 1.31. On Pompeius, Velleius, 2.1; Cicero, *In Verrem*, 2.5.181: *humili atque obscuro loco natus, plurimis inimicitiis . . . amplissimos honores est adeptus*. They also hated Scipio's friend Philus (Valerius, 3.7.5) as well as each other (Dio, 23 frag. 82).

30. Appian, 13; Plutarch, *T.G.*, 15.

31. Plutarch, *T.G.*, 9.3; 10.7; 11.1; 11.2.

32. Plutarch, *T.G.*, 13: φοβούμενοι τοῦ Τιβερίου τὴν αὔξησιν; *T.G.*, 14: ἐκ τούτου μάλιστα προσέκρουσε τῇ βουλῇ.

33. Livy, *Per.*, 58: *tot indignatibus commotus graviter senatus*.

34. Sallust, *Jugurtha*, 31.7: *quem regnum parare aiebant*; Cicero, *De Amicitia*, 41: *Ti. Gracchus regnum occupare conatus est, vel regnavit is quidem paucos menses*. See also Cicero, *Republic*, 2.49.

35. Livy, 38.51: *unum hominem caput imperii Romani*; 38.54: *regnum Scipionum*; 38.56: *perpetuum consulem et dictatorem*. Polybius, 10.40, reads like a defence against such a charge.

36. 454 Manlius and Sulpicius to Athens.

    394 Manlius and Valerius to Delphi.

    244 Manlius and Sempronius consuls when Brindisi founded.

    240 Claudius and Sempronius consuls when Greek plays first performed in Rome.

    229 Fulvius in first Illyrian War.

    215 Valerius commands against Macedon, followed by Sulpicius

and Sempronius. Political zenith of Gracchan families 215–209 coincides with aggressive posture against Macedon.
205 Valerius and Sulpicius to Pergamum.
201 Claudius and Sempronius to Greece and Asia.
200 Claudius and Sulpicius command against Macedon.
189 Fulvius and Manlius command in Greece and Asia, support settlements favourable to Pergamum.
187 Sempronius and Sulpicius defend Fulvius' eastern policy.
184 Claudius to Greece and Macedon.
173 Claudius and Valerius to Greece and Macedon.
172 Valerius report favourable to Pergamum, hostile to Macedon.
171 Licinius, Mucius, Valerius, Claudius, Manlius command against Macedon.
170 Hostilius and Claudius command against Macedon.
169 Claudius and Sempronius censors to stiffen the war effort.
167 Licinius to Pergamum.
165 Sempronius to Pergamum.
164 Sulpicius to Pergamum.
161 Sempronius to Syria.
149 Licinius, Manlius and Hostilius to Asia.
This list of eastern missions is neither exhaustive nor water-tight. Naturally there are counter-examples. But the cumulative weight of the evidence is irresistible.

37. Cicero, *De Amicitia*, 37: *non enim paruit ille Ti. Gracchi temeritati sed praefuit; nec se comitem illius furoris sed ducem praebuit*; Valerius, 4.7.1; Plutarch, *T.G.*, 8, 20 (wrongly naming Nasica, then in exile, as the inquisitor).
38. Livy, 23.7; 27.3; Cicero, *De Lege Agraria*, 2.93.
39. Cicero, *De Officiis*, 3.51–3, quoting Antipater: *hominibus consulere debeas et servire humanae societati*; 3.91; Plutarch, *Cleomenes*, 2, 10–11. Panaetius succeeded Antipater as head of the Stoa in 129.
40. Cicero, *Republic*, 2.1; Polybius, 6.10; 6.45–9.
41. Livy, 34.31.
42. Polybius, 6.9.
43. Cicero, *De Officiis*, 2.78–80: *qui se populares volunt... labefactant fundamenta rei publicae... nostros Gracchos nonne agrariae contentiones perdiderunt?*
44. Plutarch, *Agis*, 5.

CHAPTER SEVEN — MASSACRE ON CAPITOL HILL
1. Appian, 14; Plutarch, *T.G.*, 16; Livy, *Per.*, 58; Dio, 24, frag. 83; Orosius, 5.9; Florus, 2.2; Victor, 64. Only Dio names Appius and Gaius, but despite the latter's youth there is no reason to doubt him.
2. Cicero, *Catiline*, 4.4. Dio, 5, frag. 22, states that in the earlier republic repeated tribunates were both illegal and common-place, which hardly clarifies the matter.
3. Gaius returned, Plutarch, *T.G.*, 20.

4. Appian, 10, 13-14:   συνεκάλει τοὺς ἐκ τῶν ἀγρῶν . . . ἐπὶ τὸν ἐν τῷ ἄστει δῆμον κατέφευγε. The notorius imprecision of the Roman calendar may have left this year's elections less conveniently timed than usual.

5. Plutarch, *T.G.*, 16; Dio, 24, frag. 83; see above, p. 42.

6. Plutarch, *T.G.*, 16; see above, p. 44.

7. Plutarch, *T.G.*, 16 (half the seats); Dio, 24, frag. 83 (all of them); Pliny, *N.H.*, 33.34. But Livy, *Per. 58: legem agrariam ferret adversus voluntatem senatus et equestris ordinis*; Velleius, 2.3: *senatus atque equestris ordinis pars melior et maior inruere in Gracchum.*

8. Velleius, 2.2; Appian, 34.

9. Plutarch, *T.G.*, 16; *T.G.*, 8, mentions a pamphlet written by Gaius; Dio, 24, frag. 83.

10. Appian, 14; Plutarch, *T.G.*, 16. Appian explicitly states that two tribes voted for Tiberius. None of the arguments, based on uncertain conjectures about voting procedure, adduced to show that this was really a legislative not an electoral assembly carries conviction.

11. Each tribe chose ten tribunes, but to be elected a candidate had to be chosen by a majority of tribes. So he could be chosen by the first two and still be uncertain about eventual success.

12. Appian, 14; Plutarch, *T.G.*, 16: ταπεινὸς καὶ δεδακρυμένος; Gellius, 2.13.

13. Appian, 15; Plutarch, *T.G.*, 16-17; Obsequens, 27; Victor, 64; Valerius, 1.4.2. Of the great temple, built by the kings, nothing remains except some foundations under the Palazzo Caffarelli.

14. Appian, 15; Plutarch, *T.G.*, 17-18. Only Plutarch reports this first stage of the senate's debate, but the sequence is still clear. This argument was reported by Flaccus (presumably the consul of 125), then came the diadem incident, the escalation of the riot, and the final exchange between Scaevola and Nasica. The temple of Faith was on the Capitol near the temple of Jupiter (Cicero, *De Officiis*, 3.104).

15. Plutarch, *T.G.*, 20; Gracchus was always followed by 3,000 or 4,000 supporters (Gellius, 2.13).

16. Appian, 15; Plutarch, *T.G.*, 19; Victor, 64; Florus, 2.2. Sources agree that the gesture was misunderstood. Tiberius was not demanding a diadem. But he was fomenting trouble; Velleius, 2.3: *concientem paene totius Italiae frequentiam*; Orosius, 5.9: *seditiones populi accenderet.*

17. Valerius, 7.5.2; Cicero, *Brutus*, 107: *[Nasicam] cum omnibus in rebus vehementem tum acrem in dicendo*; 212; *De Officiis*, 1.109. See above pp. 47 and 52.

18. Speech of Nasica in Valerius, 3.2.17: *quoniam consul, dum iuris ordinem sequitur, id agit, ut cum omnibus legibus Romanum imperium corruat, egomet me privatus voluntati vestrae ducem offero: qui rem publicam salvam esse volunt me sequantur*; Appian, 16; Plutarch, *T.G.*, 19.

19. The robe was about his head (Appian and Plutarch) rather than his left arm (Velleius, 2.3, and Valerius, 3.2.17). The irrational had now taken command.

20. Several accounts of the fight are here reconciled as nearly as possible. Plutarch, *T.G.*, 19 (naming Satureius and L. Rufus); Cicero, *Ad Herrenium*, 4.68 (quoting the vivid eye-witness account); Appian, 16; Orosius, 5.9; Velleius, 2.3; Diodorus, 34.7; Livy, *Per.*, 58; Valerius, 1.4.2; Obsequens, 27; Victor, 64; Florus, 2.2. All sources emphasize the makeshift wooden weapons, and with Plutarch's assertion that nobody was killed with iron this confirms the quasi-religious atmosphere. The analogy with a pig is based on Badian's restoration of C. Gracchus, frag. 18 (*O.R.F.*, 179): *qui pro suilla humanam hostiam trucidet*. The location of the murder is not clear; other than in Cicero it seems that Tiberius was trying to get away and may even have reached the main Capitoline approach (Velleius) or one of the stairways (Orosius).

21. Plutarch, *T.G.*, 20; this was at the order of the aedile Lucretius, hence nicknamed Vespillo, or corpse-bearer (Victor, 64; Valerius 1.4.2).

22. Appian, 2: ξίφος δὲ οὐδέν πω . . . . . οὐδὲ φόνον ἔμφυλον; Plutarch, *T.G.*, 20: πρώτην ἐν Ῥώμῃ στάσιν . . . . . αἵματι καὶ φόνῳ πολιτῶν διακριθῆναι; Velleius, 2.3: *inde ius vi obrutum, potentiorque habitus prior, discordiaeque civium ferro diiudicatae.*

23. Cicero, *Republic*, 1.31: *cur in una re publica duo senatus et duo paene iam populi sint? nam, ut videtis, mors Ti. Gracchi et iam ante tota illius ratio tribunatus divisit populum unum in duas partis*; Appian, 17; the thought is echoed in Livy, 2.44, referring to earlier disputes: *duas civitates ex una factas.*

24. Plutarch, *T.G.*, 20; Cicero, *Brutus*, 212: *qui ex dominatu Ti. Gracchi privatus in libertatem rem publicam vindicavit*; *Pro Milone*, 72; *Philippic*, 8.13; Valerius, 4.7.1; Plutarch, *T.G.*, 21 and Diodorus, 34.7, quoting Homer, *Odyssey*, 1.47:

ὡς ἀπόλοιτο καὶ ἄλλος ὅ τις τοιαῦτά γε ῥέζοι.)

25. Florus, 2.2; Diodorus, 34.5; Plutarch, *Comparison*, 6: ἀρετῇ πεπρωτευκέναι; Appian, 17: ἀρίστου βουλεύματος ἕνεκα, βιαίως ᾳὐτῷ προσιών.

26. Dio, 24, frag. 83; Cicero, *De Haruspicum Responsis*, 41; Velleius, 2.2. Aristotle's concept of περιπέτεια, the reversal of fortune underlying all great tragedy, is evident in these judgements.

CHAPTER EIGHT — A SHOWDOWN WITH SCIPIO

1. Appian, 16; Plutarch, *T.G.*, 19–20; Livy, *Per.*, 58; Orosius, 5.9; Victor, 64; Velleius, 2.6; Valerius, 6.3.1d.

2. Justinian, *Digest*, 49.15.4; 50.7.8. His cousin Q. Scaevola was son-in-law to Laelius (Cicero, *Republic*, 1.18); and he had helped the young Rutilius (Cicero, *De Officiis*, 2.47).

3. Cicero, *In Verrem*, 2.4.108; Diodorus, 34.33.

4. Cicero, *De Domo*, 91; *Pro Plancio*, 88; *In Verrem*, 2.4.108; Diodorus, 34.10; Obsequens, 27a; Valerius, 1.1.1.

5. Valerius, 7.2.6; Plutarch, *T.G.*, 21.
6. Plutarch, *T.G.*, 21; Cicero, *De Oratore*, 2.285.
7. Appian, 18; Velleius, 2.4. The rebellion lasted four years (Appian, *Mithridates*, 62; coins of Aristonicus, *G. & C.*, 284). The idealized City of the Sun (Strabo, 14.1.38) derived perhaps from the Utopian romance of Iambulus (Diodorus, 2.55–60).
8. Asia's first official year as a Roman province was 134–133 (coin of Ampius, *G. & C.*, 12). Popillian decree on Pergamum (*O.G.I.S.*, 435; Sherk, 11) is dated between 16 October and 11 December. Both this and Nasica's mission look like hurried reactions before the scale of the revolt had become clear, and so are best assigned to 133. On Nasica, see Plutarch, *T.G.*, 21; Valerius, 5.3.2e; Victor, 64; Cicero, *Pro Flacco*, 75; probably the same as the embassy of five in Strabo, 14.1.38.
9. Cicero, *De Amicitia*, 69, 73.
10. Cicero, *De Amicitia*, 37; Valerius, 4.7.1.
11. Velleius, 2.7: *asperrime saevierant*; Sallust, *Jugurtha*, 31; Plutarch, *T.G.*, 20. See above, p. 80.
12. Plutarch, *C.G.*, 1; *O.R.F.*, 177.
13. Orosius, 5.7; Florus, 1.34: *triumphus tantum de nomine*; Pliny, *N.H.*, 33.141.
14. Cicero, *Tusculans*, 4.40; Pliny, *N.H.*, 7.122. Rupilius in Sicily, see Valerius 6.9.8, 9.12. ext 1.
15. Cicero, *Philippic*, 11.18; Livy, *Per.*, 59.
16. Justin, 36.4.
17. Degrassi, 467, 468 in Campania; 469, 470, 471, 472 (three) in the Vallo di Diano; the later 474 from Pisaurum. Carcopino deduced a pattern of job rotation within the commission from the varying order of names, but since the order never varies on the original stones this theory lacks conviction.
18. Cicero, *Republic*, 1.31; Livy, *Per.*, 59; Gellius, 1.6; *O.R.F.*, 107.
19. Degrassi, 454: *primus fecei ut de agro poplico aratoribus cederent paastores*. The stone, found near Polla, is unsigned but the identification is probable; see Wiseman, *Papers of the British School at Rome*, 1964, 1969.
20. Cicero, *Brutus*, 96, 103–106, 159, 221, 296, 333; *De Oratore*, 1.40, 3.28.
21. Cicero, *Laws*, 3.35; *Ad Fam.*, 9.21.
22. Cicero, *Laws*, 3.35; *De Amicitia*, 39.
23. Cicero, *De Oratore*, 2.170; *De Amicitia*, 96; Livy, *Per.*, 59; *O.R.F.*, 178.
24. Velleius, 2.4: *si is occupandae rei publicae animum habuisset, iure caesum*; *O.R.F.*, 131-2. For popular reaction, see Velleius: *omnis contio adclamasset*; Valerius, 6.2.3: *contio violenter succlamasset*; Victor, 58: *obstrepente populo*; Plutarch, *T.G.*, 21.
25. Justin, 36.4: *intentior praedae quam bello . . . poenas inconsultae avaritiae sanguine dedit*; Orosius, 5.10: *effugit et dedecus et servitutem*; Eutropius, 4.20; Florus, 1.35; Strabo, 14.1.38; Livy, *Per.*, 59; Velleius, 2.4; Valerius, 3.2.12.

26. Horace, *Satires*, 2.1.62–68; Cicero, *Republic*, 1.31.
27. The new commissioners were probably elected together (Appian, 18). Velleius, 2.6, and Victor, 65, are misleading only because set in a different context. On Fulvius, see Cicero, *Brutus*, 108; Plutarch, *C.G.*, 10, 14. On his family, Livy, 26.15; 41.27; 42.28.
28. As note 25. The Perperna family was new to Rome and its first known member served under Claudius in 168. For the auction (but misdated to 132), see Pliny, *N.H.*, 33.148–9: *erudita civitate amare etiam, non solum admirari, opulentiam externam.*
29. Degrassi, 473 (three) from near Aeclanum. To be dated 130–129, before the commissioners lost their judiciary powers. Livy, *Per.*, 59.
30. Livy, *Per.*, 59; Appian, 18–19.
31. *Scholia Bobiensia*, 118; Cicero, *Republic*, 1.31–32: *concitatis sociis et nomine Latino, foederibus violatis, triumviris seditiosissimis . . .* ; 3.41: *Asia Ti. Gracchus perseveravit in civibus, sociorum nominisque Latini iura neglexit ac foedera;* 6.12: *dictator rem publicam constituas oportet.*
32. Cicero's remark about Asia (last note) does not refer to the land question. It could well be a complaint that the Asian treasure was used primarily to benefit Romans not allies. It certainly does not prove that the allies were excluded from the benefits of land reform. Nor do the references in the Bronze Land Law to 'public land given and assigned by the commissioners to a Roman citizen' (*C.I.L.*, 1.585, lines 3, 15). In fact the law does also refer to Latin rights on the public land (lines 29, 31).

    Plutarch's silence is equally inconclusive. No doubt Roman settlers had first claim, and the likeliest view is that poor Italians had residual and theoretical rights to benefit which few of them ever realized in practice. See above, p. 62.
33. Appian, 19; *O.R.F.*, 133. Scipio bitterly deplored the corrupting effect of Eastern music and manners, presumably to make an analogy with the Asian money that was paying for land reform. Similarly Livy, 39.6, on Asian furniture, music and gastronomy.
34. The senate presumably acted through a redefinition of the rights of the allies rather than an actual repeal of the law. Appian, 19; Plutarch, *Sayings of Scipio*, 22; *O.R.F.*, 132.
35. Appian, 20; Cicero, *De Amicitia*, 12; Plutarch, *C.G.*, 10; Orosius, 5.10.

CHAPTER NINE — GAIUS TAKES UP THE CAUSE
1. Plutarch, *T.G.*, 2 (above, p. 2); Dio, 25, frag. 85; Valerius, 8.10.1.
2. Plutarch, *C.G.*, 1; Appian, 21.
3. Plutarch, *T.G.*, 21; *C.G.*, 15, 17. But Nepos (in Plutarch, *T.G.*) links Gaius to the daughter of Brutus, so also Ampelius, 19.4, 26.2. So presumably Licinia's mother married Brutus after the death of Crassus, and then Licinia married Gaius. Her mother was probably a Clodia or Claudia (Cicero, *Ad Att.*, 12.22.2), but she need not have been a close relative of Appius Claudius.
4. *O.R.F.*, 190; Plutarch, *C.G.*, 15 (his son); 19 (Misenum); 12 (house

on Palatine); 13 (letters of Cornelia).

5. Plutarch, *Moralia*, 798 F.
6. *O.R.F.*, 177-8; see above, pp. 103-12.
7. Plutarch, *C.G.*, 10; Appian, 20. Sempronia also named in Livy, *Per.*, 59; Orosius, 5.10; and with Gaius in *Scholia Bobiensia*, 118. Carbo in Cicero, *De Oratore*, 2.170; *Ad Fam.*, 9.21.3; *Ad Q. fratrem*, 2.3.3.
8. Plutarch, *C.G.*, 10; Appian, 20. Absence of inquiry, Cicero, *Pro Milone*, 16; Livy, *Per.*, 59; Velleius, 2.4; Valerius, 5.3.2d. On Laelius, see *O.R.F.*, 121, as emended by Badian: *eum morbus tum removit*. On Metellus, Valerius, 4.1.12.
9. Velleius, 2.1; Valerius, 6.4.2.
10. Cicero, *De Amicitia*, 39-41.
11. Appian, 21; Dio, 24, frag. 84; Livy, *Per.*, 59. Other consuls may have shouldered the judicial function rejected by Tuditanus in 129.
12. *Liber Coloniarum*, printed in Blume and Lachmann, *Die Schriften der Römischen Feldmesser*. It uses such phrases as *limitibus Gracchanis quadratis* or *lege Sempronia adsignata*. Yet land hunger was still not abated, and demand still exceeded supply (Appian, 21): ὁ δῆμος ἐν ἐλπίδι τέως τῆς γῆς γενόμενος ἠθύμει. Bradford, *Ancient Landscapes*, gives striking aerial pictures of Roman land patterns.
13. Plutarch, *C.G.*, 1: τί δῆτα, Γάιε, βραδύνεις; εἷς μὲν ἡμῖν ἀμφοτέροις βίος, εἷς δὲ θάνατος, ὑπὲρ τοῦ δήμου πολιτευομένοις πέπρωται. A less rousing version in Cicero, *De Divinatione*, 1.56, Valerius, 1.7.6. Sulla became quaestor at 30, and M. Antonius at 29.
14. Velleius, 2.6: *idem occupavit furor*; Florus, 2.3: *statim et mortis et legum fratris sui vindex*; Appian, 21; Gaius in *O.R.F.*, 188: *verum peto a vobis non pecuniam sed bonam existimationem atque honorem*.
15. On the knights, see above, pp. 10, 24, 88, and Chapter 11.
16. Cicero, *Republic*, 4.2: *quam commode ordines discripti, aetates, classes, equitatus in quo suffragia sunt etiam senatus, nimis multis iam stulte hanc utilitatem tolli cupientibus, qui novam largitionem quaerunt aliquo plebei scito reddendorum equorum.*
17. Livy, *Per.*, 99; Cicero, *Pro Murena*, 40: *equestri ordine restituit non solum dignitatem sed etiam voluptatem* (the law was renewed in 67).
18. Senate Decree on Pergamene Land (Sherk, 12) dated by fragments of the names of consuls. But Magie and Mattingly date it to 101. On Fulvius, see Obsequens, 28a.
19. Cicero, *Brutus*, 109; *De Officiis*, 3.47; *O.R.F.*, 180.
20. Latin voting rights, Livy, 41.8. On Perperna, see Valerius, 3.4.5.
21. Appian, 21: ὡς μείζονι χάριτι περὶ τῆς γῆς οὐ διοισομένους; 34: ὡς κοινωνοὺς τῆς ἡγεμονίας ἀντὶ ὑπηκόων ἐσομένους; right of appeal, Valerius, 9.5.1.
22. Appian, 21: Plutarch, *C.G.*, 2; *O.R.F.*, 195; Valerius, 9.5.1.
23. Appian, 34; Livy, *Per.*, 60; Plutarch, *C.G.*, 15, 18; Ammianus,

15.12.5; Obsequens, 30; Velleius, 2.6.
24. Plutarch, *C.G.*, 2; Victor, 65: *pestilentem Sardiniam*; the senate's unhelpfulness may confirm that Orestes was a friend of Gaius.
25. Plutarch, *C.G.*, 2; Livy, *Per.*, 60; Obsequens, 30; Orosius, 5.11. Heichelheim finds grain prices high until 121.
26. Livy, 27.10, 41.8; Cicero, *Brutus*, 170; *Ad Herennium*, 4.22: *perfidiosae Fregellae, cuius nitor urbis Italiam nuper inlustravit*; 4.13; 4.37.
27. Plutarch, *C.G.*, 3: συνωμοσίας; Obsequens, 30: *coniuraverunt*; Livy, *Per.*, 60; Velleius, 2.6; Cicero, *Pro Plancio*, 70; *In Pisonem*, 95: *Opimius qui praetor et consul maximis rem publicam periculis liberarat*; Victor, 65: *Asculanae et Fregellanae defectionis*; Asconius, 17: *ceteros quoque nominis Latini socios male animatos.* On the odious Fregellan traitor Numitorius, see Cicero, *De Finibus*, 5.62; *Philippic*, 3.17; *De Inventione*, 2.105. Opimius refused a triumph (Valerius, 2.8.4; Ammianus, 25.9.10).
28. Plutarch, *C.G.*, 2; Diodorus, 34.24; Victor, 65; *O.R.F.*, 180.
29. *O.R.F.*, 181-2: *versatus sum in provincia quomodo ex usu vestro existimabam esse.*
30. Strabo, 14.1.38; Cicero, *In Caecilium*, 69; Appian, 22; Appian, *Mithridates*, 57. See above, p. 152.
31. Velleius, 1.15.
32. Plutarch, *C.G.*, 3; Victor, 65.
33. *O.R.F.*, 181, 183.
34. Plutarch, *C.G.*, 3; Appian, 21: περιφανέστατα αἱρεθείς.

CHAPTER TEN — REVOLUTIONARY POWER
1. Plutarch, *C.G.*, 3: ἀπάντων πρῶτος; Cicero, *Brutus*, 125-6: *quam ille facile tali ingenio, diutius si vixisset, vel paternam esset vel avitam gloriam consecutus! eloquentia quidem nescio an habuisset parem neminem. grandis est verbis, sapiens sententiis, genere toto gravis*; 333; *Pro Fonteio*, 39.
2. Plutarch, *C.G.*, 3-4; Livy, *Per.*, 60; Velleius, 2.6; Dio, 25, frag. 85; *O.R.F.*, 177.
3. Cicero, *De Haruspicum Responsis*, 43: *C. autem Gracchum mors fraterna, pietas, dolor, magnitudo animi ad expetendas domestici sanguinis poenas excitavit*; Plutarch, *Comparison*, 5; *C.G.*, 3.
4. Plutarch, *C.G.*, 4.
5. Appian, 21: εὐθὺς ἐπεβούλευε τῇ βουλῇ; Diodorus, 34.24-5; Dio, 25, frag. 85; Velleius, 2.6.
6. Velleius, 2.6: *longe maiora et acriora repetens.* For Gracchan supporters and opponents, see above, pp. 41 and 180.
7. Plutarch, *C.G.*, 4; Diodorus, 34.25.
8. Cicero, *Pro Rabirio Perduellionis*, 12: *legem ne de capite civium Romanorum iniussu vestro (populi) iudicaretur*; *In Catilinam*, 4.10; *In Verrem*, 2.5.163 (flogging); Plutarch, *C.G.*, 4 (exile); *Scholia Ambrosiana*, 271.
9. Speeches of Gaius, *O.R.F.*, 184-5; Plutarch, *C.G.*, 4; Diodorus,

34.26; Velleius, 2.7 (mistakenly naming Rupilius too, who was already dead); Cicero, *De Domo*, 82; *Pro Cluentio*, 95; *Brutus*, 128; *Republic*, 1.6; *Laws*, 3.26.

10. Livy, *Per.*, 60: *ut senis et triente frumentum plebi daretur*; price also given in *Scholia Bobiensia*, 135, and Cicero, *Pro Sestio*, 55; Plutarch, *C.G.*, 5; Appian, 21; Victor, 65; Florus, 2.3. The Roman peck or *modius* equals 0.93 of a British peck, or 1.86 gallons.

11. Florus, 1.43: *Baleares insulae piratica rabie maria corruperant*; Orosius, 5.13; Livy, *Per.*, 60. On Fabius, Plutarch, *C.G.*, 6.

12. Velleius, 2.6; Livy, 30.26; 31.4; 31.50: *annona pervilis binis aeris in modios*; Polybius, 2.15, reckoning 4 obols (equal to 6.67 old asses) for a *medimnus* of 5 *modii*; Pliny, *N.H.*, 18.17.

13. Cicero, *In Verrem*, 2.3.214.

14. Granaries, Plutarch, *C.G.*, 6; Festus, 392. Free distribution was begun by Cicero's enemy Clodius in 58.

15. Orosius, 5.12; Diodorus, 34.25; Ampelius, 26.2.

16. Florus, 2.1: *quid tam aequum quam inopem populum vivere ex aerario suo? sed . . . emptio frumenti ipsos rei publicae nervos exhauriebat, aerarium.* Cicero, *De Officiis*, 2.72; *Tusculans*, 3.48; *Pro Sestio*, 103 (speech delivered in 56).

17. Cicero, *Tusculans*, 3.48; *Pro Fonteio*, 39; *Scholia Bobiensia*, 96; *O.R.F.*, 186-7.

18. Diodorus, 34.25; Appian, 22; Plutarch, *C.G.*, 5. Gaius first used the open forum for speeches, Crassus had already started using it for counting votes (see above, p. 44). For Gaius' extravagant platform manner, see above, p. 3.

19. Plutarch, *C.G.*, 6: μοναρχική τις ἰσχύς; Diodorus, 34.25: ἐπὶ τοσοῦτο προέβη δυναστείας; Velleius, 2.6: *nihil denique in eodem statu relinquebat*.

20. Seneca, *De Beneficiis*, 6.34.2.

21. Appian, 21, 24; Velleius, 2.6; *Fasti triumphales*.

22. Degrassi, 269, identifies Fannius as the son of Marcus not of Gaius, despite Cicero, *Brutus*, 99. See also Plutarch, *T.G.*, 4; Cicero, *Brutus*, 100-1; *De Amicitia*, 3; *Ad Att.*, 12.5b.3; 16.13b.2. Opimius a candidate, Plutarch, *C.G.*, 11.

23. Plutarch, *C.G.*, 8; Appian, 21. For the election of 449 and the Trebonian law of 448, see Livy, 3.64-5: *ut . . . usque eo rogaret dum decem tribunos plebei faceret.*

CHAPTER ELEVEN — VISION OF EMPIRE

1. Livy, 9.46: Dionysius, 6.13; Victor, 32; Valerius, 2.2.9; Pliny, *N.H.*, 15.19.

2. Dionysius, 4.18; Cicero, *Pro Roscio Comoedio*, 42: *si a censu spectas, eques Romanus est*; see above, page 10. For the 100,000d. minimum, see Horace, *Ep.*, 1.1.57-62, and Porphyrion, ad loc.; Seutonius, *Caesar*, 33.1; Pliny, *N.H.*, 33.32; and probably Livy, 24.11 (a million old asses in 214). Cato suggested raising the number holding the public horse to 2200 (*O.R.F.*, 37).

3. Livy, 5.7: *quibus census equester erat, equi publici non erant adsignati, equis se suis stipendia facturos promittunt*; dishonoured men could be deprived of their public horses and made to pay for their own (Livy, 27.11); Livy, 34.31: *vos a censu equites legitis*; similarly Polybius, 6.20: πλουντίνδην.' For a self-made knight, see Valerius, 4.7.5; for the more common hereditary status, Cicero, *Pro Plancio*, 32; for the gold rings, Livy, 23.12.
4. See above, pp. 10 and 120.
5. Cicero, *Pro Cluentio*, 150: *[equites] qui summum locum civitatis aut non potuerunt ascendere aut non petiverunt*; 153-4: *illam vitam tranquillam*, the quiet life of the knights contrasted with the glories and dangers of the senate: *Pro Plancio*, 17: *eo cursu qui semper patuerit hominibus ortis hoc nostro equestri loco . . . omnes tecum equitum Romanorum filii petiverunt.*
6. Livy, 21.63; Cicero, *In Verrem*, 2.5.45; Asconius, 93.
7. Livy, 23.48; 34.21.
8. Livy, 25.3; 39.44; 43.16; 45.18.
9. The companies, Livy, 23.48-9; Polybius, 6.17; Cicero, *Ad Fam.*, 13.9.2 (the giant Bithynian company). For the knight as company promoter and director, Cicero, *Pro Plancio*, 32: *maximarum societatum auctor, plurimarum magister*; 23: *flos enim equitum Romanorum, ornamentum civitatis, firmamentum rei publicae, publicanorum ordine continetur*; *Pro Rabirio Postumo*, 3: *Curtius, princeps ordinis equestris fortissimus et maximus publicanus*. The Puteoli building contract (Degrassi, 518) illustrates the use of pledges.
10. Livy, 43.16; see above, p. 25.
11. Cicero, *De Officiis*, 2.75: *expilatio direptioque sociorum*.
12. On Tubulus, Cicero, *De Finibus*, 2.54; 4.77; 5.62. On Aquillius, Appian, 22, and above pp. 126 and 152.
13. Appian, 22: ἀθρόως τὴν βουλὴν καθηρήκοι; Plutarch, *C.G.*, 5-6: ἀπέκοψε τῆς τῶν συγκλητικῶν δυνάμεως; Florus, 2.1; Livy, *Per.*, 60; Diodorus, 37.9; 34.27; 34.25; Velleius, 2.6; 2.13; 2.32; Tacitus, *Annals*, 12.60; Pliny, *N.H.*, 33.34.
14. Appian, Velleius, Plutarch and Diodorus all make the law's application quite general: τὰ δικαστήρια μετέφερε; *iudicia transferebat*; (οἱ συγκλητικοί) μόνοι γὰρ ἔκρινον τὰς δίκας; τὸ δικάζειν ἀφελόμενος. The multiplicity of courts is attested by Polybius. 6.17; Cicero, *Brutus*, 106: *quaestiones perpetuae hoc (Carbone) adulescente constitutae sunt*; *De Finibus*, 2.54 (a praetor judging *inter sicarios* in 142); *Pro Rabirio Postumo*, 14 (new courts a common phenomenon by 100). The theory that only the exortion court existed or was transferred must be rejected.
15. See above, p. 132.
16. Cicero, *Pro Cluentio*, 151: *hanc ipsam legem, ne quis iudicio circumveniretur, C. Gracchus tulit*; 148: it covered any magistrate or senator who conspired *quo quis iudicio publico*

condemnaretur; 104 and 114, showing that for *receiving* bribes a senator would be charged under the extortion law *de pecuniis repetundis*.

17. Plutarch, *C.G.*, 5; *Comparison*, 2; *T.G.*, 16 (attributing it to Tiberius); Livy, *Per.*, 60.
18. Appian, 22: ἀντιλαμβάνοντες παρ' αὐτῶν ὅ τι θέλοιεν.·
19. Cicero, *In Verrem*, 1.51-52; 2.1.26; and pseudo-Asconius ad loc.
20. Bronze Extortion Law (*C.I.L.*, 1.583, as revised by Mattingly, *J.R.S.*, 1969), lines 12-13, 16-17: [*praetor*] *facito utei CDL viros legat, quei in hac civitate* (the positive qualification· is here missing) . . . *dum ne quem eorum legat quei tribunus plebis . . . siet fueritve, queive in senatu siet fueritve . . . .*
21. Bronze Law, lines 23 and 74, cites two previous laws on the subject, that of Piso in 149 and another passed by M. Junius, otherwise unknown. Line 23 cites a law of Rubrius, perhaps the colonial law also passed in 123 (above, p. 162), which still permits the bronze law to date from 123 or later. But if it was Gracchan, as seems most likely, it must date from 123, probably from before September (see line 7), and perhaps from immediately after the elections. If it was later then the Junian law could be that of 123. The precise balance between the judiciary and the extortion legislation will remain a subject for dispute.
22. Bronze Law, lines 13, 17. Appian, 22:'ἀξίωσιν also suggests selection by wealth. Bronze Land Law, line 37, selects judges from the first class; could Gaius Gracchus have done the same?
23. Pliny, *N.H.*, 33.34: *hoc tertium corpus in re publica*; Cicero, *In Verrem*, 2.3.94: *cum equester ordo iudicaret*; 2.3.168: *si publicani, hoc est si equites Romani iudicarent*. Junius, a friend of Gaius Gracchus, defends the dignity of the knights (Pliny, *N.H.*, 33.36).
24. Varro, in Nonius Marcellus, 728: *equestri ordini iudicia tradidit ac bicipitem civitatem fecit discordiarum civilium fontem*.
25. Livy, 40.51 (new *portoria* and *vectigalia*); 27.10 (freedom tax); 29.37 (salt tax); Cicero, *In Verrem*, 2.3.12-15 (Sicilian tithes).
26. Cicero, *Tusculans*, 3.48: *patronum aerarii*; Velleius, 2.6: *nova portoria*; *O.R.F.*, 188: *ut vectigalia augeatis*.
27. Cicero, *Pro lege Manilia*, 14: *maximis vestris vectigalibus*; see above, p. 75. On state revenue, see Plutarch, *Pompey*, 45.
28. Gaius, *Dissuasio Legis Aufeiae*, *O.R.F.*, 187-8.
29. Appian, *Mithridates*, 57; *Civil Wars*, 5.4. Presumably the Aufeian proposal to ratify Aquillius' settlement was delayed until 124 to allow for Aquillius' trial first. See above page 126. Only some such reconstruction can reconcile Gaius' Asian tax law of 123 with the fact that Asia had already been paying taxes to the Romans (see Velleius, 2.38, and Senate Decree on Pergamene Land, above, p. 121).
30. Cicero, *In Verrem*, 2.3.12: *censoria locatio constituta est, ut Asiae lege Sempronia*, contrasted with the fixed tribute paid by Spain or the locally farmed tithes of Sicily; Appian, *Civil Wars*, 5.4; *Fronto ad Verum*, 2.1; *Scholia Bobiensia*, 157, and perhaps Bronze Land Law, 82, indicate possibility of remission.

31. Cicero, *In Verrem*, 2.3.94; Diodorus, 34.2.31; Appian, 22.
32. Cicero, *Pro lege Manilia*, 17: *firmamentum ceterorum ordinum*; 18-19, explains how Rome's entire credit and financial system came to depend on the massive investments made in Asia by publicans and many other enterprising businessmen. When Asia stumbled, banks in the forum closed their doors: *fidem concidisse*.
33. L. Crassus, in Cicero, *De Oratore*, 1.225: *eripite nos ex faucibus eorum*; Florus, 2.1: *vectigalia subprimebat*; Diodorus, 34.25: δίκαιον μῖσος.
34. Cicero, *In Verrem*, 1.38; Livy, *Per.*, 70: Rutilius was *invisus equestri ordini* because he defended Asia *a publicanorum iniuriis*; the new courts convicted many other innocent senators (Velleius, 2.13).

CHAPTER TWELVE — THE TIDE TURNS

1. Plutarch, *C.G.*, 6. Fabius was presumably the consul of 121 and so the son of Fabius Aemilianus.
2. Sallust, *Jugurtha*, 27: *lege Sempronia provinciae futuris consulibus Numidia atque Italia decretae*; Cicero, *De Domo*, 24; *De Provinciis Consularibus*, 3; 37; *Pro Balbo*, 61; *Ad Fam.*, 1.7.10.
3. Immunity from veto, Cicero, *De Provinciis Consularibus*, 17; 36. We know that the senate tried to assign meaningless duties to the consuls of 59, foreseeing that one of them would be Caesar; presumably there were precedents (Seutonius, *Caesar*, 19). On 113, see Tacitus, *Germany*, 37; Livy, *Per.*, 63; Appian, *Celtic Wars*, 13.
4. Sextius, Domitius and Fabius triumphed; Aix was founded in 122, Narbonne in 118. Domitius built the road through Narbonne (Degrassi, 460a).
5. Plutarch, *C.G.*, 5; Diodorus, 34.25; perhaps also Asconius, 68: *plures leges quibus militiae stipendia minuebantur*. In fact 17 had been the normal recruiting age (Livy, 25.5).
6. Plutarch, *C.G.*, 6; 7; *Comparison*, 2; Appian, 23; Degrassi, 458.
7. Crawford, *Roman Republican Coinage*. See above, p. 51. It is difficult to accept Crawford's suggestion that in one year Gaius' reforms raised the annual cost of keeping one legion in the field from 600,000*d.* to 1,500,000*d.*
8. Livy, *Per.*, 60: *tulit legem agrariam, quam et frater eius tulerat*; Velleius, 2.6: *dividebat agros*; Plutarch, *C.G.*, 5; 9 (rent payable); Siculus Flaccus, in Thulin's *Corpus Agrimensorum* 100, 129 (but his 200-acre limit should be disbelieved). On persistent land hunger, see Appian, 21, and above, p. 117. The Bronze Land Law (*C.I.L.*, 1.585) was passed in 111 and we have a copy carved on the back of the bronze extortion law already discussed (above, p. 148); it enshrines Gaius Gracchus' definition of what public land was immune from distribution (lines 1, 3, 4, 6, 13, 22): *exceptum cavitumve nei divideretur*. On C. Crassus, see Victor, 65; it could be a mistaken reference to P. Crassus who had been a commissioner long before, but it is not easy to see how such an

error could have got into this context.

9. Florus, 2.3; Orosius, 5.12: *maxime legis agrariae causa*; Ampelius, 19.3. Both Gracchi linked fundamentally to land reform, Cicero, *De Officiis*, 2.80 (quoted above, p. 83); *De Lege Agraria*, 1.21; 2.10; *In Catilinam*, 4.4: *C. Gracchus agrarios concitare conatus est*. It is curious that Appian makes no mention of land in his account of Gaius' actual tribunate, having stressed it so much beforehand.

10. Livy, *Per.*, 60: *effecit ut complures coloniae in Italia deducerentur*; Appian, 23; Plutarch, *C.G.*, 6; 8 (Taranto and Capua); 9 (better class of settlers); *Comparison*, 2; Victor, 65 (Taranto and Capua); Velleius, 1.15 (Taranto and Scolacium); Pliny, *N.H.*, 3.99, and Strabo, 6.3.4 (Taranto). On Capua see Cicero, *De Lege Agraria*, 2.81, perhaps exaggerating to make a point. On Fulvius see Fraccaro, *Opuscula*, 2.77, and the Peutinger Table.

11. Bronze Land Law (note 8 above), line 22.

12. Plutarch, *C.G.*, 10. On Lepidus, Livy, 39.55 and 41.13.

13. Legislation firmly dated to 123 (Velleius, 1.15; Orosius, 5.12; Eutropius, 4.21). Livy, *Per.*, 60, Plutarch, *C.G.*, 10, and Appian, 24, are indeterminate, and it is difficult to believe that any controversial Gracchan law was passed in 122.

14. Latin vote, Livy, 25.3. Population estimates from Brunt, *Manpower*. Latin rights discussed in Sherwin White, *Citizenship*, and Badian, *Clientelae*.

15. Appian, 23: τοὺς Λατίνους ἐπὶ πάντα ἐκάλει τὰ ʽΡωμαίων . . .; similarly Plutarch, *C.G.*, 8 and 9; Cicero, *Brutus*, 99: *orationem de sociis et nomine Latino*. Plutarch, *C.G.*, 5 and Velleius, 2.6, are confused accounts rather than evidence of earlier, more sweeping proposals. For Italian excitement, see Appian, 34-5.

16. Livy, 43.3.

17. Bronze Extortion Law, 76-8. Asconius, 3: *ius Latii, ut petendo magistratus civitatem Romanam adipiscerentur*. See Sherwin-White, *J.R.S.*, 1972, 92-6.

18. Plutarch, *C.G.*, 10: θορυβώδης καὶ μισούμενος ὑπὸ τῆς βουλῆς ἄντικρυς; Livy, *Per.*, 61: *socius eiusdem furoris*; Velleius, 2.6: *aeque prava cupientem . . . socium regalis potentiae*.

CHAPTER THIRTEEN — END OF AN ERA

1. Plutarch, *C.G.*, 8.

2. Cicero, *Brutus*, 109; Diodorus, 37.10; Livy, 23.2; Bronze Land Law, line 29; he became consul in 112, censor in 109; Suetonius, *Tiberius*, 3: *patronus senatus*.

3. Appian, 23.

4. Appian, 24, the reference to Fulvius going to Carthage could indicate an earlier visit. In 122 he stayed in Rome (Plutarch, *C.G.*, 10-11).

5. Plutarch, *C.G.*, 8-9; Appian, 23.

6. Gaius called his colony Junonia (Plutarch, *C.G.*, 11; Solinus

27.11). Velleius, 2.6: *novis coloniis replebat provinciis* and 2.7: *extra Italiam colonias posuit* suggest that other settlements abroad were planned. Carthage was the first outside Italy (Velleius, 2.7). For Corinth, see Bronze Land Law, line 96. The Gallic war brought settlements at Aix and Narbonne while Metellus rounded off his Balearic conquests by settling Romans from Spain (? half-breeds) in Palma and Pollentia (Strabo, 3.5.1).

7. Plutarch, *C.G.*, 9; Appian, 24: ὁ δὲ τοῦ δημοκοπήματος ἐκπεσών. Gaius a triumvir, Sallust, *Jugurtha*, 42; Livy, *Per.*, 60.

8. Appian, 24; Bronze Land Law, 60: *neive unius hominis nomine, quoi ex lege Rubria quae fuit colono . . . agrum quei in Africa est dare oportuit licuitve, amplius iug. CC in (singulos ? . . .) data adsignata fuise iudicato*; *Fronto ad Verum*, 2.1; Aerial photographs in Bradford, *Ancient Landscapes*, confirm the 200-acre pattern.

9. Bronze Land Law, 49 ff, confirms and rationalizes tenure of land in Africa. Appian, 24; *Libyan Wars*, 136.

10. Appian, 24; *Libyan Wars*, 135; Zonaras, 9.30; Cicero, *De Lege Agraria*, 1.5, 2.51.

11. Plutarch, *C.G.*, 11; Appian, 24; *Libyan Wars*, 136; Orosius, 5.12; Obsequens, 33.

12. Livy, 1.6.

13. Appian, 24: συνεκάλουν ἐξ ὅλης Ἰταλίας; so Solinus, 27.11: *Carthago colonis Italicis data*. Roman citizens in Eutropius, 4.21 and Orosius, 5.12.

14. Plutarch, *C.G.*, 12; speech *de legibus promulgatis* in *O.R.F.*, 190–2; (frag. 52 as emended by Badian: *quod vinum*). The rapacity of Roman nobles at their allies' expense is endorsed by Diodorus, 34.33.5. Gaius is surely referring to his own son (Plutarch, *C.G.*, 15: τὸ παιδίον) and Tiberius' sons are all dead. Daughters do not count, for Sempronia lived yet, not to mention Cornelia.

15. Sallust, *Ad Caesarem*, 8: *ut ex confusis quinque classibus sorte centuriae vocarentur*. Compare Cicero, *Pro Murena*, 47; *confusionem suffragiorum . . . aequationem gratiae, dignitatis*. Debts, Nonius, 728: *in spem adducebat non plus soluturos quam vellent*.

16. Cicero, *Brutus*, 100; *O.R.F.*, 144–5.

17. Plutarch, *T.G.*, 2; Pliny, *N.H.*, 33.147.

18. Cicero, *Brutus*, 99–100; *O.R.F.*, 143–4: *si Latinis civitatem dederitis . . . nonne illos omnia occupaturos putatis?*

19. Plutarch, *C.G.*, 9. See above, p. 42–3. Sallust, *Jugurtha*, 69, refers to the beating and execution of a junior commander who was a Roman citizen (Appian, *Numidian Wars*, 3). Legal practice not always matched theory away from home.

20. Appian, 23; Plutarch, *C.G.*, 12. For law of 126 see above, p. 121–2.

21. The rejection of his bills is not directly attested, but must immediately follow the decree of Fannius and surely preceded the elections.

CHAPTER FOURTEEN — DAGGERS IN THE FORUM

1. Cicero, *De Finibus*, 4.66: *quae hic rei publicae vulnera imponebat, eadem ille sanabat; Brutus*, 109.
2. Plutarch, *C.G.*, 12.
3. Plutarch, *C.G.*, 12: ὅσον αὐτοῖς σκότος ἐκ τῶν αὐτοῦ περικέχυται πολιτευμάτων; Appian, 35.
4. Plutarch, *C.G.*, 13; Orosius, 5.12; Florus, 2.3; Victor, 65.
5. Appian, 24; Plutarch, *C.G.*, 13.
6. Degrassi, 475, ignoring the speculations of Carcopino since this stone is nothing to do with the Italian land commission. Carthage abandoned, Appian, *Libyan Wars*, 136; Bronze Land Law, 59: *lege Rubria quae fuit*.
7. Cicero, *Brutus*, 128; *Post Reditum in Senatu*, 38, 37; *Ad Quirites*, 11, 6, 9.
8. Cicero, *De Oratore*, 2.106, 165, 170.
9. Sallust, *Jugurtha*, 40; Cicero, *Brutus*, 127-8.
10. For Plautius, see *O.R.F.*, 195.
11. For Tubero, see Cicero, *Brutus*, 117; *De Amicitia*, 37.
12. For Postumius, **see** Plutarch, *T.G.*, 8. For Cato, also Scipio's nephew, see Cicero, *Brutus*, 108; *De Amicitia*, 39. For Metellus, see *O.R.F.*, 194. Scaurus encouraged Opimius, (Victor, 72), and as consul in 115 Scaurus placed a ban on the praetor Decius Subulo, who had unsuccessfully prosecuted Opimius for murder in 120; see Badian, *J.R.S.*, 1956.
13. Scaevola in Justinian, *Digest*, 24.3.66: *Gracchi culpa ea seditio facta esset*.
14. Sallust, *Jugurtha*, 42.
15. Plutarch, *C.G.*, 13; Diodorus, 34.28a; Appian, 24.
16. As above, also Orosius, 5.12; Victor, 65; Florus, 2.3; and similarly from now on.
17. In Diodorus' hostile account, Gaius demands the death of Antyllius; not so in Plutarch (see also *Comparison*, 5) or Appian.
18. Orosius: *signum belli*; Plutarch: ὁ δὲ Ὀπίμιος . . . παρώξυνε τὸν δῆμον ἐπὶ τὴν ἄμυναν. Note on timing: Plutarch begins the action on the Capitol at first light, ἕωθεν ; after the storm the senate is summoned ἅμα δὲ ἡμέρᾳ, here taken to mean 'when it was full day', i.e. later that morning, rather than 'next morning', which would hardly match the consul's sense of urgency.
19. Cicero, *In Catilinam*, 1.4: *uti L. Opimius consul videret ne quid res publica detrimenti caperet*; similar formulae in *Pro Milone*, 70; Sallust, *Catiline*, 29; *speech of Philippus*, 22; different wording in Cicero, *Philippic*, 8.14; Plutarch, *C.G.*, 14: σῴζειν τὴν πόλιν ὅπως δύναιτο καὶ καταλύειν τοὺς τυράννους.
20. Cicero, *Laws*, 3.8: *salus populi suprema lex esto; Pro Milone*, 11: *silent enim leges inter arma nec se exspectari iubent*; 70; *In Catilinam*, 4.10.
21. Cicero, *De Oratore*, 2.132-4; *De Partitione*, 106: *ne sceleratissimum quidem civem sine iudicio iure ullo necare potuisti*.
22. Plutarch, *C.G.*, 14. Cicero, *In Catilinam*, 1.4, claims that no night

intervened, but should be disbelieved in view of Plutarch's detailed account. Cicero was only trying to hurry up the senate of his day.

23. Plutarch, *C.G.*, 15. No brother is known, so perhaps a cousin is meant, such as L. Crassus, the brilliant orator who in his youth showed strong Gracchan sympathies, prosecuting Carbo and founding the colony of Narbonne. Licinia could hardly go to the house of her diehard step-father Brutus. The senate summoned Gaius for having disrupted a tribune's meeting in the forum (Victor, 65).

24. Gracchan slaves, Florus, Victor. Offer of freedom, Appian, Orosius. Opimius' slaves, Plutarch, Ampelius 26. Temple of Diana, Appian, Orosius, later in Plutarch.

25. Metellus, Lentulus and many others, Cicero, *Philippic*, 8.14; *In Catilinam*, 4.14; Valerius, 5.3.2f. Brutus, Orosius and Ampelius, 19, 26.

26. Tactical details in Orosius. Lentulus lived to go into exile (Valerius 5.3.2f).

27. Alternative versions in Plutarch, *C.G.*, 16; Appian, 26; Orosius, 5.12. Or they were strangled while rallying the troops (Velleius, 2.6). Cicero, *De Domo*, 102, Livy, *Per.*, 61 and Diodorus, 34.29–30, also refer.

28. Plutarch, *C.G.*, 16; *Comparison*, 4: ὅλως πλείονα τοῦ μή τι δρᾶσαι πρόνοιαν ἢ τοῦ μὴ παθεῖν ἔχων ἑωρᾶτο (a Socratic as well as a Stoic precept); Orosius, 5.12 (temple of Minerva). Gaius' last speech, Cicero, *De Oratore*, 3.214: *quo me miser conferam? quo vortam? in Capitoliumne? at fratris sanguine redundat. an domum? matremne ut miseram lamentantem videam et abiectam?* Also *O.R.F.*, 196; imitated by e.g. Cicero, *Pro Murena*, 88.

29. Gaius crippled, see Victor, 65: *talum intorsit*; Orosius, 5.12: *aegre pervenit*. Pomponius was a Roman knight (Velleius, 2.6) and held the gate (Victor and Valerius, 4.7.2); P. Laetorius, named Licinius in Plutarch, held the bridge until overpowered, then stabbed himself and leapt into the river (Valerius and Victor). Velleius gives the bridge scene to Pomponius, Plutarch to them both.

20. Appian, Velleius, Orosius, Diodorus, 34.29. Valerius, 6.8.3. Alternatively he may have died at his own or his enemies' hand (Victor, Plutarch). The slave may have been called Euporus or Euphorus (Valerius, Velleius, Victor). On the grove of Furina, see Cicero, *De Natura Deorum*, 3.46.

31. Plutarch, *C.G.*, 17; Septimuleius came from Anagnia (in Latium) (Cicero, *De Oratore*, 2.269); he was called Vitellius (Diodorus, 34.29); and had been a friend of Gaius (Valerius, 9.4.3, Diodorus, Victor); gold was given for Fulvius' head too (Appian, 26). See also Pliny, *N.H.*, 33.48; Orosius, Florus; Livy; Obsequens, 33.

32. Plutarch; Appian; Orosius: *consul sicut in bello fortis fuit ita in quaestione crudelis* (but Gaius' headless corpse was sent to

Cornelia in Misenum); Velleius, 2.6–7: *mira crudelitate...
crudeles quaestiones... visa ultio privato odio magis quam
publicae vindictae data*; Cicero, *De Domo*, 102. For Scaevola and
Licinia, see note 13 above.

33. Velleius, 2.7 (the boy was only 17); Plutarch; Appian; Orosius.
Gaius' friend Herennius died in similar fashion (Valerius, 9.12.6).

34. Plutarch, *C.G.*, 18–19; Seneca, *Ad Helviam*, 16.6.

CHAPTER FIFTEEN — THE FATAL LEGACY

1. Plutarch, *C.G.*, 17; Appian, 26; Cicero, *Pro Sestio*, 140;
Augustine, *City of God*, 3.24–5; Degrassi, 827–8; Varro, *L.L.*,
5.156; Obsequens, 34 (possibly relating to 121). The founding of
the temple, Plutarch, *Camillus*, 42).

2. Marius was consul 107, 104–100, and 86; Sulla dictator 81–79;
Pompey and Crassus were consuls in 70 and 55; Caesar consul in
59, returned from Gaul to launch civil war in 49, died in 44; after
the defeat of Antony, Augustus formally established the
constitutional basis of empire in 27.

3. Cicero, *De Oratore*, 1.38: *eloquentissimos audisse Ti. et C.
Sempronios... diserti et omnibus vel naturae vel doctrinae
praesidiis ad dicendum parati*; *De Officiis*, 2.43; *De Provinciis
Consularibus*, 18; (above, p.   ). Other citations for eloquence
collected in *O.R.F.*

4. Cicero, *Pro Fonteio*, 39: *nostrorum longe ingeniosissimi atque
eloquentissimi*; *De Haruspicum Responsis*, 41: *secutus est C.
Gracchus: quo ingenio, qua eloquentia, quanta vi, quanta
gravitate dicendi, ut dolerent boni...* ; Cicero, *De Legibus*, 3.20:
*C. vero Gracchi ruinis et iis sicis, quas ipse se proiecisse in forum
dixit, quibus digladiarentur inter se cives*; *De Finibus*, 4.66
(above, p.   ).

5. Livy, *Per.*, 58, 60, 61; Orosius, 5.10.10: *scelerata familia ad
perniciem patriae suae nata*; 5.12: *C. Gracchus... magna
reipublicae pernicies*; Dio, 25, frag. 85.3: ἐπίφθονος
καὶ τοῖς στασιώταις; 'Cicero' (authorship dubious) *ad
Herennium* 4.38: *tumultus domesticos et intestinos*; 4.22; 4.42.

6. Cicero, *De Officiis*, 2.43 (above, p.   ); *Pro Plancio*, 88: *quibus
ducibus improbos cives res publica vicit armatis*; *De Oratore*,
2.165: *si consul est, qui consulit patriae, quid aluid fecit
Opimius?*; 2.169; Valerius, 6.3.1d: *viguit in nostra civitate
summa nobilitas ac spes amplissima. sed quia statum civitatis
conati erant convellere, insepulta cadavera iacuerunt.*

7. Florus, 2.5: *bicipitem ex una fecerant civitatem*; Cicero,
Republic, 1.31; Varro, in Nonius Marcellus, 728; (above, pp.
and   ).

8. Livy, 9.46: *in duas partes discessit civitas; aliud integer populus,
fautor et cultor bonorum, aliud forensis factio tenebat*; similarly
Sallust, *Jugurtha*, 41: *omnia in duas partis abstracta sunt, res
publica dilacerata*; and Cicero, *Pro Sestio*, 96: *duo genera semper
in hac civitate*; (above, pp.   and   ).

9. Florus, 2.1-2: *species aequitatis*; Cicero, *In Catilinam*, 1.3-4; Sallust, *Jugurtha*, 16, 42, 31, 5: *tunc primum superbiae nobilitatis obviam itum est*; a similar interpretation is quoted in Cicero, *Ad Herennium*, 4.31.

10. Machiavelli, *Discourses*, 1.37; Appian, 17 (above, p. 97); Velleius, 2.7.1; Sallust, *Jugurtha*, 42: *et sane Gracchis cupidine victoriae haud satis moderatus animus fuit*.

11. Appian, 27: νόμου ἀρίστου καὶ ὠφελιμωτάτου, εἰ ἐδύνατο πραχθῆναι; Plutarch, *Comparison*, 5.4-5. The Gracchi went too far in trying to serve their countrymen (Plutarch, *Agis*, 2.4); but if only the two brothers had come to prominence together then their joint power would have been irresistible (Plutarch, *T.G.*, 3).

12. Appian, 32-3; Valerius, 3.8.6; 9.7.1; 9.15.1; Victor, 62, 73; etc.

13. Cicero, *Ad Herennium*, 4.67: *inulti iacent Gracchi*; *Pro Sestio*, 140; Velleius, 2.7.

14. Tacitus, *Annals*, 1.53; 4.13; 6.16; 6.38. A Sempronia, talented but unchaste wife of D. Brutus (consul 77), figures briefly in the conspiracy of Catiline; so do two Fulvii, while a Fulvia helped to undermine it (Sallust, *Catiline*, 17, 23, 25, 26, 28, 39, 40). On L. Caesar, see Cicero, *In Catilinam*, 4.13.

LISTS OF CONSULS
AND OTHER SENIOR MAGISTRATES

These lists, and the family trees that follow, illustrate the remarkable continuity of the great Roman families and, in particular, the relative dominance around 215 and again around 179 of the families associated with the Gracchan movement: Claudius, Fulvius, Mucius, Licinius, and, less conspicuously, Alerius, Sulpicius and Hostilius.

Censors are shown in CAPITALS.

Dictators and masters of cavalry are in *italics*, and marked 'd' or 'mc'.

Where more than two consuls are shown the others are replacements in cases of death or voided elections.

A man's second and later consulates are marked 'ii', 'iii', etc.

Forenames are abbreviated as follows:

A.	Aulus	L.	Lucius	Ser.	Servius
Ap.	Appius	M.	Marcus	Sex.	Sextus
C.	Gaius	M'.	Manius	Sp.	Spurius
Cn.	Gnaeus	P.	Publius	T.	Titus
D.	Decimus	Q.	Quintus	Ti.	Tiberius

			(I)		*216–209*	
216		C.	Terentius	Varro		*(Battle of*
		L.	Aemilius	Paullus ii		*Cannae)*
	d	*M.*	*Iunius*	*Pera*		
	mc	*Ti.*	*Sempronius*	*Gracchus*		
	d	*M.*	*Fabius*	*Buteo*		
215		L.	Postumius	Albinus	iii	
		Ti.	Sempronius	Gracchus		
		M.	Claudius	Marcellus	ii	
		Q.	Fabius	Maximus	iii	
214		Q.	Fabius	Maximus	iv	
		M.	Claudius	Marcellus	iii	
		M.	ATILIUS	REGULUS		
		P.	FURIUS	PHILUS		

213		Q.	Fabius	Maximus
		Ti.	Sempronius	Gracchus ii
	d	*C.*	*Claudius*	*Centho*
	mc	*Q.*	*Fulvius*	*Flaccus*
212		Q.	Fulvius	Flaccus iii
		Ap.	Claudius	Pulcher
211		Cn.	Fulvius	Centumalus Maximus
		P.	Sulpicius	Galba Maximus
210		M.	Claudius	Marcellus iv
		M.	Valerius	Laevinus ii
	d	*Q.*	*Fulvius*	*Flaccus*
	mc	*P.*	*Licinius*	*Crassus Dives*
		L.	VETURIUS	PHILO
		P.	LICINIUS	CRASSUS DIVES
209		Q.	Fabius	Maximus v
		Q.	Fulvius	Flaccus iv
		P.	SEMPRONIUS	TUDITANUS
		M.	CORNELIUS	CETHEGUS
		(II)		*180-174*
180		A.	Postumius	Albinus
		C.	Calpurnius	Piso
		Q.	·Fulvius	Flaccus
179		Q.	Fulvius	Flaccus
		L.	Manlius	Acidinus Fulvianus
		M.	AEMILIUS	LEPIDUS
		M.	FULVIUS	NOBILIOR
178		M.	Iunius	Brutus
		A.	Manlius	Vulso
177		C.	Claudius	Pulcher
		Ti.	Sempronius	Gracchus
176		Cn.	Cornelius	Scipio Hispallus
		Q˙	Petillius	Spurinus
		C.	Valerius	Laevinus
175		P.	Mucius	Scaevola
		M.	Aemilius	Lepidus ii
174		Sp.	Postumius	Albinus Paullulus
		Q.	Mucius	Scaevola
		Q.	FULVIUS	FLACCUS
		A.	POSTUMIUS	ALBINUS

		III	*147-121*
147	P.	Cornelius	Scipio Africanus Aemilianus
	C.	Livius	Drusus
	L.	CORNELIUS	LENTULUS LUPUS
	L.	MARCIUS	CENSORINUS
146	Cn.	Cornelius	Lentulus *(Carthage &*
	L.	Mummius	Achaicus *Corinth destroyed)*
145	Q.	Fabius	Maximus Aemilianus
	L.	Hostilius	Mancinus
144	Ser.	Sulpicius	Galba
	L.	Aurelius	Cotta
143	Ap.	Claudius	Pulcher
	Q.	Caecilius	Metellus Macedonicus
142	L.	Caecilius	Metellus Calvus
	Q.	Fabius	Maximus Servilianus
	P.	CORNELIUS	SCIPIO AFRICANUS AEMILIANUS
	L.	MUMMIUS	ACHAICUS
141	Cn.	Servilius	Caepio
	Q.	Pompeius	
140	C.	Laelius	Sapiens
	Q.	Servilius	Caepio
139	Cn.	Calpurnius	Piso
	M.	Popillius	Laenas
138	P.	Cornelius	Scipio Nasica Serapio
	D.	Iunius	Brutus Callaicus
137	M.	Aemilius	Lepidus Porcina *(Ti. Gracchus*
	C.	Hostilius	Mancinus *quaestor)*
136	L.	Furius	Philus
	Sex.	Atilius	Serranus
	AP.	CLAUDIUS	PULCHER
	Q.	FULVIUS	NOBILIOR
135	Ser.	Fulvius	Flaccus
	Q.	Calpurnius	Piso
134	P.	Cornelius	Scipio Africanus Aemilianus ii
	C.	Fulvius	Flaccus
133	P.	Mucius	Scaevola *(Ti. Gracchus*
	L.	Calpurnius	Piso Frugi *tribune)*

132	P.	Popillius	Laenas	
	P.	Rupilius		
131	P.	Licinius	Crassus Dives Mucianus	
	L.	Valerius	Flaccus	
	Q.	CAECILIUS	METELLUS MACEDONICUS	
	Q.	POMPEIUS		
130	L.	Cornelius	Lentulus	
	M.	Perperna		
	Ap.	Claudius	Pulcher	
129	C.	Sempronius	Tuditanus	*(Death of*
	M'.	Aquillius		*Scipio)*
128	Cn.	Octavius		
	T.	Annius	Rufus	
127	L.	Cassius	Longinus Ravilla	
	L.	Cornelius	Cinna	
126	M.	Aemilius	Lepidus	*(C. Gracchus*
	L.	Aurelius	Orestes	*quaestor)*
125	M.	Plautius	Hypsaeus	
	M.	Fulvius	Flaccus	
	CN.	SERVILIUS	CAEPIO	
	L.	CASSIUS	LONGINUS RAVILLA	
124	C.	Cassius	Longinus	
	C.	Sextius	Calvinus	
123	Q.	Caecilus	Metellus Baliaricus	*(C. Gracchus tribune)*
	T.	Quinctius	Flamininus	
122	Cn.	Domitius	Ahenobarbus	*(C. Gracchus tribune ii)*
	C.	Fannius		
121	L.	Opimius		
	Q.	Fabius	Maximus Allobrogicus	
		IV	*Praetors for 215 and 179*	
215	Ap.	Claudius	Pulcher	
	Q.	Fulvius	Flaccus	
	Q.	Mucius	Scaevola	
	M.	Valerius	Laevinus	
179	Cn.	Cornelius	Scipio Hispallus	
	P.	Mucius	Scaevola	

| Q. | Mucius | Scaevola |
| C. | Valerius | Laevinus |

THE GRACCHAN FAMILIES

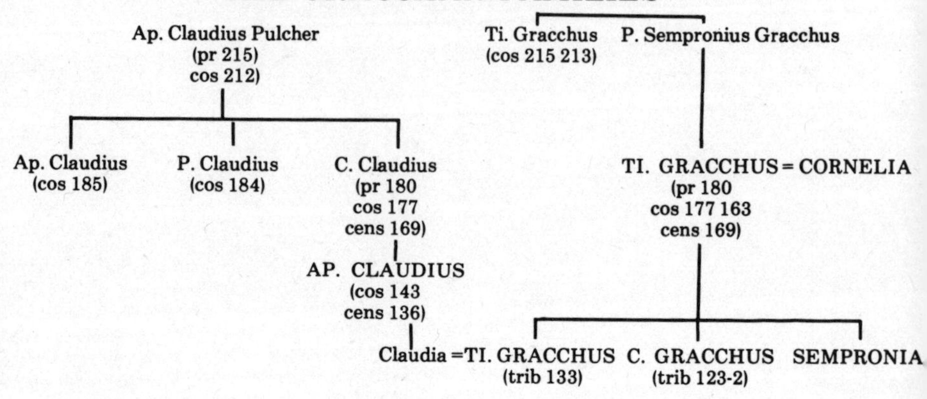

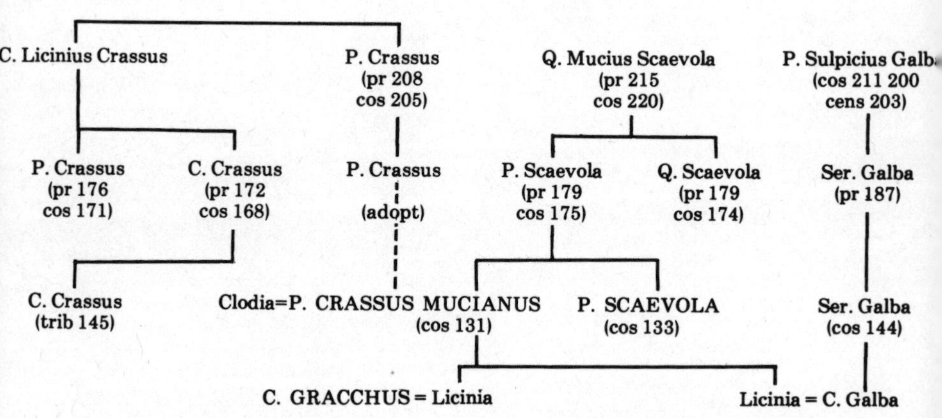

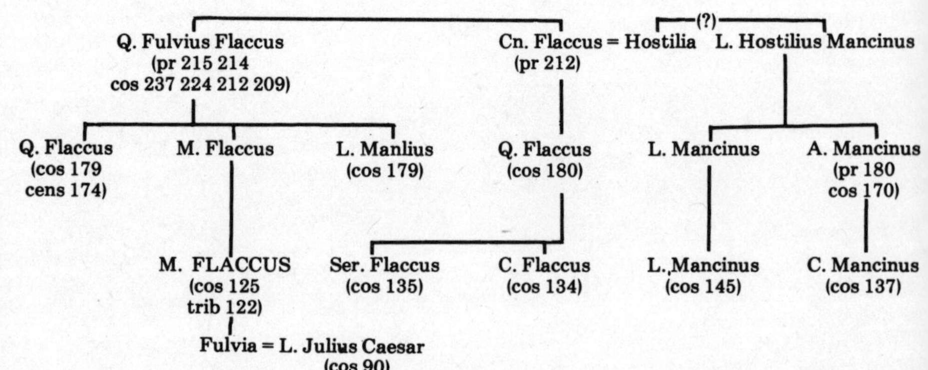

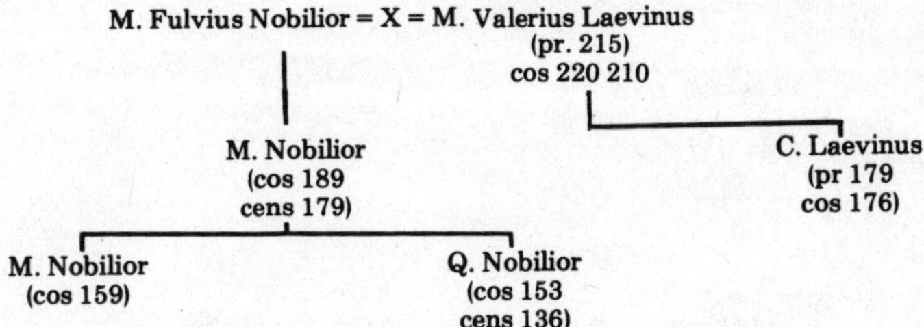

M. Fulvius Nobilior = X = M. Valerius Laevinus
(pr. 215)
cos 220 210

M. Nobilior
(cos 189
cens 179)

C. Laevinus
(pr 179
cos 176)

M. Nobilior
(cos 159)

Q. Nobilior
(cos 153
cens 136)

THE SCIPIO FAMILIES

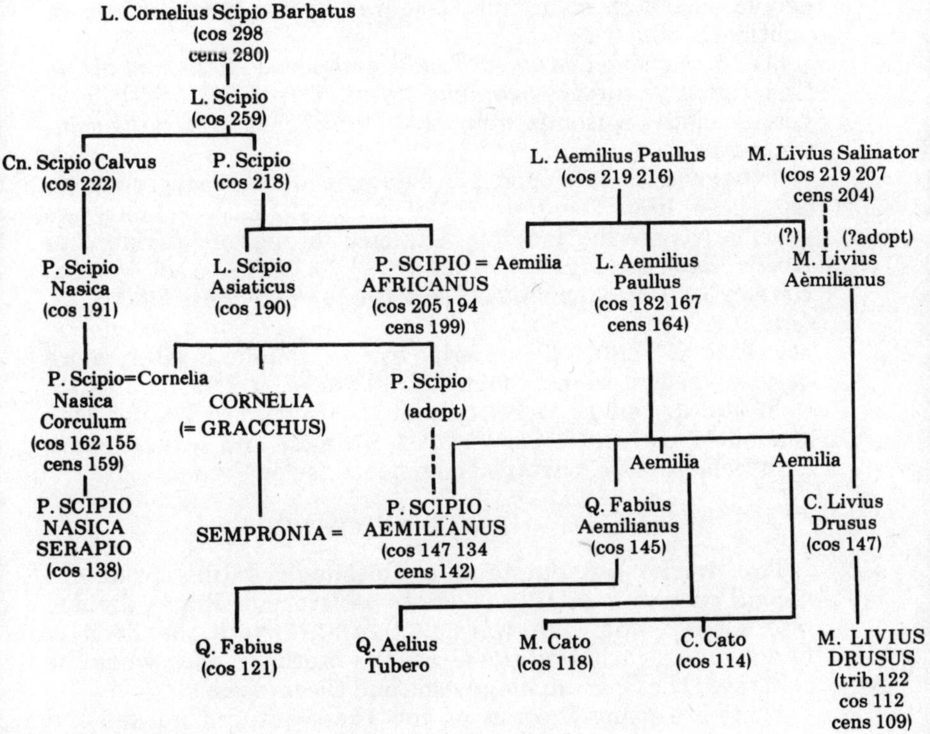

L. Cornelius Scipio Barbatus
(cos 298
cens 280)

L. Scipio
(cos 259)

Cn. Scipio Calvus
(cos 222)

P. Scipio
(cos 218)

L. Aemilius Paullus
(cos 219 216)

M. Livius Salinator
(cos 219 207
cens 204)

(?)   (?adopt)

P. Scipio
Nasica
(cos 191)

L. Scipio
Asiaticus
(cos 190)

P. SCIPIO = Aemilia
AFRICANUS
(cos 205 194
cens 199)

L. Aemilius
Paullus
(cos 182 167
cens 164)

M. Livius
Aèmilianus

P. Scipio=Cornelia
Nasica
Corculum
(cos 162 155
cens 159)

CORNELIA
(= GRACCHUS)

P. Scipio
(adopt)

Aemilia   Aemilia

P. SCIPIO
NASICA
SERAPIO
(cos 138)

SEMPRONIA =

P. SCIPIO
AEMILIANUS
(cos 147 134
cens 142)

Q. Fabius
Aemilianus
(cos 145)

C. Livius
Drusus
(cos 147)

Q. Fabius
(cos 121)

Q. Aelius
Tubero

M. Cato
(cos 118)

C. Cato
(cos 114)

M. LIVIUS
DRUSUS
(trib 122
cos 112
cens 109)

SELECT BIBLIOGRAPHY

I—LATIN WRITERS

CICERO, advocate and statesman in the first century B.C., wrote speeches and treatises on politics, philosophy and rhetoric which contain countless vivid references to historic events and people, although sometimes coloured by his own forensic or political needs.

LIVY'S massive history of Rome, composed at the end of the first century, survives complete from 218 to 167, with later years briefly epitomized in the *Periochae* and *Oxyrhynchus* summaries.

CATO and VARRO portray the agricultural background to republican life. The histories of SALLUST and VELLEIUS are valuable, as are the anecdotes scattered through the *Memorable Deeds and Sayings* of VALERIUS MAXIMUS, the *Natural History* of the elder PLINY, and the *Attic Nights* of AULUS GELLIUS.

Useful, if confused, material can be found in later, more derivative historians, such as FLORUS, OROSIUS, JUSTIN, OBSEQUENS and EUTROPIUS, and the *Lives of Famous Men* attributed to AURELIUS VICTOR. ASCONIUS and several much later Scholiasts left detailed commentaries on Cicero.

II—GREEK WRITERS

Two works are outstanding, although dating from the second century A.D. APPIAN wrote a history of Rome, divided into foreign and civil wars. PLUTARCH wrote the lives of famous men, including the Gracchus brothers, with whom he compared the Spartan kings Agis and Cleomenes.

There are many theories of how these authors worked and what primary sources they used. Appian is more 'serious', and it used to be fashionable among scholars to prefer his account to Plutarch's whenever they clashed. But in fact many discrepancies can be attributed to their totally different interests. Both were very selective and sometimes quite confused about the facts or their significance. It is often impossible to accept either account as it stands, and necessary to hunt for some bedrock of fact by judging each case on its merits. Plutarch's other essays and studies sometimes help.

POLYBIUS gives an almost eye-witness account of how second-century Rome came to power; his history is carefully observed and quite fascinating in its detail. There are important fragments of the histories of DIODORUS (first century B.C.), the later DIO CASSIUS, and his Byzantine epitomist ZONARAS. STRABO'S geography is a mine of information.

III—OTHER SOURCE MATERIAL

BROUGHTON, *Magistrates of the Roman Republic*, collects full lists of magistrates in every year, from written work and inscriptions, and gives references for all their known activities.

MALCOVATI, *Oratorum Romanorum Fragmenta* (cited by page as *O.R.F.*) collects all known passages of speeches made by the Gracchi, Scipio Aemilianus, and many lesser figures.

DEGRASSI, *Inscriptiones Latinae Liberae Rei Publicae*, is the most useful collection of Latin inscriptions. The old and many-volumed *Corpus Inscriptionum Latinarum (C.I.L.)*, especially the second edition of volume one, is the basic collection. WARMINGTON'S *Archaic Inscriptions* (Loeb Classical Library: Remains of Old Latin, IV) gives translations and texts of many inscriptions, including the bronze land and extortion laws.

SHERK, *Roman Documents from the Greek East*, is the most modern selection of relevant Greek inscriptions. DITTENBERGER'S *Sylloge Inscriptionum Graecarum (S.I.G.)*, the *Orientis Graeci Inscriptiones Selectae (O.G.I.S.)*, and many other specialized collections are also important.

CRAWFORD, *Roman Republican Coinage*, is the most modern and comprehensive collection and interpretation of Roman coins.

GREENIDGE and CLAY, *Sources for Roman History, 133-70 B.C.* (cited *G. & C.*) conveniently collects many relevant passages from Greek and Latin authors, and some inscriptions and coins. LEWIS and REINHOLD, *Roman Civilisation Sourcebook*, gives much of the ancient evidence in translation.

IV—MODERN BOOKS

Cambridge Ancient History, viii, 218-133, ix, 133-44; the
  fullest general history but old-fashioned in approach.
SCULLARD, *Roman World, 753-146*, modern and reliable.
MARSH, *Roman World, 146-30* (revised by Scullard).

SCULLARD, *From the Gracchi to Nero.*

BRUNT, *Social Conflicts in the Roman Republic;* the most illuminating short history.

GELZER, *The Roman Nobility* (translated by Seager); an epoch-making analysis.

SHERWIN-WHITE, *The Roman Citizenship.*

TAYLOR, *Roman Voting Assemblies.*

TAYLOR, *Party Politics in the Age of Caesar;* stimulating and useful for the Gracchan period.

NICOLET, *L'ordre Equestre à l'Époque Républicaine;* the most detailed survey of the knights.

HILL, *The Roman Middle Class.*

SMITH, *The Failure of the Roman Republic.*

FRANK, *Economic Survey of Ancient Rome,* i.

HEICHELHEIM, *Ancient Economic History,* iii.

BADIAN, *Publicans and Sinners;* trenchant examination of the capitalists and their political role.

BADIAN, *Roman Imperialism in the Late Republic.*

BADIAN, *Foreign Clientelae (264-70);* the political impact of foreign and Italian affairs.

BRUNT, *Italian Manpower (225-14).*

MAGIE, *Roman Rule in Asia Minor.*

SCULLARD, *Scipio Africanus, Soldier and Politician.*

LIDDELL HART, *A Greater than Napoleon: Scipio Africanus.*

SCULLARD, *Roman Politics (220-150).*

TOYNBEE, *Hannibal's Legacy.*

ASTIN, *Scipio Aemilianus;* detailed modern narrative, including the crisis of Tiberius Gracchus.

GRUEN, *Roman Politics and the Criminal Courts (149-78).*

BOREN, *The Gracchi;* a useful short biography.

EARL, *Tiberius Gracchus, a Study in Politics;* excellent on personalities.

NICOLET, *Les Gracques, Crise Agraire et Révolution à Rome;* excellent on economic and ideological background.

CARCOPINO, *Autour des Gracques* (with appendix by Nicolet); highly controversial but stimulating study of special problems, notably land and colonies.

RIDDLE, *Tiberius Gracchus, Destroyer or Reformer of the Republic;* excerpts from ancient and modern comments.

SEAGER, *The Crisis of the Roman Republic;* invaluable collection of important articles (some mentioned below).

WALBANK, *Historical Commentary on Polybius.*

GABBA, *Appian Civil Wars,* modern edition with notes.

LUGLI, *Itinerario di Roma Antica;* latest and fullest guide to the city's topography.

V—SOME IMPORTANT ARTICLES

TAYLOR, 'Forerunners to the Gracchi' (*Journal of Roman Studies,* 1962).

LINTOTT, 'Imperial Expansion and Moral Decline in the Roman Republic' (*Historia,* 1972).

CRAWFORD, 'Money and Exchange in the Roman World' (*J.R.S.,* 1970).

BADIAN, 'From the Gracchi to Sulla'; review of historical work done 1940-59 (Seager's *Crisis*).

BOREN, 'The Urban Side of the Gracchan Economic Crisis' (Seager's *Crisis*).

BADIAN, 'Tiberius Gracchus and the Beginning of the Roman Revolution'; the most important individual study (*Aufstieg und Niedergang der Römischen Welt*).

BRISCOE, 'Supporters and Opponents of Tiberius Gracchus' (*J.R.S.,* 1974).

NAGLE, 'The Failure of the Roman Political Process in 133' (*Athenaeum,* 1970-1).

SHOCHAT, 'The Lex Agraria of 133' (*Athenaeum,* 1970).

TAYLOR, 'Was Tiberius Gracchus' Last Assembly Electoral or Legislative?' (*Athenaeum,* 1963, with further discussion by Earl and Taylor in 1965 and 1966).

GRUEN, 'The Political Allegiance of P. Mucius Scaevola (*Athenaeum,* 1965).

MATTINGLY, 'The Date of the S.C. de Agro Pergameno (*American Journal of Philology,* 1972).

BRUNT, 'The Equites in the Late Republic'; a penetrating analysis (Seager's *Crisis*).

BALSDON, 'The History of the Extortion Court at Rome, 123-70' (Seager's *Crisis*).

BADIAN, 'Lex Acilia Repetundarum' (*A.J.P.,* 1954).

MATTINGLY 'The Two Republican Laws of the Tabula Bembina'; new text and discussion of the bronze land and extortion laws (*J.R.S.,* 1969-70).

SHERWIN-WHITE, 'The Date of the Lex Repetundarum and its Consequences' (*J.R.S.,* 1972).

EWINS, 'Ne Quis Iudicio Circumveniatur' (*J.R.S.,* 1960).

HALL, 'Appian, Plutarch and the Elections of 123' (*Athenaeum,* 1972).

N.B.; the above books and articles will give ample reference to earlier studies.

INDEX OF PERSONS

(Romans are normally listed by family NAMES, then surnames, then dates. Offices held are abbreviated: dict., cens., cos., pr., trib., for dictator, censor, consul, praetor, tribune. Also P.M. for high priest (*pontifex maximus*) and P.S. for leader of the senate (*princeps senatus*). Forenames abbreviated as on p. 229. Tiberius and Gaius Gracchus are cited as T.G. and C.G.; Scipio Aemilianus as Scipio. The index covers the text only.

ACILIUS
M'.— Glabrio (trib. ? 133): 148-9.
AELIUS
— (Aelian and Fufian laws, c. 147): 43.
Q. — Tubero (Scipio's nephew): 78, 181.
Aemilia (m. Scipio Africanus): 29.
Aemilianus: see Cornelius, Fabius.
AEMILIUS
M. — Lepidus (cos. 187, 175, P.M. 180-52, P.S. 179-52): 161.
M. — Lepidus Porcina (cos. 137): 48-9.
M. — Lepidus (cos. 78): 194.
L. — Paullus (cos. 219, 216): fell at Cannae, 29, 166.
L. — Paullus (cos. 182, 168): victor of Pydna, 6, 25-6, 29, 32, 41-2, 44, 49, 103
M. — Scaurus (cos. 115, P.S. 115): 181.
Agis IV (king of Sparta 244-1): 82-3.
Alexander the Great (king of Macedon 336-23): 4, 14, 16, 19, 50.
Andriscus (rebel 149-8): 29.
ANNIUS
T. — Luscus (cos. 153): opposes T.G., 77-8, 105.
T. — Rufus (cos. 128): land reform, 105.
Antiochus III the Great (king of Syria 223-187): 16-18, 32.
Antiochus IV Epiphanes (king of Syria 175-63): 3-4.
Antipater of Tarsus (Stoic philosopher c. 133): 81.
ANTIUS
M. — Briso (trib. 137): 48, 68.
ANTONIUS
M. — ('Mark Antony', cos. 44, 34): 100, 152.
Antyllius (died 121): 183-4.
APPULEIUS
L. — Saturninus (trib. 103, 100): 198.
AQUILLIUS
M'.— (cos. 129): Asian settlement, trial, 126, 145, 151-2, 180.
Ariarathes V (king of Cappadocia 163-130): 107.
Aristonicus (Pergamene rebel 133-0): 77, 102, 108.
Attalus III (king of Pergamum 138-3): bequest to Rome, 75-6, 84-5, 94, 102-3, 107.
Augustus (C. Octavius, 'Octavian', emperor 31-14 A.D.): ix-x, 68, 96, 195-6.
AURELIUS
L. — Cotta (cos. 144): 45, 180.
L. — Orestes (cos. 126): in Sardinia, 118, 122, 125.
M. — (emperor 161-80 A.D.): 130.
Blossius of Cumae (Gracchan philosopher): 2, 59, 77, 80-1, 92, 102.
Brutus: see Junius.

CAECILIUS
L. — Metellus (cos. 251, 247): 133.
Q. — Metellus Macedonicus (cos. 143): at war, 29, 31, 34, 42, 50; and Scipio, 46, 49-50, 107, 110, 115; and T.G., 77-8; censor (131), 78, 104, 107; and Asia 121; opposes C.G., 180, 188.
Q. — Metellus Baliaricus (cos. 123): 133.
L. — Metellus (cos. 119 or 117): 181.
Caepio: see Servilius.
CALPURNIUS
L. — Bestia (cos. 111): anti-Grachan 179-81.
Q. — Piso (cos. 135): 48.
L. — Piso Frugi (trib. 149, cos. 133): 33, 49; extortion law, 44, 88, 144, 146; consul, 50, 52; opposes C.G., 135, 180.
Caracalla (emperor 211-7 A.D.): 163.
Carbo: see Papirius.
Carneades (philosopher c. 155): 32, 81.
CASSIUS
L. — Longinus Ravilla (trib. 137, cos. 127): voting law, 47-9, 68; censor, 125.
Claudia (sister to P. Claudius, cos. 249): 20.
Claudia (m. T.G.): 41, 46.
Claudia (or Clodia, m. Crassus and Brutus): 41, 114, 180.
CLAUDIUS
Ti. — Asellus (trib. 140): opposes

Caepio and Scipio, 47.
Ap. — Caecus (cos. 307, 296): 45.
Ap. — Centho (pr. 175): 24.
M. — Marcellus (cos. 166, 155, 152): 34.
C. — Nero (cos. 207): victor of Metaurus, 13-14.
Ti. — Nero (cos. 202): 15.
Ap. — Pulcher (cos. 212): 13.
C. — Pulcher (cos. 177): 23, 41; censor (169) and knights, 24-5, 27, 143.
Ap. — Pulcher (cos. 143, P.S. 136): Gracchan leader, 41, 45, 47, 49, 58, 60; opposes Scipio, 45-6, 104; censor (136), 52; augur, 60; land commissioner, 73, 104; candidate again (133), 85-6, 102; and Licinia, 114; dies, 107.
Ap. — Pulcher (cos. 130): 108.
Clausus, Attius (Ap. Claudius Sabinus, cos. 495): 45.
Cleomenes III (king of Sparta 235-19): 82-3.
Clodia: (see Claudia).
Cornelia (mother of Gracchi): 1, 2, 22, 28-9; and C.G., 114, 130-1, 182; and Scipio, 115; later life, 191, 198.
CORNELIUS
P. — Lentulus (cos. 162, P.S. 125): 126; opposes C.G., 180, 188-9.
L. — Lentulus Lupus (cos. 156, P.S. 131): 107.
L. — Scipio Barbatus (cos. 298): 12.
L. — Scipio (cos. 259): 12.
P. — Scipio (cos. 218): 13.
P. — Scipio Africanus (cos. 205, 194, P.S. 199-83): 1, 3-5, 12-19, 31, 79, 118, 124, 191; victor of Zama (202), 15; trials, 18-19, 68; and Gracchus, 21-2, 25; and Aemilianus, 29.
L. — Scipio Asiaticus (cos. 190): victor of Magnesia (190), 16-18; trial, 18.
P. — Scipio (augur): 29, 80.
P. — Scipio Africanus Aemilianus (cos. 147, 134): family, 6, 19, 26, 29, 115, 166; in Spain and Africa (151-48): 29, 34, 42; consul, sacks Carthage (146), 28-32, 42-3, 72; political activity (to 137), 44-9, 90; friends, 37, 45, 49, 78, 102, 138, 181; enemies, 45-9, 104, 107, 110; and Numantine affair, 37-9; consul again, sacks Numantia (133), 37, 48, 51, 72, 76, 86, 103, 114; hostile to Gracchans (133-1), 97, 100, 105-6, 108; champions Italians, 109-12; 'dictator', 110, 112, 185; death (129), 112, 115-6, 128; knights, 120; aftermath, 116-7, 124, 159, 167.
P. — Scipio Nasica Corculum (cos. 162, 155, P.M. 150-41, P.S. 147-41):

26, 31-2.
P. — Scipio Nasica Serapio (cos. 138, P.M. 141-33): 47, 49, 52; opposes T.G., 73-4, 78, 94-6, 101, 182, 185, 197; exiled, dies, 101-3, 106.
L. — Sulla (dict. 81-79): 128, 194.
Crassus: see Licinius.
CURIATUS
C. — (trib. 138): corn and levy disputes, 47, 51-2.
CURIUS
M'. — Dentatus (cos. 290, 275, 274): 5.

DECIUS
P. — Subulo (trib. 120): prosecutes Opimius, 186.
Diogenes of Babylon (Stoic philosopher c. 155): 81.
Diophanes of Mytilene (tutor of T.G.): 2, 80, 102.
Drusus: see Livius.
Eudemus (Pergamene ambassador, 133): 76-7.
Eumenes II (king of Pergamum 197-59): 18, 22, 76.

FABIUS
Q. — Maximus Verrucosus ('Cunctator', cos. 233, 228, 215, 214, 209, P.S. 209-3): 5, 15.
Q. — Maximus Aemilianus (cos. 145): 6, 34, 43, 45, 49.
Q. — Maximus Servilianus (cos. 142): 34, 46.
Q. — Maximus Allobrogicus (cos. 121): 115, 133, 156; consul 171, 173, 178-9.
FANNIUS
C. — (cos. 122): 28, 138-9, 162; and C.G., 166, 173-6, 178, 180.
M. — (coinage officer, ? 123): 159.
Flamininus: see Quinctius.
FLAMINIUS
C. — (trib. 232, cos. 223, 217): 30, 142.
FUFIUS
— (Fufian law, c. 147): 43.
FULVIUS
Q. — Flaccus (cos. 179): 22-3.
Ser. — Flaccus (cos. 135): 52.
C. — Flaccus (cos. 134): 50, 52.
M. — Flaccus (cos. 125, trib. 122): Gracchan leader, 41, 93, 101, 108, 121, 125, 128; and Scipio, 106, 112, 115, 169; land commissioner, 108, 159; consul, franchise bill, 88, 121-5, 164-5, 175; in Gaul, 123, 126, 128, 138, 157, 161, 187; supports C. G., 147, 165, 178, 181; tribune, new franchise bill, 138-9, 162-5; against Drusus, 167-71, 176; Carthage dispute, 171, 179, 182-4; last

preparations, 186-7; death 187-91, 197; son-in-law, 199.
Q. — Flaccus (son of last): 188, 191.
M. — Nobilior (cos. 189): 22.
Q. — Nobilior (cos. 153): 44, 52, 69.
FURIUS
L. — Philus (cos. 136): 37, 48.

GABINIUS
A. — (trib. 139): voting law, 47.
Galba: see Sulpicius.
Gracchus: see Sempronius.
Hannibal (Carthaginian general, 221-202); 1, 4-6, 9, 12-16, 19-20, 28, 31, 54, 142, 162, 194, 198.

HORATIUS
— Cocles (guards bridge, 508): 190.
HOSTILIUS
A. — Mancinus (cos. 170): 24.
L. — Mancinus (cos. 145): against Scipio, 30, 37, 45.
C. — Mancinus (cos. 137): Numantine affair, 35-7, 48, 98, 100, 107.
L. — Tubulus (pr. 142): bribed, 145.
Jugurtha (king of Numidia, 118-04): 194, 197.

JULIUS
L. — Caesar (cos. 90): franchise law, 199.
C. — Caesar (dict. 49-44): ix, 7, 25, 195; land, 61; Gaul, 76, 157; death and funeral, 92, 100.
JUNIUS
D. — Brutus Callaicus (cos. 138): 47-9; marriage, 114; opposes C.G., 180, 189.
M. — Pennus (trib. 126): aliens law, 121-2.

LAELIUS
C. — Sapiens (cos. 140): 37, 44, 49, 100, 115, 121, 138; consul, land bill, 46, 54, 60; against Gracchans, 80, 102, 106.
LAETORIUS
P. — (friend to C.G.): 190.
Laevinus: see Valerius.
Lentulus: see Cornelius.
Lepidus: see Aemilius.
Licinia (wife of C.G.): 41, 114, 187-9, 191.
LICINIUS
— (slave to C.G.): 3.
C. — (trib. 493): 59.
S. — (trib. 138): levy dispute, 47, 59.
P. — Crassus Dives (cos. 205, P.M. 212-183): 60.
P. — Crassus (cos. 171): 24, 60.
C. — Crassus (trib. 145): 44, 59, 160.
P. — Crassus Dives Mucianus (cos.

131, P.M. 132-0): Gracchan leader, 41, 44, 49, 80, 100, 104; supports land law, 52, 58-61; land commissioner, 101, 104; consul, to Asia, dies, 77, 86, 103-4, 107-8; daughters, 114, 180.
L. — Crassus (cos. 95): 188 . (?); prosecutes Carbo 194.
M. — Crassus Dives (cos. 70, 55): 194.
L. — Lucullus (cos. 151): 34.
C. — Stolo (trib. 376-67): reforms, 59, 86.
LIVIUS
C. — Drusus (cos. 147): 166.
M. — Drusus (trib. 122, cos. 112): opposes and defeats Gracchan bills, 165-71, 174-7, 181; his own laws, 168, 174, 178.
M. — Drusus (trib. 91): 194.

MAMILIUS
C. — Limetanus (trib. 109): 180.
Mancinus: see Hostilius.
MANLIUS
— Torquatus ('Mallius', cos. 165 or 164): 41, 69.
Cn. — Vulso (cos. 189): 22, 31.
A. — Vulso (cos. 178): 68.
Marcellus: see Claudius.
MARCIUS
Q. — Rex (pr. 144): 32.
MARIUS
M. — (of Teanum): 172.
C. — (trib. 119, cos. 107, 104-0, 86): 193-4.
Masinissa (king of Numidia 202-149): 124.
Menelaus of Marathus (tutor to C.G.): 80, 173.
Metellus: see Caecilius.
Micipsa (king of Numidia 148-118): 124.
MINUCIUS
M. — Rufus (trib. 121, cos. 110): opposes C.G., 179, 181, 183.
Mithridates V Euergetes (king of Pontus and Lesser Armenia, 150-120): 107, 152.
MUCIUS
Q. — (trib. 133?): replaces Octavius, 73, 89, 92.
P. — Scaevola (cos. 175):23.
Q. — Scaevola (cos. 174): 23.
P. — Scaevola (cos. 133, P.M. 130-115): Gracchan leader, 41, 49-50, 81, 145; consul, supports land law, 52, 58-61; death of T.G., 93-5; aftermath, 100-2, 107, 110; abandons C.G., 182, 191.
MUMMIUS
L. — Achaicus (cos. 146): sacks Corinth, 30-1; censor, 46.

Nabis (king of Sparta, 207-192): 82.
Nasica: see Cornelius.
Nero: see Claudius.
Nicomedes II (king of Bithynia 149-128): 107, 151.
Octavian: see Augustus.

OCTAVIUS
Cn.— (cos. 165): dies (162), 26, 68.
M. — (trib. 133): opposes T.G., 65-70; deposed, 70-3, 78, 83, 89; threatened by C.G., 131.
OPIMIUS
L. — (pr. 125, cos. 121): at Fregellae 124; election defeat, 138; consul, opposes C.G., 171, 173, 178-9, 183-4; ultimate decree, 184-6; destroys Gracchans, 187-91, 193, 196-7; temple of Concord, 192; prosecuted (120), 180-1, 186, 193; convicted (109), 180, 198.
Panaetius Of Rhodes (Stoic philosopher, 144-09): 45, 81.

PAPIRIUS
C. — Carbo (trib. 131, cos. 120): Gracchan leader, 41-2, 49, 116; tribune, attacks Scipio, voting law and re-election bill, 47, 86, 105-6, 115, 138-9, 180; land commissioner, 107-8, 159-60, 180; turns against C.G., 180-1, 196; suicide, 105, 194.
Paullus: see Aemilius.
Pericles (Athenian leader, 463-429): 163.
PERPERNA
M. — (father of next): expelled, 122.
M. — (cos. 130): in Asia, 108, 126.
Perseus (king of Macedon 179-68): 24, 26, 32.
PERSIUS
C. — (scholar): and Fannius, 174.
Phalaris (tyrant of Acragas, 570-54): 173.
Philip V (king of Macedon 221-179): 16, 21-2, 32.
Philocrates (slave of C.G.): 190.
Pisistratus (Athenian tyrant, 560-27): 173.
Piso: see Calpurnius.
PLANCIUS
Cn. — (aedile 54): 142.
PLAUTIUS
M. — Hypsaeus (cos. 125): attacked by C.G., 122, 181.
Polybius (Achaean leader, 193-168: and historian): 5-6.
POMPEIUS
Q. — (cos. 141): consul, in Spain, 34, 36-7, 46-9; opposes T.G., 77-9, 104; censor (131), 78, 104, 107.
Q. — Magnus ('Pompey', cos. 70, 55.

52): 194.
POMPONIUS
— (friend to C.G.): 189-90.
POPILLIUS
C. — Laenas (cos. 172, 158): in Egypt, 3-4.
M. — Laenas (cos. 139): 34, 48.
P. — Laenas (cos. 132): persecutes Gracchans, 102-3; exiled, 132, 181, 185; recalled, 179, 193.
PORCIUS
M. — Cato (cos. 195, cens. 184): 18, 30-1, 44, 49, 59 (and cited).
C. — Cato (cos. 114): supports T.G., 41-2, 116; coinage officer, 159; ? opposes C.G., 181.
POSTUMIUS
Sp. — Albinus (cos. 110): 181.
L. — Megellus (cos. 294): 68.
Ptolemy VIII Euergetes Physcon (king of Egypt 170-116): 2.
Pulcher: see Claudius.
Pylaemenes (king of Paphlagonia c. 131): 107.
Pyrrhus (king of Epirus, 307-272): 4, 16.

QUINCTIUS
T. — Flamininus (cos. 198): 16, 32, 82.
T. — Flamininus (cos. 123): 158.
Romulus (first king of Rome, 753-16): 170.

RUBRIUS
— (trib. 133): 89.
C(?) — (trib. 123): Carthage law, 162.
Rufus (murders T.G.): 95.
RUPILIUS
P. — (cos. 132): and Gracchans, 102-3; in Sicily, 50; suicide, 103.
RUTILIUS
P. — Rufus (cos. 105): 100, 126, 154.

SATUREIUS
P. — (trib. 133): strikes T.G., 95.
Saturninus: see Appuleius.
Scaurus: see Aemilius.
Scaevola: see Mucius.
Sempronia (m. Scipio): 26, 29, 115, 198.
SEMPRONIUS
Ti. — Gracchus (cos. 238): 20.
Ti. — Gracchus (cos. 215, 213): 20-1.
P. — Gracchus (father of next): 20.
Ti. — Gracchus (trib. 187, pr. 180, cos. 177, 163, cens. 169): early career and Scipio, marriage, 1, 18-19, 21-2; in Spain, 22, 29, 33-4, 36, 38; consul, in Sardinia, 23; censor and knights, 24-5, 143; later career, Eastern missions, 26, 29, 68, 76, 80; death, character, 26-7, 38, 186.

Ti. and C.—Gracchus ('The Gracchi', collective references): birth and family, 1-2, 12, 19, 26-7, 29, 191; historical role, ix-xii, 7, 14, 30, 48, 140; character studies, 2-3, 27; associated families, 21, 23, 41, 49, 80; Greek influence, 80-4; honoured, 191; unavenged, 198; aims and achievement, 64, 122, 163, 192-9.

Ti. — Gracchus (trib. 133): *Early Career (to 134), 28-52;* augur, Carthage, 28-30, 44; marriage (c. 140), 41, 46; quaestor (137) and Numantia, 35-9, 48, 50; aims and motives, 38-40, 50, 58, 84, 98; supporters, 41, 49-50, 58-60, 80, 86-7, 99, 116, 131; elected tribune, 39, 52; *Tribune (133), 53-99;* land problem, 46, 51, 53-8; land bill, 53, 58-62; debated, 62-6; amended, 69; vetoed, 66-70; deposition of Octavius, 70-3; bill carried 73; land commission, 73-4; second land (judicial) law, 74; Pergamum legacy, bill for its distribution, 74-7, 83-4, 102, 110; proposal for Pergamene cities, 76; growing opposition, 'monarchy', 77-9, 83-6, 101, 116, 163; re-election campaign, 85-90, 106, 133, 138; further laws proposed, 88-9; riot and death, 92-6, 183-5; achievement, 42, 96-9; aftermath, 100-9, 116-9, 128; and allies, 110-1; and knights, 88, 120; pretended son, 198.

C. — Gracchus (trib. 123, 122): *Early Career (to 124), 100-127;* and brother (133), 58, 85-6, 95, 114; marriage, 41, 114; 'quiet period', 100, 103, 106, 112-8; quaestor (126) and Sardinia, 118, 122-6, 128, 133; Italians, 109-11, 121-2, 126, 172; land, 73, 104, 108, 110, 114, 117, 159; knights, 121; grain, 124; Plautius, 122, 181; Asia and Aquillius, 121, 126, 145, 151-2; aims and motives, 89, 99, 113-15, 118-19, 125-6, 130-1, 140, 144-6, 173; talents, 113-15, 129-30, 195; return and election, 125-7; *First Tribunate (123), 128-162;* chronology, 129, 136, 156, 163; bill on deposed magistrates, 131; law on capital punishment and Popillius 132, 146, 185; grain law, 133-6; granaries, 134; quasi-regal power, 137-9, 156; re-elected 86, 138-9; judiciary proposals and background, 44, 88, 120-1, 136-7, 140-5; judiciary law, 145-50, 153; conspiracy law, 146-7; extortion/bronze/Acilian laws, 148-9, 164; tax reforms, 151; Asian taxation law, 75, 151-4; law on consular provinces, 157; military reforms, 158; Spanish corn, 156; roads, 158; land law, 61, 117, 159-60, 168; colonization laws, 160-1, 168; Rubrian law on Carthage, 160-2; legislative achievement, 154-5, 162; economic success, 159; *Second Tribunate (122), 162-178;* franchise bill, 82, 163-5, 167, 171-3; Carthage, 30, 167-71; growing opposition, 166-9; and Fulvius, 165, 181; moves home, 171; voting and debt proposals, 172-3; struggle and defeat, 172-6; re-election campaign, 171, 173-4, 177-8; *Out of Office (121), 179-191;* enemies, 126, 131, 179-82; supporters, 181-2; Carthage dispute, 179, 182-4; last preparations, and death, 186-91, 197.

C. — Gracchus (pr. 33 A.D.): 199.

C. — Tuditanus (cos. 129): 112.

Septimuleius: 191.

SERTORIUS

Q. — (rebel in Spain, 83-72): 194.

SERVILIUS

Cn.— Caepio (cos. 141): 50, 125.

Q. — Caepio (cos. 140): 34, 47, 49.

Servius Tullius (king of Rome 578-535): 10.

SEXTIUS

L. — Sextius Lateranus (trib. 376-367): 59, 86.

Spartacus (rebel slave 73-1): 194.

Sphaerus philosopher c. 230): 82.

Sulla: see Cornelius.

SULPICIUS

Ser.— Galba (pr. 187): 22.

Ser. — Galba (cos. 144): 34, 41, 45, 49; trial, 44, 52, 90.

C. — Galba (m. Licinia): 41, 180.

TERENTIUS

C. — Varro (cos. 216): 5.

Tubulus: see Hostilius.

Tuditanus: see Sempronius.

TULLIUS

M. — Cicero (cos. 63): 135, 185, 194-6.

VALERIUS

C. — Laevinus (cos. 176): 23.

Vettius (friend of C.G.): 103, 115.

VILLIUS

C. — (executed 132): 102.

Viriathus (Spanish leader 147-39): 29, 34, 47.

Zeno (Stoic philosopher 313-263): 81.